☜ **W9-ADO-221**

Environmental Problems in the Soviet Union & Eastern Europe

Selected Papers from the Third World Congress
for Soviet and East European Studies
Washington, D.C.
30 October–4 November 1985

Sponsored by the
INTERNATIONAL COMMITTEE
FOR SOVIET AND EAST EUROPEAN STUDIES
and the
AMERICAN ASSOCIATION
FOR THE ADVANCEMENT OF SLAVIC STUDIES

General Editor   R. C. Elwood   *Carleton University*

EDITORIAL COMMITTEE MEMBERS

Environmental Problems in the Soviet Union & Eastern Europe

Edited by Fred Singleton

Lynne Rienner Publishers   Boulder & London

Published in the United States of America in 1987 by
Lynne Rienner Publishers, Inc.
948 North Street, Boulder, Colorado 80302

and in the United Kingdom by
Lynne Rienner Publishers, Inc.
3 Henrietta Street, Covent Garden, London WC2E 8LU

Library of Congress Cataloging-in-Publication Data

Environmental problems in the Soviet Union and
    Eastern Europe.

    Selected papers from the Third World Congress for
Soviet and East European Studies, held in Washington, D.C.,
Oct. 30–Nov. 4, 1985, sponsored by the International
Committee for Soviet and East European Studies and the
American Association for the Advancement of Slavic Studies.
    Bibliography: p.
    Includes index.
    1. Environmental protection—Soviet Union—Congresses.
2. Environmental protection—Europe, Eastern—Congresses.
3. Environmental policy—Soviet Union—Congresses.
4. Environmental policy—Europe, Eastern—Congresses.
I. Singleton, Frederick Bernard. II. World Congress
for Soviet and East European Studies (3rd : 1985 :
Washington, D.C.) III. International Committee for
Soviet and East European Studies. IV. American
Association for the Advancement of Slavic Studies.
TD171.5.S65E58   1987   333.7'0947   87-4930
ISBN 1-55587-059-7 (lib. bdg.)

Printed and bound in the United States of America

The paper used in this publication meets the
requirements of the American National Standard
for Permanence of Paper for Printed Library
Materials Z39.48-1984. ♾

Contents

Tables

Figures

Foreword

The articles selected for publication in this volume were chosen from among those presented at the Third World Congress for Soviet and East European Studies held in Washington, D.C., from 30 October to 4 November 1985. The Congress, which was sponsored by the International Committee for Soviet and East European Studies and the American Association for the Advancement of Slavic Studies, attracted over 3,000 scholars from forty-one countries. This figure represents a twofold increase over the number of delegates who attended either the first congress in Banff, Canada, in 1974 or the second congress in Garmisch-Partenkirchen, West Germany, in 1980 and reflects the revival of Slavic studies throughout the world.

More than 600 papers were formally presented or distributed at the Washington congress. From among the substantial number submitted for possible publication in this series, the editorial committee has selected 160 to appear in fifteen volumes. Five volumes are being published in the social sciences; three by Cambridge University Press and two by Lynne Rienner Publishers. Five volumes devoted to history and literature are being published by Slavica Publishers, while the remaining five in education, law, library science, linguistics, and aspects of Eastern European history are appearing as part of established series or as special issues of scholarly journals. The titles of all these publications will be found at the end of this volume.

As general editor for the third congress I should like to express my sincere appreciation to Donald W. Treadgold, the program chairman, and Dorothy Atkinson, executive director of the AAASS, who were responsible for the efficient organization of the Washington congress; to Oskar Anweiler and Alexander Dallin, the past and current presidents of the International Committee, for encouraging the publication of these proceedings; and to Roger Kanet, the general editor for the first two congresses, whose advice has been invaluable to his successor. Thanks also are owed to the congress participants who submitted their papers for consideration, to the editorial committee that selected those to be published, and to the editors of the various volumes.

R. C. Elwood
General Editor

FRED SINGLETON

1

Introduction

All societies are responsible for some degree of disruption to the natural environment that they occupy. Evidence of soil erosion, arising from the destruction of the natural vegetation mantle, can be found in habitats occupied by Stone Age communities of thousands of years ago; and, from Biblical times onward, the encroachments by the deserts in Africa and the Middle East can be attributed directly to human activity. The problem has become more acute, however, in the last two hundred years and has now reached crisis proportions. We are steadily destroying the natural resources on which human life depends and are reaching a point where, if we do not destroy the earth in the insanity of a nuclear "big bang," we shall do it by slower means as we undermine the basis from which we draw our means of subsistence. The escalation in the rate of destruction may be attributed primarily to the population explosion that began in Western Europe and North America with the Industrial Revolution, and which has now spread to Asia, Africa, and Latin America.

As the pressure of the expanding population made increasing demands on the world's natural resources, so ever larger areas were exploited to satisfy immediate human needs. In the industrial societies, rising aspirations for higher material standards fueled expansionist tendencies as new sources of food and raw materials were sought. The exploitation of the land already under cultivation was intensified when new technologies made higher yields possible. Often, however, more intensive methods of farming, which produced quick returns in the short run, resulted in long-term damage to the soil; and the increasing use of chemical fertilizers and insecticides has led to the pollution of rivers and lakes.

No society is free from the evil of putting short-term economic advantage before the long-term goal of preserving the natural resources of the earth for the use of future generations. The rational use of resources can be achieved only if society cooperates with nature and finds a balance in which reasonable human needs are satisfied without destroying the environment. The Communist world for a long time held the view that it could handle these problems in a more intelligent way than could its capitalist rivals. The assumption was that the pursuit of private profit through the mechanism of the so-called free market was the main cause of the despoliation of the earth. The industrial nations of the western world, having laid waste their own environments, reached out to their imperial possessions in the tropical world, enslaving its peoples and plundering its natural resources. The examples of the creation of the dust bowl in Oklahoma in the 1930s, the destruction of African environments and ways of life by the enforcement of one-crop agriculture, and the destruction of equatorial forests in Brazil can be cited. The self-confident assertion in the program of the Communist party of the Soviet Union (CPSU), at its twenty-second congress in 1961, that "communism elevates man to a tremendous level of superiority over nature and makes possible a greater and fuller use of its inherent forces" was an echo of Marx's own boasts about the conquest of nature. Engels's cautionary disclaimer—"We will not flatter ourselves too much with our victories over nature. For every victory, it takes its vengeance upon us"—has been ignored.

There are signs, however, that leaders of the Soviet Union and the nations of Eastern Europe are now beginning to realize that their system does not possess a magic key that enables them to unlock the riches of nature without paying a price in terms of environmental damage. The old attitude, which regarded all wealth as being the creation of human labor, and of ignoring the intrinsic wealth provided by nature in the calculations of Marxist cost-accounting, is now giving way to a sober realization that environmental management is a complex process that cannot be conducted in terms of mechanistic formulae. During the last twenty years, as Elizabeth Koutaissoff illustrates in her survey of Soviet literature on the environment, genuine attempts have been made to grapple with some of the problems not only by empirical research and by practical measures of amelioration, but also through the education system, in training young citizens to respect nature. There have even been attempts to adjust the ideological framework of Marxism to relate it to the newly perceived problems. Criticisms of Soviet theory and practice, which previously had appeared only in *samizdat* literature, and which often resulted in penalties for those who voiced them, now appear in official literature. One can hope that under Gorbachev this tendency will continue. Philip Pryde, while pointing out the discrepancy between Soviet theory and practice in environmental questions, concludes that some progress is being made. The abandonment by the Gorbachev regime in 1986 of the grandiose schemes for water transfer, involving large-scale river diversions inherited from the Stalin era, suggests that the results of environmental monitoring studies are at last beginning to have an influence on the decision makers.

It is now becoming accepted that misuse of the environment is as much a feature of the communist world as it is of the advanced capitalist countries and of the Third World. Recognition is also dawning that control of the environment is a problem that can only be satisfactorily tackled on an international plane. The participation of the Soviet Union and the German Democratic Republic (GDR) in international discussions on the pollution of the Baltic, the work of the Centre for Combatting Oil Pollution in the Mediterranean (based in Malta and including all littoral nations except Albania), and the attempt in collaboration with Western ecologists to build a new "Great Wall of China" in the form of a forest shelter belt to halt the advance of the desert are all recent examples of international cooperation in this field.

The divorce between words and deeds in the Soviet Union and Eastern Europe is nowhere more glaring than in the environmental field. The tone was set by the Soviet Union in its early days. Among the factors that help to explain this are the urgent imperatives of the industrialization drive, which overrode all other considerations, the inexperience of the managers, the cumbersome and highly compartmentalized bureaucracy, and the sheer geographical size of the Soviet Union. There was little to encourage a conservationist mentality and much to predispose people to put a high priority on the achievement of a greater volume of production as a single-minded objective. The fact that the Soviet Union covered 22.5 million square kilometers—one-sixth of the earth's surface—most of which was sparsely populated and economically underdeveloped, produced an expansionist attitude of mind. The "moving frontier," which was so important a concept in the nineteenth-century United States, as the settlers moved across the great plains and over the Rockies to California, had its counterpart in the spread of Soviet industrialization into Siberia and Central Asia. If ecologically damaging techniques were used to exploit the timber resources of the world's largest area of coniferous forest, it did not seem to matter, as there was always the remaining 900 million hectares of coniferous forest that would provide timber for the next generation. As Brenton Barr demonstrates in Chapter 6, although the scientific evaluation of timber resources had made great progress since World War II, the utilization of timber resources is still dictated by planning objectives that "are essentially related to the current fulfillment of production goals and not to relatively long-term considerations such as preservation of the forest, sustained yield management, environmental protection, etc." He also has drawn attention to "delays in the introduction of rigorous planning in wood processing, plus the chaotic actions of numerous non-forestry ministries and agencies." Unfortunately, these faults afflict many other areas of Soviet economic development and frequently render ineffective the efforts of conservationists who are advocating a more rational use of natural resources.

The expansion of agricultural production has normally been achieved by bringing new land into cultivation, rather than by the intensification of agriculture on existing farmland by the use of improved techniques. This prodigal attitude to land use received a sharp shock when Khrushchev's virgin lands scheme in Kazakhstan threatened to create a dust bowl similar to that which U.S. capitalism produced in Oklahoma and Texas in the 1930s. As Ihor Stebelsky has shown in Chapter 5, despite the claims made for the success of "Stalin's plan for the transformation of nature," mismanagement of the soil has been as damaging during the Soviet period as it was under the tsars, and although there has been some improvement since the disasters of the Khrushchev era, the Soviet Union has not been able to halt the evils of soil degradation and increasing salinity, which arise from the inefficient application of modern techniques and wasteful methods of irrigation. Despite the fact that a high proportion of Soviet agricultural land is in semiarid areas, the directors of agricultual policy have failed to learn any lessons from countries with similar climatic conditions. It may be that part of the answer lies in Professor Stebelsky's last sentence: ". . . the individuals who work the soil continue to lack vested interest in the land and fail to bear personal responsibility for soil erosion."

The question of who is responsible for preventing environmental damage lies at the heart of many of the problems that arise in collectivist societies. Although Soviet law provides penalties for those who willfully pollute the environment, which include the power to close down offending factories, the machinery of enforcement is inadequate, and those who attempt to rouse public opinion in protest against environmental misuse may themselves incur penalties. Milka Bliznakov draws attention to the multiplicity of decision makers involved in, for example, the construction of new towns in Siberia. She decides that the problem is "inherent in the institutional structure of the Soviet Union." Although the teams of planners started their work with high hopes of building communities that would harmonize with nature and avoid damage to the fragile balance of nature in this unique environment with its great extremes of climate, she concludes sadly that many projects "would probably remain dreams on paper, while blocks of prefabricated housing continue to be erected, disregarding natural or man-made beauty." It may not be realized that the design of the railroad settlements was handled by six transportation institutes, sixty-four design organizations, several ministries, regional and city governments, local Party organizations, and administrative institutes. With this welter of authorities, it is not surprising that it is hard to apportion responsibility for any mistakes that may be made. Similar bureaucratic confusion exists in such matters as the planning and design of hydroelectric dams, allocation of resources to new industrial projects, management of preserved lands, and almost any other aspect of Soviet life where society and nature interact.[1]

The inability to identify those responsible for environmental mistakes is equally difficult where there are transgressions of laws intended to prevent pollution. It is almost unheard of for a factory in full production to be closed because of violations of antipollution laws, and if fines are imposed on individual managers, they are derisory in amount and are, in any case, usually not paid in person by the official who is held to be responsible. When, for example, the head of the Borislav Drilling Operations Administration was found to be responsible for emptying 2,000 cubic meters of polluted water into the Shchepilsk River, causing the death of thousands of fish, he was fined twenty-five rubles.[2]

The rapid expansion of industry into Siberia in the last few decades, and especially the developments associated with the Baikal-Amur Mainline (BAM) railway, can be compared in some respects to the westward movement of the center of gravity of the U.S. economy, which began over a century ago. It has thrown up similar environmental issues. The threat to Lake Baikal is well known, but there are many other lesser-known examples where the balance of nature has been adversely affected by the insensitivity of the planners. This is apparent in the monotonous uniformity of some of the new towns along the line of BAM, which are described by Milka Bliznakov as having no identity and being undistinguishable from new Soviet towns in other parts of the country. The enthusiasm of some of the young architects, as well as the initiative of local residents improvising and adapting to their surroundings, occasionally gleams through the usual dullness imposed by the centralized bureaucracy.

The wide-open spaces of Siberia can absorb a vast amount of industry, with its concomitant pollution, while still leaving most of the country unspoiled, but the situation is more serious in the more densely populated countries of Eastern Europe. The postwar demand for industrialization has been pushed forward, for the most part, with total disregard for the environment. Indeed, as John Kramer points out, in Poland funds specifically earmarked for environmental protection have been diverted to industrial production, and low priority is given in new construction plans to the provision of antipollution facilities. It is sad to report that most Poles in positions of authority and many ordinary citizens accept the sentiments expressed in *Zycie Warszawy* in November 1982: "Environmental pollution is the price that has to be paid for industrial development and the development of civilization." A similar situation exists in Czechoslovakia where antipollution laws exist, they are seldom enforced (see Chapter 9). As in the Soviet Union, the enforcement machinery is inadequate, lacking trained personnel, technical equipment and, above all, the political will to act.

Public concern about the despoliation of the environment can on rare occasions be mobilized, usually when a direct and obvious threat to public health is perceived. In Poland this broke the surface during the heady days when Solidarity (*Solidarność*) was in the ascendant; the authorities were unable to withstand the pressure and were forced to take action. The Polish Ecology Club, founded in September 1980, succeeded in closing some factories; and the Green Movement, associated with Rural Solidarity, made tentative moves to make contact with the semilegal Green movements in Czechoslovakia and the GDR, as well as with the established ecology groups in Western Europe.

For a time, the voices that castigated environmentalists as being enemies of socialism were stilled. After the imposition of martial law in December 1981, the movements associated with *Solidarność*)were steadily crushed, and the po-faced bureaucrats reassumed their old positions. All was not totally lost, however, and even in official circles there is some grudging acceptance that something must be done—when the economic situation improves. There is, perhaps, an element of hypocrisy in the lip service paid to the existence of an environmental problem—it is the tribute vice pays to virtue—but it is at least an improvement, if only a cosmetic one, on the old attitude that socialism had solved the problem.

The persecution of dissidents who draw attention to the environmental shortcomings of the regimes varies from country to country and from time to time. In Czechoslovakia, in the 1980s, the cases of Pavel Křivka and Pavel Škoda show the extent to which the authorities will go to suppress those who attempt to publish the facts concerning environmental misuse.

In Yugoslavia, the ecological movement is given freer rein to criticize and to warn the authorities of ecological disasters, and there are some examples of protest movements achieving some success—as, for example, with the campaign to stop the construction of a nuclear power station near the Adriatic resort of Zadar. However, although the Greens are not regarded as enemies of the people, they are frequently ignored by local governments and by the workers in self-managed factories, who are likely to regard the priority of increased production as being a more important objective than the protection of the environment. Occasionally, the federal authorities may be persuaded to act when, as in the case of the Tara Gorge in Montenegro, international pressures reinforce the arguments of local ecologists (see Chapter 10).

The transnational aspect of pollution is beginning to receive attention. Although Poles cannot publicly refer to the fact that water-borne pollution enters their country from the Soviet Union via the Bug River, the two governments have entered into an agreement to clean up the river. It is permitted to discuss openly the threat to Wrocław's water supply from the pollution of the headwater of the Oder, which rises in Czechoslovakia. Yugoslavia participates in the organization concerned with combatting pollution in the Mediterranean, as does Poland, the German Democratic Republic (GDR), and the Soviet Union on international action to control pollution in the Baltic Sea.

The shock resulting from the disaster at Chernobyl in April 1986 produced some response in official circles in Eastern Europe, and had a much more profound effect on the unofficial "Green" movements. Protests in Yugoslavia in May 1986 prompted the authorities to shelve plans for an additional nuclear reactor, which had been under discussion during the previous two years; and there is some doubt about the implementation of the nuclear power station program in Poland. The Soviet Union, however, has declared that it intends to continue its program, and the world's largest nuclear power station, at Ignalina in Lithuania, will be opened on schedule. Czechoslovakia and the GDR are also pushing ahead with their plans. The remark of Dr. Günter Flack, a leading scientific adviser in the GDR, is typical of the complacent attitude of East European officials. Little more than a week after the Chernobyl disaster, he stated that "in principle Chernobyl is safe," and that there was no need to modify the GDR's nuclear program. One of the reasons for this attitude is that the plans for industrial expansion, which in all East European societies form the keystone of their economic policies, depend upon cheap and abundant supplies of electricity. The alternatives to nuclear power all involve the use of techniques that, at least in the short run, are more visibly damaging to the environment than nuclear power. The chapter on Czechoslovakia draws attention to the pollution that comes from using the abundant supplies of lignite, which produces sulfurous fumes when used to generate electricity. The GDR also suffers from the consequences of burning lignite. Even hydroelectricity generation gives rise to environmental damage when huge areas of farm land are flooded behind power dams. It is perhaps because of these factors that even the Green movements are sometimes unsure of their response to the problems of providing "clean" power supplies.

There are some bright spots in an otherwise depressingly gloomy picture. The Soviet Union established nature reserves (*zapovedniki*) during the inter-war years; and in the postwar period, game reserves, biosphere reserves, and national parks have been established, to protect endangered species of fauna and flora and to safeguard landscapes of special beauty and scientific interest. The practice often falls short of the ideal, and the conflicts of interest between industry, agriculture, tourism, and even of education (see Chapter 4), on the one hand, and conservation of nature, on the other, are often resolved in ways that are environmentally undesirable. In Yugoslavia, national parks are well established in Croatia and Slovenia, but the position is less satisfactory in some other republics.

The overall picture that one gleans from a study of the problems in the Soviet Union and Eastern Europe as a whole—and the material presented in this book represents a very small corner of a vast subject—is that, while the old attitudes that refused to recognize that socialist societies are capable of committing ecological atrocities are being abandoned, a coherent new approach has not yet emerged. The Greens are no longer seen as enemies of socialism, but they are often regarded as irrelevancies, who may be ignored. Perhaps the Communist authorities should pay heed to Tito's statement that no country can call itself truly socialist that fails to protect its environment.

Notes

1. See Chapter 4.
2. See Craig Zum Brunnen, "Water Pollution Problems," in F. Singleton, ed., *Environmental Misuse in the Soviet Union* (New York: Praeger, 1976) 35.

ELISABETH KOUTAISSOFF

Survey of Soviet Material on Environmental Problems

The Soviet Union is a vast and geographically varied country, and for this and other reasons field work there is difficult to organize; however, the amount of published data o n environmental problems is overwhelmingly abundant. Indeed, concern for the environment is as widespread in the Soviet Union as it is elsewhere. Much of this rapidly proliferating literature is theoretical, even more of it is very technical, but the present survey will deal mainly with what could be termed case studies. They provide vivid illustrations of the manifold adverse effects of anthropogenic factors impinging on nature and the measures taken by the state and individuals to mitigate the consequences.

For a long time, the idea of an impending ecological crisis was resisted by the Soviet authorities. The vastness of the country helped to conceal the damage done to nature; more important, the rapid and relentless building of the material and technical basis of communism was such an overriding practical priority for the Party (CPSU) that it could not be halted even though the consequences of industrialization, urbanization and the technoscientific revolution were coming into conflict with nature's capacity to cope with air, water, and soil pollution, and the wasteful exploitation of natural resources was driving the extractive industries far into the Arctic.

Apart from the *practical* need to build the material and technical basis of communism, there were *ideological* reasons to

11

resist the idea that an ecological crisis could threaten a socialist country. It had long been asserted that adverse anthropogenic factors are inherent only in the capitalist mode of production, the aim of which is the maximalization of profits and not concern for nature; environmental degradation was just one case of the contradictions besetting capitalist methods of production. As for socialist countries, they had already replaced the irrational and wasteful production of material goods by a planned and rationally managed economy; they were in the process of achieving planned social development and were seeking ways to manage the biosphere and eventually to control earthquakes, weather, and climate. Stalin's grandiose postwar schemes for the transformation of nature illustrate the Promethean utopianism implicit in Marxism.

Another of its assumptions, namely that natural resources as such have no value and acquire value only when drawn into production by human labor, has now been modified and brought in line with the Marxist theory of value by adding to present and past labor (embodied in machinery and the infrastructure) future labor as well, i.e., work needed to maintain the productivity of the environment and the health of future generations. This form of work has become known as *prirodookhranitel'naia deiatel'nost'* (nature protection activity).

The reluctant admission that natural resources were neither free nor inexhaustible and that the technoscientific revolution was increasing its impact on both nature and human societies prompted the journal *Voprosy filosofii* to start, in the early 1970s, a series of round table discussion articles on humanity, society, and nature. The first articles on *Obshchestvo i priroda*, published in 1973, were followed in 1974 by another series entitled *Nauka i global'nye problemy sovremennosti*. At these and ensuing conferences and in theoretical publications concerned with both the impact and the meaning of the technoscientific revolution, discussions widened and the question was raised whether science itself had become a force of production; eventually, discussions came to embrace biological and social factors in human evolution. After a long period of emphasis on the importance of social factors in the evolution of human societies—of "social heredity"—practically to the exclusion of the biological ones, Soviet writers now increasingly accept the view that human beings themselves are part of nature. If the present fragmentation of both natural and social sciences could give way to a greater integration of disciplines, possibly to a unified program of research involving a variety of scientists and institutes, there would arise a new science of sozology or global ecology. Had not Marx and Engels predicted that natural science would encompass the science of human beings to the same extent as the science of human beings would encompass natural science, there would be a *single* science.

Within the contradictory unity of organism and environment in the course of their interaction, mutual optimal adaptation rests largely with the more active and highly organized form of matter that affects the less organized. In general, the flow of matter and energy brought about by human activities must be made to harmonize with the natural circulation of matter and energy within the biosphere as a whole. A conscious management of both the biosphere and social processes involves their optimal compatibility, i.e., symbiosis. Soviet writers reject any limits to growth because changes in technology are bound to push such limits ever farther. This is a case of dialectics of contradictions between the finite and infinite. The latter is achieved through an endless alternation of finite states that in one way or another contain and manifest the infinite. The prospect of infinite human progress consists not in an exponential increase in production, consumption, and population growth, but in a rational regulation of all the components of human activity that correspond to concrete possibilities at any stage of development of the human society and its environment.[1] A rational and conscious interaction between humanity and nature is the essence of the noosphere. The term *noosphere*, first coined by LeRoy and Teilhard de Chardin in 1928, was introduced into Russian usage by V. I. Vernadskii who defined it as a new geological era brought about by human thought and labor, which transform the biosphere in the interests of a conscious, united humankind.

To achieve a rational management of the biosphere, a better understanding of ecosystems is needed and more appropriate technology has to be devised and introduced into production. Furthermore, tremendous psychological barriers will have to be overcome. These include not only the belief that the bounties of nature are free and inexhaustible, but also the lack of general understanding of to what extent ecological changes affect the entire planet. The study of these very complex problems has been concentrated since 1976 at the All-Union Scientific Research Institute of Systems Analysis of the State Committee for Science and Technology.

More recently, yet another aspect of man-nature relations has come to the fore, namely that nature is more than a storehouse of raw materials; it is also a place of escape from the strains and stresses of life in the "concrete jungle" of modern man's urbanized "grey environment"—so much so that in 1978, at the Pushchino Biological Research Center, the first conference was held on "the Protection of Nature—the Psychological Aspects." It considered methods of estimating the risks of technogenic factors on human physical and mental health and ways to promote a nature conservation mentality with the help of the mass media.[2] (Incidentally, Pushchino is one of the first *ecopolises* in the Soviet Union. It is a small town on the banks of the Oka—a tributary of the Volga—with a protected area comprising a national park, birch groves, meadows, and two unspoiled ravines.)[3]

Managing the biosphere is still hampered by our inadequate understanding of nature's self-regulating and self-renovating processes (slow and uncertain in the harsh North), of the concatenation of cause and effects that may be long-term, complex, and unpredictable like mutations, and the effect of supersonic aircraft, rockets, and nuclear tests on the ozone layer of the stratosphere and, hence, even on the climate. It is hampered too by lack of cooperation between countries; social ecology may require changes in such spheres of social consciousness as law and morality. Will humanity's very strength generate higher standards of wisdom and ethics? Time and again, a streak of eschatological aspirations creeps into Soviet writings even when grappling with urgent and highly practical problems of global ecology. In this they are not alone—many Western futurists also start with economics and end by calling for a new morality.

Be that as it may, all the theorizing reflects the very basic practical problem of how to achieve further economic growth without accelerating the likely irreversible destruction of nature. A new Russian word, *prirodopol'zovanie*, encapsulates this desire to reconcile development and conservation; it has its parallel in the English neologism *ecodevelopment*. Both convey an anthropocentric attitude: nature is not sacred as God's creation, nor is there any hint of "animal rights." This search for a conciliation of the demands of an expanding economy and finite resources has engendered in the Soviet Union, as elsewhere in the 1970s, a flurry of remedial activities: endeavors at international cooperation in the field of conservation, laws on the protection of nature, a revival of protected nature reserves, and environmental education on a large scale. However, on the negative side many difficulties remain, exacerbated by unfavorable climatic conditions.

The Global Aspect

The global dimensions of the ecological crisis prompted UNESCO to convene in September 1968 its first conference on *Man and the Biosphere*, and in 1972 it issued its program known as MAB. In 1972, the Stockholm Conference on the Human Environment set up the United Nations Environmental Program (UNEP). Although the Soviet Union did not attend the Stockholm conference (in protest at the GDR not having been invited), it did join UNEP. In 1975, the State Committee for Science and Technology, jointly with the Presidium of the Academy of Sciences of the Soviet Union and the Ministry of Foreign Affairs, set up a committee to collaborate with the UNESCO MAB program. This committee has its headquarters at the Institute of Evolutionary Morphology and Animal Ecology of the Academy of Sciences. Since 1979, the long-established journal *Priroda* has regularly published articles relating to the MAB program, especially section 8, "Conservation of Natural Areas and Their Genetic Material," and its two subsections, namely 8a—the organization of biosphere reserves, and 8b—research into species and their productivity in a given area.[4]

Soviet representatives have taken part in many international conferences and collaborate with other countries in joint projects such as the United States-Soviet Union studies on the arctic flora and fauna and the impact of the oil industry on the fragile tundra vegetation.[5] The Soviet Union has also hosted several conferences sponsored by the International Union for the Conservation of Nature (IUCN), UNESCO, and UNEP, e.g., that of IUCN (of which the Soviet Union has been a member since 1956) in Ashkhabad in 1978, the Intergovernmental Conference on Education and Environment in Tbilisi in 1977, the second meeting of Infoterra (a UNEP information bulletin set up by the Stockholm conference that became operational in 1979), the first International Congress on Biosphere Reserves in Minsk in 1983, and the twenty-seventh Geological Congress in Moscow, 1984—a result of which was the establishment of a UNESCO-UNEP-Soviet international center in the Crimea to train specialists in the fields of geology and environment.[6]

At the June 1984 Munich conference on air pollution, the

Soviet Union was one of the countries that undertook to reduce, during the forthcoming decade, the emission of sulfur oxides by 30 percent even though the Soviet Union is a "net importer" of acid rain from the West, estimated at an annual five million tons of sulfur compounds.[7]

The Soviet Union is also a cosignatory to various conventions, among which probably the most important are the Marine Protection Agreement concluded in 1976 by the states bordering the Baltic Sea and the one signed in 1972 by the CMEA countries. In this connection, a seminar of specialists from CMEA countries was held in Sochi in November 1984 to discuss the establishment of a bank of ecological, physiological, and genetic data on land and water systems in the vicinity of atomic power stations and the elaboration of mathematical models of the effect of atomic power stations on the surrounding biota for the purpose of long-term forecasting.[8]

Legislation, Administration, and Research

Within the Soviet Union, the volume of legislation concerning the environment has increased dramatically. There had been earlier decrees to restrict hunting or limit the emission of toxic substances, but in the 1960s and 1970s these decrees became more numerous and more specific. In October 1960, the Supreme Soviet of the Russian Soviet Federated Socialist Republic (RSFSR) passed a law "On the Preservation of Nature in the RSFSR" designed to preserve the productivity of cultivated lands, combat wind and water erosion, establish purification systems to prevent the pollution of rivers, and to stop the floating of loose logs downstream. It listed various provisions to regulate the methods of felling trees in forests, especially on slopes, and to protect wildlife and natural beauty spots. The decree also confirmed support for the All-Union Society for the Protection of Nature, enjoined research into methods of nature conservation, the teaching of conservation measures in schools, and appropriate propaganda by the mass media. However, the decree seems to have had little effect, for five years later the Presidium of the Supreme Soviet of the RSFSR issued a decree along the same lines (26 October 1965). In its preamble, it listed numerous and persistent malpractices such as excessive lumbering, the polluting of rivers and lakes by untreated sewage and industrial wastes, the floating of loose timer, overfishing, and the wasteful extractions of ores of which much never got to the surface or remained lying around the mines. Various ministries and, in particular, the Moscow and Leningrad city soviets were instructed to enforce the measures prescribed by the 1960 law.

By 1972, it was felt that all-union comprehensive legislation was needed. A detailed decree was issued by the Supreme Soviet of the Soviet Union on 20 September 1972, followed by that of the Central Committee of the CPSU and the Council of Ministers of the Soviet Union on 29 December 1972, instructing various ministries to take relevant measures and, furthermore, to include in their future plans definite proposals for the protection of nature. Of particular significance was the inclusion of such plans into the general plans (both annual and long-term) elaborated by the State Planning Committee (GOSPLAN); for this purpose, it was to set up a special committee. Yet another committee was to be set up jointly by the State Committee for Science and Technology, the Academy of Sciences, GOSPLAN, the State Committee for Construction (GOSSTROI), the Ministry of Health, the Ministry of Agriculture, and the Department of Hydrometeorological Services in collaboration with other ministries and representatives of Union republic councils of ministries for the purpose of elaborating, in the course of 1973–1974, a prognosis of possible changes in the biosphere during the next twenty or thirty years.[9]

For the first time the tenth five-year plan (1976–1980), in its chapter on scientific and technical developments, included a special section on the elaboration and implementation of measures for the protection of the environment and the rational use and reproduction of natural resources. A similar clause was included also in the eleventh five-year plan (1981–1985) and funds were allocated for the purpose.[10] The introduction of conservation measures into quinquennial plans makes it necessary to effect complex and detailed calculations of the costs of the damage done to the environment and that of preventing or mitigating it. For example, air pollution affects human health and results in medical expenses and loss of labor when workers are on sick leave; it reduces the yield of crops and, in the long run, that of forests; it also increases the expenditure on the maintenance of buildings. Plans have to take into account the cost of installing air and water purification systems and also the running costs of maintaining them. There may be cases when projects that are economically advantageous, but ecologically disastrous, have to be modified, relocated, and even scrapped, as was the case with the proposals to build dams on the Pechora, the rivers of the Kamchatka Peninsula, and on the island of Sakhalin.[11]

It should be also mentioned that article 18 of the 1977 constitution states that "in the interests of the present and future generations the necessary steps are taken in the USSR to protect and make scientific, rational use of the land and its mineral and water resources, flora and fauna, to preserve the purity of air and water, ensure the reproduction of natural wealth, and improve the human environment." There are further references to the protection of nature in articles 67, 73, 131, and 147.

Among the specific enactments of the Supreme Soviet and the decrees of the Central Committee of the Party and the Council of Ministers are those prescribing measures to be taken for the protection of the Caspian Sea from oil pollution (25 September 1968), the Volga and Ural Rivers from untreated sewage (13 March 1974), and the Black and Azov Seas from both pollution and overfishing (15 March 1974). Other decrees deal with the recultivation of lands damaged by mining, peat extraction, and geological surveys (2 June 1976); the prevention of air pollution (15 June 1980); the protection of wild animals, including breeding grounds and migration routes (25 June 1980); and the utilization of secondary (waste) raw materials (8 December 1984). Confirming and expanding earlier regulations regarding the exploitation of forests, the Supreme Soviet passed a detailed law on the protection of forests and the rational utilization of forest resources (17 June 1977). Relevant, and often more specific, laws and regulations have been introduced in the Union Republics with Estonia leading the way since 1957.[12] Even this incomplete list of enactments reveals the multiplicity and complexity of environmental problems.

To implement and enforce the growing volume of environmental legislation, a vast network of committees has been set up. The Supreme Soviet has a Commission for the Protection of Nature that coordinates the activities of the all-union ministries in this field. The Presidium of the Council of Ministers has its Commission on Environmental Protection and Rational Use of Natural Resources. GOSPLAN has a Department for Nature Conservation that coordinates the plans submitted to it by the all-union ministries and the councils of ministers of the Union Republics, so too has the State Committee for Science and Technology (GKNT). More specialized functions are carried out by the Soviet State Committee for Hydrometeorology and the Protection of the Environment (GIDROMET) with its network of observation posts responsible for monitoring and controlling air pollution. The Ministry of Land Melioration and Water is responsible for water purification plants and the Ministry of Fisheries for the maintenance of fish stocks and the protection of the continental shelf. The Ministry of Agriculture has a department for the Protection of Nature, Nature Reserves, and Hunting; it is also responsible for supervising the chemical and biological methods of pest control. The Ministry of Health has a network of sanitary-epidemiological inspectorates to control water pollution. The State Committee for Forestry supervises the rational exploitation of forests and their protection from fires and insect pests. The ministry in charge of safety precautions in industrial and mining enterprises is also responsible for a rational (as opposed to wasteful) exploitation of mineral deposits. Last, Union Republic authorities and local soviets must ensure that adequate conservation measures are enforced within their respective territories.[13]

The very multiplicity of authorities sharing in the task of monitoring and protecting the state of water, air, land, and wildlife and for applying conservation laws allows for many loopholes and lack of coordination. Moreover, the various committees and subcommittees dealing with the environment are also part of larger units, e.g., ministries whose main objective is to fulfill their production plans, not to help solve the environmental problems of some other ministry. Thus the State Committee for Forestry is not competent to deal with the utilization of (waste) forest byproducts or the state of the streams and rivers flowing through its forests. No mining enterprise is responsible for the *total* utilization of *all* the metals present in the ore, but only for its major component. For instance slag heaps, which could provide adequate gravel for surfacing roads or rubble for the manufacture of building materials, disfigure the countryside and take up thousand of hectares of land,[14] while even beauty spots like the Zhiguli Hills along the Volga are being damaged by the quarries of GOSSTROI.[15] This is partly a problem of geography—slag heaps accumulate around mines and, unless their rubble can be used locally, transport costs for moving such bulky material are uneconomical. An exception to this is in the Ukraine where efforts to make use of this waste have been successful.[16]

In the early 1970s, the economists K. G. Gofman, M. Ya. Lemeshev, and the biologist N. F. Reimers calculated that only 1 percent of the total weight of resources used was incorporated in the final product. The rest was burned to provide energy, evaporated in steam, smoke, and gases, or was discarded as waste. Later estimates put the coefficient of utilization at 5 to 10 percent which still means that 90 to 95 percent of the resources withdrawn from nature are irretrievably lost.[17]

Lack of coordination engenders not only inefficiency, but deliberate delays and malpractices; thus, according to D. L. Kartvelishvili, president of the Council of Ministers of the Georgian SSR, the ferroalloy works at Zestafoni were among the worst air polluters in the region. Complaints from workers and local residents poured into the local Party committee, the district soviet, and right up the bureaucratic ladder to the central authorities in Tbilisi. As a result, the possibility and cost of reconstructing the plant were discussed 289 times by different planning, construction, engineering, financial, and conservation committees. Eventually, the entire managerial staff of the plant, as well as the district officials, were sacked—apparently not only for incompetence, but also for deliberate obstruction and cover up, while at long last a smoke abatement system was installed at the cost of ten million rubles.[18]

Kartvelishvili quotes another example of damaging inefficiency due to the fragmentation of responsibilities in the case of the Black Sea littoral in Georgia. Building enterprises (including road builders) removed sand and gravel from the beaches for their construction work. Meanwhile, the fast flowing coastal rivers were being dammed for electricity generation, thus stopping the resupply of sand and gravel to the beaches, the area of which began to shrink. As a result, during storms the high waves rolled over the narrow beaches up to the water front, flooding and even washing away buildings. Local soviets and enterprises were each responsible for the upkeep of just their own stretch of coastline, and no single authority was responsible for the maintenance of its entire length until 1981 when a scientific-industrial *ob"edinenie* (unit), the first of its kind, was set up to make a study of storms and wave patterns. It suggested the construction of fifty-meter-wide boulder and gravel jetties at strategic points to break up the force of the surge and, in the long run, allow offshore currents to spread the material over the shrunken beaches.[19]

Even the organization of nature reserves is hampered by this fragmentation. For instance, there is a strong case to establish a nature reserve on the North Pacific islands, e.g., the Komandors, with their seal-breeding grounds. The establishment of a reserve depends on the Chief Hunting Administration of the RSFSR whereas marine wildlife comes under the Ministry of Fisheries of the USSR. As a result, since 1976 when the proposal was first put forward, no decision has been taken.[20]

The Cost of Maintaining a Sustainable Environment

More damaging than the tangle of authorities responsible for the protection of nature are the high financial costs of maintaining a sustainable environment. Older plants have no purification systems or else they are obsolete and recurrently out of service. In new plants, installation of these systems averages up to 11 percent of the capital costs and may be more, e.g., at the famous Shchekino chemical works they were as high as 40 percent; running costs may also turn out to be considerable.[21]

The economic costs of pollution may be eventually even higher. Several studies have been made at the Central Economic Mathematical Institute of the Academy of Sciences of the USSR (AN SSSR) by N. F. Fedorenko and his team, at the Institute of Economics of the AN SSSR by T. S. Khachaturov and his team, the Council for the Protection of Nature of GOSPLAN by V. N. Leksin, the Ukrainian Academy of Sciences, and the Voroshilov branch of the Economics Institute of the same academy, as well as by its Odessa section.[22]

Even the cheapest and simplest smoke abatement installation costs 1,000 to 3,000 rubles; the scrubber types are more expensive, ranging from 5,000 to 12,000 rubles, while electrofilters may cost 100,000 to 300,000 rubles. Combatting gas pollutants is more expensive, and prices may range from eighty to a hundred million rubles in the case of coal-fired power stations. Some of the costs can be recuperated from the sulfur retrieved, but the more thorough the purification the higher the costs. Coal and oil-fired power stations are reputed to be among the major air polluters responsible for 70 percent of sulfur oxides and 40 percent of the nitrogen compounds released into the atmosphere with paper mills, cement plants, and iron works coming a close second. Since 1976, a number of research institutes and enterprises such as *Energogazoochistka* have been working on the problem and have designed smoke abatement techniques, which achieve a 99 percent purification, and also on various methods to reduce the amounts of toxic gases by using absorbents based on ionized liquids, ammonia, limestone, magnesite, etc. This has reduced the level of pollution in 1984 to 88 percent of what it had been in 1976 despite increased industrial activity.[23]

Water from power station cooling systems is not contaminated with toxic substances, but it upsets the temperature regime of the waterways into which it is discharged and this affects living organisms. Nowadays, 70 percent of all power stations recycle this water after cooling it in reservoirs; it can then be used to breed trout and other warm-water fish. Some of the water is lost through evaporation, so the cycle is not entirely closed.

Atomic power stations are less polluting and many have been built in the European part of the Soviet Union. Some muted concern has been voiced regarding their safety,[24] but no official report has been published on the nuclear waste disaster that apparently occurred in the late 1950s in the Urals.[25] Emphasis is on safety precautions.[26] However, another unforseen danger to the environment may be caused by electromagnetic fields generated by high tension transmission cables, which are said to affect vegetation below them, while their proliferation might even alter the earth's magnetic field.[27]

Some income can be derived from the reuse of pollutants and, if prevention of damage is taken into account, calculations show that the average saving on dust could amount to 60 to 100 rubles per ton, on sulfur oxides 150 to 300 rubles per ton, on carbon oxides 27 to 70 rubles per ton, and on nitrogen oxides up to 350 rubles per ton.[28] Unfortunately, such theoretical calculations of overall costs of pollution and of the income obtained from the recovery and reuse of waste concern the economy as a whole whereas, for an individual plant, expenditure on antipollution measures is great and income from recycling very small. So it is cheaper for a polluting plant to pay fines than to install or modernize its purification systems; moreover, the fine is paid by the enterprise, not by the manager. Numerous cases are reported in the Soviet press of enterprises setting aside sums for the payment of fines and unashamedly including them in their annual and even longer-term financial plans. The regulation issued jointly by the State Committee for Labor and the Central Committee of Trade Union (29 May 1978) on loss of bonuses seems to have had little effect.

Sometimes, the worst offenders are major enterprises whose products are urgently needed by the country—therefore they have enough clout to circumvent the law. Not in distant Georgia or the backwoods of Siberia, but within the boundaries of Moscow itself, the well-known Dinamo electric engineering works still runs an antiquated and polluting foundry, and has managed for years to postpone the injunction of the sanitary inspectorate ordering its closure or complete reconstruction, which would inevitably interrupt the production flow of the plant's important electrical appliances.[29] Increasingly, voices are raised for strengthening the laws, making deliberate pollution a criminal offense, or at least making fines payable by managers personally.

The high cost of cleaning up old industries is not the only problem; damage to nature can be done by "savings" in the case of new industries. Thus for the construction of a dam and power station on the Zeia River, a tributary of the Amur, a large area of forest had to be flooded. Financially, it was worthwhile to fell only the best trees and leave the rest to rot at the bottom of the newly formed lake; the decaying trees absorbed the oxygen needed by fish while chips of broken twigs and bark clotted their fins, causing their death. Moreover, because of a shortage of tractors, the area began to be flooded before the cut logs were removed. Now they are floating on the surface and drift into the estuaries of the smaller rivers, polluting what was previously the spawning grounds of many varieties of fish, and in stormy weather, these logs are a danger to motorboat rudders. The irony is that in distant Leningrad, specialists in fish farming were drawing up plans to breed valuable fish species in the new Zeia lake, including the *omul*, which lives only in the purest of fresh waters.[30]

Also because of lower costs, as well as out of concern for the health of miners, open-pit mining has become widespread in the Soviet Union where up to two-thirds of all ores are extracted in this way. It may be quite acceptable in the underpopulated and agriculturally unproductive regions of Siberia, but is something of a disaster when iron ore is mined in the Kursk Magnetic Anomaly in the country's black earth belt, since open-pit mining damages ten times more land than underground mining. Already, 25,000 hectares of fertile land have been lost to agriculture and another 5,000 will be destroyed every five years. Because ore deposits slope vertically to a depth of 500 meters, heaps of rubble 50 to 80 meters high pile up along the trenches; topsoil, even if it is saved, cannot be stored for any amount of time, with the result that only 1 percent of the area has been recultivated. Even with better techniques, hardly 10 to 15 percent could be made usable again.[31]

Land, Forest, and Wildlife

In general, loss of agricultural land had become a serious problem in the Soviet Union. Of its total area of 22.4 million square kilometers, only 27 percent is suitable for agriculture since vast areas in the north lie in the permafrost belt and many southern regions are dry steppe or desert. Of the 6.1 million square kilometers of agricultural land, about 2.27 million square kilometers or 227 million hectares are arable. Between 1965 and 1971, 12 million hectares were diverted to nonagricultural use such as urban settlement, roads, airfields, strip mining, and huge reservoirs for hydropower stations that supply about 14 percent of the country's electricity. Another 40 to 50 million hectares are likely to be lost to agriculture before the year 2000. Because of these losses (and also the slow but steady increase in population), the ratio of arable land per inhabitant has fallen from 0.94 hectares in 1960 to 0.82 in 1980. In mountainous Georgia, it is down to 0.17 hectares.[32]

Since loss of agricultural land is caused by economic development, economic considerations might help decelerate these losses either if a price were set on the land alienated or if, at least, rehabilitation were made obligatory. A detailed land register (cadastre), now being compiled in the Soviet Union includes information on soil fertility; this work, started in the Lithuanian SSR in 1957, has been completed in several, but not all, Union Republics. When land is taken from collective or state farms, the industrial enterprise pays compensation commensurate with its value. This varies widely from 110 to 120 rubles per hectare in the arid regions of Kazakhstan or subarctic Iakutiia to 18,000 rubles per hectare in sunny Moldavia.

It has also been proposed that compensation be based on the value of the topsoil at the rate of 0.8 to 0.9 rubles per cubic meter. Depending on the thickness of this fertile layer, its total amount over one hectare is in the range of 2,000 to 4,000 cubic meters. The price of stripping, storing, and respreading it after mining operations have been completed, could cost up to 2,500 rubles per hectare if properly done, which is not always the case. The Scientific Research Institute on Prices has proposed that (under the tenth five-year plan, 1976–1980) enterprises pay six kopeks compensation per unit of produce (e.g., per ton of coal mined), but this does not take into account the fact that recultivated land is of poorer quality than it was previously; a fairer compensation should be much higher, anything up to fifty-five kopeks. Some enterprises, like the Kamysh-Burkun iron-mining combine in the Crimea, pay compensation "in kind" by returning one hectare of recultivated land for every one previously alienated.[33]

The shrinking area of agricultural land makes recultivation

an urgent problem. Considerable research has been done both in the methods of stripping and preserving topsoil and in finding plant species that would grow on impoverished recultivated land. The first studies in this field were designed to stabilize the surface of dusty ash and cinder wastes accumulating at coal-burning power stations. Among the pioneers in the search for annual and perennial plants and of methods of planting them and getting them to grow by adding enough topsoil, peat, and adequate fertilizers was the Laboratory (now the Department) of Industrial Botany of the University of the Urals where such experiments were started in the late 1950s. They were later expanded, in collaboration with the Ural Center of the AN SSSR, to slag heaps at coal and iron mines. Similar research has been carried out since the late 1960s and early 1970s in other research institutes, in particular for the Donets Basin (Donbas) industries by the Ukrainian Scientific Research Institute of Soil Science and Agrochemistry and Donetsk Botanical Garden using perennial grasses. On old slag heaps, some trees—elms and cherries—have been grown successfully but conifers and poplars usually die.[34]

The chances of success depend very much on the nature of the substratum. Thus land that has been disturbed by limestone or refractory clay quarries or even by coal mining holds out better prospects than slag heaps containing toxic metal salts at iron and nonferrous metal mines. Success or failure depends also on climate: in harsh northerly conditions, only a fraction of the seeds planted will germinate and only some of the seedlings take root and survive. Hence the growing worry about the destruction of the fragile tundra vegetation by the Siberian oil industry.

Even in more favorable climate conditions, the search for suitable plants is long and arduous, and up to 200 species have sometimes been tried, of which only a few undemanding natives from arid regions have prospered. Furthermore, plants tolerant of toxic salts may grow too toxic themselves to be fed to animals, so the reclaimed land can be used for recreational purposes only. Research is in progress on types of bacteria and algae (as well as on higher leguminous plants) that could contribute to soil formation. Despite many setbacks, work goes on and is becoming more rewarding; for instance, in Estonia, shrubs and even trees are now growing on former shale deposits and also in the Moscow brown coal basin.

Even more urgent than land recultivation in mining districts is the problem of reforestation throughout the country.

Indeed, the Soviet Union is fast losing its forests although the forested areas still amount to about 7.9 million square kilometers or 36 percent of its total territory. Since 1943, all forests are classified into three groups. Group 1 comprises forests where logging is allowed for "sanitary" purposes only: these forests cover an area of 194.3 million hectares or just under 16 percent of the total forested area (according to a 1973 survey) and may have been enlarged since through reforestation. They include agricultural shelter belts, green belts around towns and lakes, along rivers and roads, and on mountain slopes (especially in the Armenian, Kirgiz, and Tadzhik SSRs) and, since 1961, a wide belt (up to 150 kilometers) of pretundra forests designed to screen the interior of the country from arctic winds. Group 2 comprises small areas of carefully managed woods in the European part of the Soviet Union and plantations specifically grown for logging. Since many forests in group 1 and all in group 2 are situated in the European part of the country, they suffered badly during World War II when some twenty million hectares were felled or damaged by bombs, blast, and fire; even botanical gardens and protected areas like the Lapland Nature Reserve and Askaniia Nova were wrecked.[35] Even today these forests are not entirely immune from falling victim to planners more concerned with output than conservation. By far the largest is group 3 which covers 77 percent of the forested area and is the main source of all timber harvested in the Soviet Union. The only constraints to the overexploitation of these forests is their remoteness and the growing shortage of labor, especially in Siberia. Already along the Trans-Siberian and the BAM railways, overexploitation has reached dangerous proportions because wood is urgently needed for housing, pit props, railway sleepers, and simply for fuel.

Much reforestation is taking place in the European part of the Soviet Union, especially around urban centers. Under the tenth five-year plan, reforestation was taking place on over 2 million hectares annually. On paper, the number of hectares replanted should exceed those denuded; however, not all seedlings survive and, if the forest is left to renew itself naturally, aspen and birch displace the more valuable conifers (e.g., in Siberia, larch takes over from Siberian cedar). Cedar forests, which account for only 5.5 percent of the forested area, are particularly valuable for the quality of their wood and also for their nuts, resin, and the variety of the flora—mushrooms, medicinal herbs, and berries—sheltering in the undergrowth. Cedar nuts are rich in oil and used to be gathered in great quantities in bygone days; in 1912, up to

220,000 tons were harvested, but now that figure has fallen to barely 10,000 tons.[36]

Much of the wastefulness of the forest industry is due to transport difficulties—long hauls, lack of roads, shortage of vehicles. Therefore, although all trees are felled, only the better trunks are taken away while stumps, branches, and tops are left to rot. Often, transport organizations underfulfill their plans for moving the logs overland and floating them downstream may cause pollution when logs are not made into rafts: some logs are bound to sink at a bend of a river and obstruct the movement of others; the decaying timber piles up, reducing the flow of water and causing fish already badly affected by polluting motorboats to die. This is often the case of the numerous smaller, shallow, slow-flowing rivers that are, moreover, ice-bound for many months. The problem has become sufficiently acute for the State Committee for Science and Technology (GKNT) to have taken the matter in hand in 1981. Provisions for the protection of small rivers are outlined in the plan for 1981–1985 and up to 1990. Volunteers from the All-Union Society for the Protection of Nature organize occasional *subbotniki* (social or collective work gatherings) to clean up stretches of these rivers. Five thousand hydrological stations situated on the small rivers monitor their conditions, but the number of small rivers is over 25,000 and far in excess of the number of stations.[37] Larger rivers and sea ports fare somewhat better since sewage treatment plants are being built along landing stages and special garbage-collecting craft moor alongside incoming ships and unloading tankers to pump away waste waters and remove dry refuse, which they discharge into appropriate sewage and refuse treatment plants on shore.[38]

Much damage is done to forests by tractors dragging trees to the nearest haulage point and destroying the undergrowth. This can be avoided by the "vertical" method of felling, i.e., by cutting down a tree so that it falls vertically direct onto a truck. In the mountains of Georgia with its fine forests of oak and beech, lumberjacks descend from helicopters; they insert tiny explosive charges around the trunk of the selected tree, attach a cable lowered from the helicopter as far up the tree as possible, and as the charges blow up, the helicopter winches the tree upward and flies it to its destination. This is an expensive method but it saves building roads across mountainous terrain and prevents damage to the rest of the vegetation.[39]

To reduce the wastefulness of the forest industry, efforts are now in hand to process stumps, bark, branches, and undersize trees into hardboard, paper, and cellulose or use them as raw materials in the chemical industry. This involves locating such industries nearer the forested areas although this may also have adverse effects on the environment; this is illustrated by the case of Lake Baikal, which is still not completely immune (despite costly purification systems) from two giant pulp and paper mills. One is situated on the Selenga River leading into the lake, and the other is actually on its shores, although it is now being converted into a furniture factory.[40]

So far, the destruction of forests has been caused by their overexploitation and by forest fires—many due to human negligence. Aerial surveillance and experiments in artificially induced rain showers are now mitigating this evil. On the other hand, acid rain is becoming a threat. The deterioration of the arctic forests on the Kola peninsula are attributed to smoke belching from the Severonikel plant situated, most unfortunately, in the vicinity of the Lapland Nature Reserve. The withering of conifers (which are particularly vulnerable to acid rain) at Norilsk is also attributed to air pollution, although the recently built purification systems may reduce the danger.[41] At Bratsk, too, a large paper mill is similarly affecting local forests.

If acid rain is still a minor problem, the disappearance of wildlife is all too evident. Its protection is not the responsibility of the State Committee for Forestry, but that of the Department for the Protection of Nature, Nature Reserves (zapovedniki) and Hunting of the Ministry of Agriculture of the USSR. Since the main objective of this ministry is to increase agricultural production, there is an inherent contradiction in entrusting it to preserve large untouched and unploughed tracts of land that could otherwise be made economically productive, the more so as the ecologically richest lands are also the most fertile. No wonder scientists and local inhabitants have a hard time preserving such areas, particularly in the more densely populated regions.

Earlier attempts to preserve wildlife were designed to limit indiscriminate hunting for the benefit of the fur trade, although some nature reserves were founded for more scientific reasons. In 1951, the Chief Administrations of the Councils of Ministers of the Union Republics, which had been responsible for their respective protected areas, were abolished with the result that the total acreage of protected areas shrank to one-tenth of what it had been. The Azovo-Silvanskii, the Crimean, and even the Belovezhskaia pushcha became *hunting* reserves. The

Commission for the Protection of Nature of the AN SSSR succeeded in rescinding the decision to abolish the Altai, Zhiguli, and Kronovskii reserves, but the stay of execution lasted only until 1961. However, by the 1970s, the importance of nature reserves was at last recognized, and since 1976 their number has been gradually increased to the present 140 or 150 of which seven have been included into the international network of biosphere reserves.[42] Among the new reserves are the largest one on the Taimyr Peninsula in the far north—1,348,000 hectares—and the first protected aquatorium in the Bay of Peter the Great off the Sea of Japan. The area of the aquatorium amounts to some 63,000 hectares and also includes the littoral and the islands—another 1,300 hectares.

On the initiative of the AN SSSR, GOSPLAN and the GKNT jointly issued (27 April 1981) guidelines on nature reserves (*zapovedniki*), dendraria (arboreta), botanical and zoological gardens, suburban and national parks, protected areas (*zakazniki*), and natural beauty spots (*pamiatniki prirody*). Nature reserves (*zapovedniki*) are given the status of scientific institutions and are usually connected with one or several research institutions. They are most strictly protected: collecting plants, fishing, and trapping are forbidden without a license from the AN SSSR or the Academy of Sciences of the appropriate republic, as is the grazing of cattle and often tourism because, even when tourists do not indulge in vandalism, they frighten away birds, trample small plants, and inadvertently disturb wildlife. In the protected areas, only certain animals and plants are protected and economic activities are strictly limited. They are open to tourists, as are national parks and natural beauty spots.

The responsibility for enforcing their protection and financing their maintenance falls on the republics or local authorities, although grants may sometimes be obtained from the state budget. Apart from the major *zapovedniki*, which come under the Department for the Protection of Nature, Reserves, and Hunting of the Ministry of Agriculture of the USSR, smaller protected areas come under a variety of authorities. Recently several ancient monasteries, founded in what was formerly inaccessible wilderness, have been made into national memorials: e.g., the group of islands in the White Sea once the site of the famous Solovetskii Monastery (which for many years after the Revolution served as a labor camp), the Kirillo-Beloozerskii on Lake Beloe, which because of its secluded site has retained some of its primeval vegetation, and Kizhi on Lake Onega (now a museum of ancient wooden buildings) where some rare plants have survived despite it becoming a tourist attraction.[43]

The total area of all the *zapovedniki* amounts to 13.2 million hectares or about 0.5 percent of the territory of the Soviet Union, although when protected areas are added the figure rises to 8 percent. Apart from the Taimyr Peninsula, there are nine others deemed sufficiently large for their purpose, namely: Kronovskii (964,000 hectares), Altaiskii (863,900 hectares), Wrangel Island (793,700 hectares), Pechoro-Il'inskii (721,500 hectares), Saiano-Shushenskii (389,000 hectares), Sikhote-Alinskii (347,000 hectares), Kavkazskii (263,500 hectares), Barguzinskii (263,200 hectares), and Krasnovodskii (262,000 hectares). Apart from the Wrangel Island being made into a *zakaznik* in 1977 and the Saiano-Shushenskii (1980), the other seven had been organized prior to 1935 but suffered from the 1951 reorganization, and not all have recovered the whole of their former territory.

Zakazniki are more acceptable economically since restrictions on human activities there are only partial, and recently their numbers have increased, especially in the Maritime Province where the inclusion of the one on Lake Khanka has brought their number to fourteen and their combined area to a million hectares.[44]

It has been estimated that large herbivores require for their survival reserves of up to 260,000 hectares while those inhabiting the tundra need four times as much because they migrate in search of food. Even in the case of plants, 40,000 to 50,000 hectares are needed if *all* species of a given region are to be preserved. In the more southerly regions, with their richer flora, up to one million hectares are needed, a suggestion hardly to the liking of the Ministry of Agriculture! When it comes to the last surviving tigers and leopards in the Sikhote-Alinskii Reserve, even greater territory is required. Since 1947, tigers are a protected species and the fine for killing one is fixed at one thousand rubles. They are protected both as an endangered species and also for a more practical reason: the destruction of tigers benefits wolves, their less agile competitors, as well as wild dogs and their crossbred offspring, who are less fearful of approaching human habitations and carry off sheep grazing even in the vicinity of settlements.[45]

In advocating both more and larger reserves, some scientists adduce economic arguments, e.g., if 2 to 3 percent of the open steppe were dotted with small woods to conserve moisture, the yield of crops would increase dramatically. Similarly, if better conservation measures were taken by fisheries along the river Ob' or along the shores of the Kamchatka, their productivity would rise by millions of rubles. The money could be used to finance an all-union research center to coordinate the fragmented research work of local institutions.

Since some reserves are small and in other protected areas (*zakazniki*) only certain species of animals or plants are protected, different places are assigned different tasks from among the sixty projects in progress. Apart from the fundamental aims of preserving models of natural ecosystems and landscapes and to conserve the gene pool of organisms, Soviet nature reserves perform other functions such as planting trees, irrigating semiarid zones, propagating endangered species, and monitoring (especially in biosphere reserves) the changes brought about by human activities. With growing urbanization, some are designed to provide facilities for mass recreation as people increasingly seek green belts and national parks to satisfy their physiological and psychological needs. Moreover, reserves contribute to the spread of environmental education.

Even small reserves, which are quite inadequate as models of virgin nature, are invaluable for scientific research and the breeding of endangered species. This is true of the Prioksko-terrasnyi, the Tsentral'no-chernozemnyi (Central Black Earth), and the Berezinskii—now all included in the international network of biosphere reserves.

The provision of biosphere reserves is a fairly novel endeavor promoted by Dr. Michel Batisse, UNESCO senior environmental adviser, to provide models of conservation allowing for rational economic development. Whereas the central core is a strictly protected area, various human activities like agriculture and forestry are permitted in the surrounding buffer zone. This zone usually houses one or more research institutions whose work consists both in the study of atmospheric, botanical, zoological, and other natural aspects of the reserve and also of the human impact—adverse or beneficent—on it and especially on its buffer zone.

All three biosphere reserves mentioned, located as they are in the long-settled regions of the European part of the country, comprise a core of fairly unspoiled countryside, but are surrounded by intense economic activities. The Prioksko-terrasnyi Reserve on the left bank of the Oka, more or less opposite the town of Pushchino, contains the Institute of Agrochemistry and Soil Science of the AN SSSR with its experimental station and 75,000 hectares of the former forest, Russkii Les, now scheduled to become a national park. Much of the forest has been cut down, but trees are now being replanted and wild boar, deer, and beaver reintroduced. This reserve played an outstanding role in rescuing the *zubr* or European bison from extinction. In the Caucasus, the last of these animals was killed in 1928 and a mere eight specimens survived World War II in the Belovezhskaia pushcha. Owing to their successful breeding in the Prioksko-terrasnyi Reserve, the number of these beasts (some crossed with American buffalo) has now risen to something like 700 and the breed reintroduced into the Caucasian Nature Reserve and some others deemed suitable. Other endangered species, such as the white crane from Iakutiia of which there remained apparently only about 300 birds, are also bred there and then returned to their former habitat, for the Prioksko-terrasnyi is far too small to support its animal population unless their numbers are kept down by export or slaughter. Among its monitoring work, this reserve checks on acid rain, the acidity of which at times reaches 5.5—4 pH affecting lichens even more than trees.[46]

An even smaller biosphere reserve, the Tsentral'no-chernozemnyi, specializes in the monitoring of the human impact on nature. This reserve consists of three plots of fairly undamaged steppe that survived because they were used only as commons for cattle grazing. Later, the experimental grounds of the Kursk Institute of Geography of the AN SSSR and those of the Institute of Agriculture and Land Protection Against Erosion were added, as well as a buffer zone comprising the slag heaps of the Mikhailov ore-enriching combine and the reservoir of the Kursk atomic power station.[47]

Somewhat larger is the Berezinskii Biosphere Reserve in Belorussia, covering an area of 76,200 hectares and stretching in a narrow band some fifteen kilometers wide for sixty kilometers along the Berezina River. It was started in 1925 as a sanctuary for beaver and later (1928) also for elk; during World War II, both the beaver and elk farms were destroyed, but have been restored since. In 1951, it suffered, like many others, by becoming a hunting reserve; 4,000 hectares of forest were cut down and the animals decimated. On the insistence of several members of the Belorussian Academy of Sciences, it was made into a local nature reserve and in 1961 it was transferred to the Department for the Protection of Nature, Nature Reserves, and Hunting of the Ministry of Agriculture of the USSR. Although roughly 60 percent of the area is marshlands criss-crossed by the Berezina and some fifty small streams, nearly 65,000 hectares are wooded; birch and aspen have succeeded pine, especially on land previously cleared for agriculture. Since 1966, efforts have been made to introduce the *zubr* as well as elk and boar. Ussuri dogs, wolves, and American mink have become pests, and hunting them is allowed in the buffer zone. About 7,000 hectares of the latter, previously collective farm fields, are now occupied by a natural history museum and scientific institutions working on various UNESCO MAB programs, including the impact of agriculture on woodlands and on air pollution.[48]

Environmental Education

Another aspect of nature reserve work is its contribution to environmental education by means of conducted tours organized by schools or members of the Societies for the Protection of Nature.

In its broadest meaning, environmental education includes television wildlife programs, press coverage, and formal education in schools and universities. The 29 December 1978 decree *O doponitel'nykh merakh po usileniiu okhrany prirody i ratsional'nomu ispol'zovaniiu prirodnykh resursov* included a paragraph ordering the building of a special pavilion at the permanent Exhibition of the Achievements of the National Economy illustrating the protection of nature and the publication of a new journal, *Priroda i chelovek*, the first issue of which came out in July 1981. In July 1979, an all-union conference took place in Minsk, which passed a number of resolutions directed at the Ministry of Education of the USSR and those of the Union Republics, the Central Committee of the Komsomol, the State Committee for Technical and Vocational Training, the Ministry of Higher and Secondary Specialized Education of the USSR and those of the Union Republics, the State Committee for Publishing and the Book Trade, the State Committee for Cinematography, and the Councils of the Societies for the Protection of Nature—all of which were called upon to disseminate ecological information and to contribute to formal and informal environmental education in their respective fields. An exhibition of posters illustrating conservation measures was held in Moscow from November 1978 to February 1979. The Soviet Union also took part in the festival of ecology films, the first of which was held in Czechoslovakia in 1979 with the award-winning Soviet film showing the deleterious effects on river runoff which results from the draining of marshes.[49] That same year, the first "red book" of endangered animal species was published by A. G. Bannikov and his team, to be followed by several others on both plants and animals in the Union Republics.

On 18 April 1979, the Ministry of Higher and Secondary Specialized Education issued a set of instructions on the introduction of courses in environmental conservation. Even faculties of social sciences were to provide courses in the methodological, philosophical, and economic aspects of *prirodopol'zovanie*. More specialized courses on dust and smoke abatement, air and water purification systems, etc., were to be taught in higher technical and secondary schools preparing engineers and technicians for industries liable to cause the emission of pollutants. Diploma projects, as well as more advanced research in environmental protection methods and devices, were to be encouraged, ranging from new types of coagulating and absorbing agents and catalysts to the designing of closed-cycle production processes. More research was to be done on the recultivation of slag heaps, fish farming, and mutagenic agents. The inextricable complexity of most environmental research projects made it advisable for several—often highly specialized institutes—to combine into interdisciplinary centers. One such federation of institutions existed already, namely the North Caucasian Regional Scientific Center, which encompassed several higher education institutions (VUZ) in the towns of Rostov, Novocherkassk, Krasnodar, Stavropol', and those of Daghestan. This center had established close relations with major industrial enterprises such as Atom-mash, Rostsel'mash, Azot, and the oil industries of the Groznyi region. As a result, gas in these oil fields is no longer flared off, but put to good use.

Among other leading institutions in the field of environmental education is the Technological Institute of Belorussia where a Chair of Nature Protection has been established. It draws up appropriate programs for other VUZ in the republic. The Ministry of Higher Education of Belorussia has organized special seminars for lecturers in this field. At the University of the Urals in Sverdlovsk, there is also a Chair of Biogeocenosis (ecosystems) and Nature Protection; it provides courses that are a part of the normal syllabus for biology and chemistry students, as well as optional ones for students in other faculties. There are also more specialized courses in the ecology of plants, animals, and soils, as was well as one on the theory of the noosphere based on the works of V. I. Vernadskii. The Department of Industrial Botany conducts experiments in recultivation on areas totalling

5,000 hectares and publishes its own journal, *Rasteniia i promyshlennaia sreda (Plants and Industrial Environment)*.

Long before the 1977 Tbilisi Intergovernmental Conference on Environmental Education, the subject was taught informally as an out-of-school activity by Komsomol and Young Pioneer organizations. At the Tbilisi conference, the Soviet Union undertook to carry out a project on the feasibility and organization of environmental studies. The faculties of natural science and of geography of the Kiev Institute of Education, in collaboration with the Central Young Naturalists' Association and the Scientific Research Pedagogical Institute of the Ukrainian SSR, inaugurated a project on "the methodology and interdisciplinary research concerning the integration of school and society in the field of environmental education." A number of schools, as well as several communities with different physical, ecological, social, and economic characteristics took part in this project conducted mainly by means of questionnaires.

Within the Academy of Pedagogical Sciences of the USSR, a Laboratory of Ecological Education (*prirodookhranitel'nogo prosveshcheniia*) was set up with a staff of ten as part of its Institute of the Content and Methods of Teaching. During the 1976–1980 five-year period, its research centered on establishing the interdisciplinary nature of environmental education, while, during the 1980–1985 period, the emphasis was on how to develop in pupils a sense of responsibility towards their environment, including moral and legal issues.

Environmental education has become an integral part of science and arts lessons, particularly those in biology, geography, and productive labor. A textbook, *Okhrana prirody (Safeguarding of Nature)* by K. V. Pashkang, was published in 1983 for use in schools where environmental education is taught as a special optional course. Early in 1980, an all-union conference on the problems of environmental education was held in Tallin, Estonia. Discussions ranged from ways of integrating the subject into the school curriculum, using it to strengthen a Marxist world view among pupils, to the need for retraining teachers by means of special refresher courses. The most imaginative papers dealt with out-of-school activities, emphasizing local conditions. Some of these activities are on a considerable scale, e.g., in Estonia and some Ukrainian towns, the young have created parks on derelict sites and planted millions of seedlings. Pupils form "green" and "blue" patrols; the greens patrol woods to detect poachers and vandals and also enforce a "month of silence" to enable birds to brood in peace; the blues keep an eye on lakes and rivers, especially on spawning grounds. They investigate possible sources of pollution by observing the proliferation of algae or by taking samples of water to be analyzed during chemistry classes.

There are also many summer "rest and work" camps and juvenile forestry and agricultural communities; some of these have become quite famous like the Berendei in Karelia and others in the Urals, Briansk Province, and in Transcarpathia. In 1979, in the RSFSR they numbered seven thousand, covering an area of 2 million hectares and attracting 300,000 youngsters annually. Belorussia even boasts a Junior Forest Academy; it is run on the lines of extension courses and has two faculties, one of silviculture and one of forest conservation. Introductory lectures are given by members of the Belorussian Technological Institute. The Ministry of Forests has organized "consultation points" for the students in its twelve forestry enterprises. In the following year, the teenagers do some practical work in the morphology and systems of forest plants. After three summers, the youngsters get a certificate that facilitates their entry into technical colleges that emphasize forestry.[50] There are, of course, excursions to natural science museums and to nature reserves, the latter a somewhat mixed blessing for nature.[51]

Conclusions

What conclusions can be drawn from this mosaic of random reports? Are environmental problems only written about or are they tackled effectively, and can the present worldwide destruction of nature be halted if not reversed? The variety and abundance of the literature on environmental problems shows the awareness by those in power of the dangers ahead and the anxiety among certain sections of the population.[52] But material progress cannot be achieved without plundering and polluting the planet. The best hope is that it will proceed with less ruthlessness, waste, and speed. Difficult choices will have to be made—agriculture in southern Russia and Central Asia desperately needs the waters of the northern and Siberian rivers—some waters will have to be diverted, but it is hoped not enough to affect the climate of the Arctic regions. The Caspian and the Aral Seas are doomed to shrink and lose their natural fish stocks, but other species may be found to succeed them. *Prirodopol'zovanie* will prevail over conservation but, one hopes it will become increasingly *ratsional'noe*—that is more cautious, better informed, and less predatory and destructive.

Postscript

The Chernobyl atomic power station disaster occurred several months after the present chapter was written. It affected the environment not only in the Ukraine and Belorussia, but even countries beyond the borders of the Soviet Union. The effects of radiation are insidious and long-term and will become fully manifest only in the years to come. Emergency measures were taken to evacuate people and livestock from the most affected zone within a radius of thirty kilometers, but were they taken soon enough and carried out quickly enough? Poultry and geese were not evacuated; how did radiation affect them? They still lay eggs, but what kind of chicks are hatching from them, and have they undergone mutations? What about wildlife and plants? Will fruit trees bear fruit in the forthcoming years, and will it be edible or still contaminated? Topsoil has been removed from the fields and buried or else ploughed in as deep as special ploughs allowed; grass mowed from meadows has been buried too. Has this achieved complete decontamination or will unforseen dangers persist in the most affected area from tiny specks of radioactive cesium or some other, perhaps yet unknown or ill-understood, material? There are so many questions that will take years to answer with any certainty.

Notes

1. E. V. Girusov, "Normativnyi aspekt ekologicheskoi nauki" in E. T. Faddeev ed., *Tsennostnye aspekty nauki i problemy ekologii* (Moscow, 1981), 236–257; also I. N. Moiseev, *Chelovek, priroda, obshchestvo* (Moscow, 1982), 215 and 225–229.

2. *Priroda* (1979), no. 10, 119.

3. O. N. Ianitskii, "Ekopolis, zhelaemoe i dostignutoe," *Sotsial'nye issledovaniia* (1985), no. 1, 67–68.

4. *Priroda* (1979), no. 1, 28–31.

5. R. A. Scriabin, "U.S.-Soviet Progress on the Protection of Northern Ecosystems: A Commentary," *Arctic and Alpine Research* (1978), no. 1, 553–557.

6. N. Gogol', "Zemli prekrasnye cherty," *Priroda i chelovek* (1985), no. 2, 18.

7. V. G. Sokolovskii, "Grani miunkhenskogo konsensusa," *Priroda i chelovek* (1985), no. 5, 42. In 1980, the emission of sulphur dioxide in the Soviet Union was estimated at 25 million tons, but since 1983 it has been reduced to 23 million tons.

8. "Pervyi mezhdunarodnyi seminar 'Metody bioindikatsii okruzhaiushchei sredy v raionakh atomnykh elektrostantsii'," *Energiia* (1985), no. 3, 62.

9. Apparently two volumes of these forecasts edited by I. P. Gerasimov were published in very small editions (possibly for internal use only) under the title *Priroda 1980* and *Priroda 1990*, and are not available in libraries in the United Kingdom or the United States. Extracts from them have been quoted by Boris Komarov (pseud.) in his *The Destruction of Nature in the Soviet Union* (White Plains, 1980).

10. There are discrepancies between the amounts allocated in the plans, i.e., 11 billion rubles for 1976–1980, and those actually spent probably due to the unavailability or shortage of the necessary technical plant or personnel. According to Z. Nuriev, "V interesakh nyneshnikh i budushchikh pokolenii," *Kommunist* (1983), no. 15, 80, 9.3 billion rubles were spent during that period and 10.3 should be spent during 1980–1985.

11. N. F. Fedorenko and N. F. Reimers, "Sblizhenie ekonomicheskikh i ekologicheskikh tselei v okhrane prirody," *Priroda* (1981), no. 9, 3–12.

12. Kh. Luik, "Upravlenie prirodopol'zovaniem v raione (opyt Estonskoi SSR)," *Voprosy ekonomiki* (1984), no. 1, 55–67.

13. T. S. Khachaturov, *Ekonomika prirodopol'zovaniia* (Moscow, 1982), 155–159.

14. According to B. N. Laskorin, 2 million hectares of agricultural land have been damaged largely through open-pit mining. See B. Ukraintsev and B. N. Laskorin, "Tretii faktor," *Priroda i chelovek* (1985), no. 4, 38.

15. B. Krylov, "Bezkar'ernaia idilliia," *Priroda i chelovek* (1985), no. 3, 28–31.

16. Ukaintsev and Laskorin, *Priroda i chelovek*, 39.

17. Iu. Iu. Tupitsia, *Ekologo-ekonomicheskaia effektivnost' prirodopol'zovaniia* (Moscow, 1980), 63; L. Eremin, "Intensivnee proizvodstvo: Intensivnee mery okhrany prirody," *Kommunist* (1985), no. 8, 52.

18. D. L. Kartvelishvili and Topuridze, "Soprichastnost'," *Priroda i chelovek* (1985), no. 2, 9–12.

19. Ibid., 12; P. A. Kaplin and L. G. Nikiforov, "Zashchita morskikh beregov ot razmyva," *Priroda* (1985), no. 1, 69–79.

20. E. E. Syroechkovskii and F. R. Shtil'mark, "Zapovedniki i zakazniki krainego Severa SSSR i perspektivy razvitiia," in E. E. Syroechkovskii, ed., *Okhrana i ratsional'noe ispol'zovanie biologicheskikh resursov Krainego Severa* (Moscow, 1983), 282.

21. O. F. Balatskii, L. G. Mel'nik, and A. F. Iakovlev, *Ekonomika i*

kachestvo okruzhaushchei sredy (Moscow, 1984), 51.

22. Balatskii et al, *Ekonomika*, 7.

23. S. D. Khodorovskaia, "Ekonomika—strazh prirody," *Energiia* (1985), no. 1, 38–40; V. V. Zhabo, "Okhrana prirody— zadacha kompleksnaia," ibid., 40–47.

24. N. Dollezhal and Iu. Koriakin, "Iadernaiia elektroenergetika: dostizheniia i problemy," *Kommunist* (1979), no. 14, 19–28.

25. Z. Medvedev, *Nuclear Disaster in the Urals* (London: Angus & Robertson, 1979).

26. A State Committee for the Supervision of Safety in Nuclear Power was set up in 1983, *Izvestiia*, 30 July and 3 August 1983; see also B. N. Laskorin, ed., *Okhrana okruzhaiuschie sredy na predpriiatiiakh atomnoi promyshlennosti* (Moscow, 1982).

27. N. M. Mamedov, "Ekologicheskaia problema i tekhnicheskie nauki," *Voprosy filisofii* (1980), no. 5, 116.

28. Khodorovskaia, *Energiia*, 18.

29. B. Antishin, "Gde zhe Vanechka?" *Priroda i chelovek* (1985), no. 4, 32.

30. Iu. Il'iashenko, "Edinichnyi topliak," *Priroda i chelovek* (1985), no. 3, 12–17.

31. V. S. Bobrinskaia, "Mozhno li sokhranit' zemli KMA?" *Priroda* (1981), no. 11, 80–88.

32. Khachaturov, *Ekonomika*, 95; Kartvelishvili and Topuridze, *Priroda i chelovek*, 10.

33. V. Gordov, "Rekul'tivatsiia i effektivnost' plodorodnykh pochv," *Voprosy ekonomiki* (1979), no. 11, 61–70; N. Feitelman, "Upravlenie prirodopol'zovaniem, *Voprosy ekonomiki* (1984), no. 3, 59–60.

34. G. M. Pikalova, "Itogi 15-letnikh nauchno-issledovatel'skikh rabot laboratorii promyshlennoi botaniki po rekul'tivatsii zemel', narushennykh promyshlennost'iu," *Rasteniia i promyshlennaia sreda* (Sverdlovsk, 1978), 5–11; I. Chernyshenko, "Zelenye terrikony," *Energiia* (1984), no. 7, 48–49; E. N. Kondratiuk, "Sokhranit' i priumnozhit'" in E. N. Kondratiuk and A. Z. Didova, eds., *Priroda vokrug nas* (Donbas, 1978), 88–90.

35. N. N. Smirnov, "Voennye razrusheniia biosfery," *Priroda* (1981), No. 9, 63; Iu. G. Noskov, "Ekologicheskie posledstviia minuvshei voiny," *Priroda* (1985), no. 3, 17.

36. G. Murashov, "Dolgii put' k kedrogradu," *Priroda i chelovek* (1985), no. 5, 34.

37. A. K. Subbotin, "Sud'ba malykh rek," *Priroda* (1981), no. 10, 2–13.

38. V. Sadovenko, "Slagaemye uspekha," *Rechnoi transport*, (1984), no. 5, 27; V. S. Chernyi, "Portovyi dvornik," in Kondratiuk and Didova, *Priroda*, 78–79.

39. Personal interview with director of the Scientific Research Institute of Forestry and the Mechanization of Sylviculture, Sochi, 1983.

40. Jean McCallister, "The Greening of Baikal? *Detente* (1985), no. 2, 9–11.

41. A. P. Poliakov, N. S. Pukhanov, and A. I. Solomakha, "Ob okhrane prirody okrestnostei goroda Norilska," in Syroechkovskii, *Okhrana*, 112; V. V. Kriuchkov, "Rekul'tivatsiia narushennykh zemel' severa," *Priroda* (1985), no. 7, 68–77; Andrew R. Bond, "Air Pollution in Norilsk: A Soviet Worst Case," *Soviet Geography* (November, 1984), 665–680.

42. V. E. Sokolov and K. D. Zykov, "Problemy zapovednogo dela," *Priroda* (1983), no. 8, 32–33; A. M. Borodin, Iu. Isakov, and V. V. Krinitskii, "The System of Nature-Protected Areas in the USSR: Biosphere Reserves as Part of the System" (paper presented at the First International Congress of Biosphere Reserves, Minsk, 1983), 122–127; B. V. Vinogradov, "Aerospace Studies of Protected National Areas in the USSR," ibid., 398–407.

43. V. E. Sokolov et al., "Problemy zapovednogo dela," *Priroda*, no. 8, 32–53; Syroechkovskii and Shtil'mark, in Syroechkovskii, *Okhrana*, 259–285; summary of the 1981 regulations on protected areas in *Priroda* (1981), no. 12, 104.

44. A. V. Zhirmunskii, "Okhrana prirody na Dal'nem Vostoke," *Priroda* (1979), no. 8, 53–71; V. M. Urosov, "V Primor'e neobkhodim natsional'nyi prirodnyi park," *Priroda* (1984), no. 7, 57–65; *Golos rodiny* (1984), no. 27.

45. Zhirmunskii, *Priroda*, 72–75; V. N. Zhivichenko, "Khishchniki, kopytnye, chelovek—gde garmoniia, a gde tragediia," *Priroda* (1984), no. 6, 45–51.

46. V. A. Kovda, A. S. Kerzhenets, A. S. Blistanov, and L. V. Zabolotskaia, "Prioksko-terrasnyi biosfernyi zapovednik," *Priroda* (1981), no. 1, 74–84.

47. A. M. Grin, V. D. Utekhin, O. S. Ignatenko, and A. M. Krasnitskii, "Tsentral'no-chernozemnyi biosfernyi zapovednik," *Priroda* (1981), no. 9, 30–40.

48. V. I. Parfenov and M. V. Kudin, "Berezinskii biosfernyi zapovednik," *Priroda* (1983), no. 6, 2–11.

49. K. N. Blagosklonov, "Eko-film—79," *Priroda* (1980), no. 2, 13–15.

50. E. Koutaissoff, "Environmental Education in the USSR," in J. J. Tomiak, ed., *Soviet Education in the 1980s* (London: Croom Helm, 1983), 85–105.

51. N. S. Aralova and K. D. Zykov, "USSR Nature Reserves: Their Role in Environmental Education" (paper presented at the First International Congress of Biosphere Reserves), 528–531; T. S. Elias, "Rare and Endangered Species of Plants: The Soviet Side," *Science*, vol. 219 (1983), 22–23.

52. Indeed, a whole session of the Supreme Soviet on 3 July 1985 was taken up by the discussion of shortcomings and downright breaches of environmental legislation, such as the continuing malpractice of starting production at new plants before the purification systems were installed. The final resolution, "On the Observance of the Demands of the Legislation on the Protection of Nature and the Rational Utilization of Natural Resources," directed the Council of Ministers—among other

measures—to elaborate a long-term state program for the protection of nature and the rational utilization of natural resources. One of the speakers, S. K. Grossu, even suggested that this ecological program be given the same prominence as those on food and energy (*Izvestiia*, 4 July 1985).

PHILIP R. PRYDE

3

The Soviet Approach to Environmental Impact Analysis

There is general agreement among geographers, biologists, and planners that the environmental impacts of proposed landscape-transforming projects should be carefully assessed prior to the start of construction. The purpose of such studies is to determine what significant adverse effects the project could have on the environment, and how such impact can be mitigated (that is, reduced in severity) or avoided.

In the United States, such studies are required on federally funded projects, under provisions of the National Environmental Policy Act (NEPA) of 1970, and are known as environmental impact studies (EIS). Many states, too, require similar reports on local projects.

Soviet Environmental Impact Studies

In recent years, the Soviet Union has shown a realization that studies of this type must be carried out if major environmental problems are to be avoided. However, there appears to be no direct equivalent of NEPA, which specifies the conditions under which environmental reports must be carried out and what they must contain. Nevertheless, various legislative acts have been passed at the all-union level that govern the use of land, water, air, fauna, and other resources. Although these do not specifically require preliminary environmental studies, all contain generalized wording about "conservation," "preservation," and "preventing harmful actions," all of which suggest that environmental considerations should be studied as part of the normal process of project planning.[1]

In addition, the 1980 Soviet statute on wildlife, "Measures for the Protection of the Animal World," includes in article 21 a provision for "the organization of scientific studies aimed at substantiating measures for the protection of the animal world."[2] However, none of the key words "mandatory," "mitigation," or "in advance" is incorporated into the wording of this section.

The Soviet constitution itself, in the latest version enacted in 1977, contains several provisions relating to natural resource conservation. Article 67 requires all citizens to conserve nature, article 42 assures the right of a healthy human environment, and article 18 calls for the rational, scientific use of the plant and animal kingdoms.[3] These sections, embodied as they are in the highest legal document of the country, provide important justification and incentive for environmental conservation in the Soviet Union.

Other actions taken at the national level include the creation of centralized commissions, directorates, and planning bodies with responsibility for the health of the Soviet environment. The most important of these is the Commission on Environmental Protection and Rational Use of Natural Resources, which is directly under the Presidium of the Soviet Council of Ministers. It functions in much the same manner as the president's Council on Environmental Quality (CEQ) in the United States, providing advice and recommendations to governmental leaders. There also exists within the State Planning Agency (GOSPLAN) the Department of Nature Conservation. The Soviet State Committee for Hydrometeorology and the Protection of the Environment (GIDROMET) is responsible for monitoring pollution and maintaining biosphere viability. Responsibility for renewable resources and preserves belongs to the Department for the Protection of Nature, Nature Reserves, and Hunting.[4]

Regardless of legal requirements, it has been clear for some time that certain major Soviet projects of the past have had unforeseen harmful consequences. Probably the best known example was the great loss of water from the Caspian Sea that followed the construction of the large dams on the Volga River, resulting in significant problems for navigation, agriculture, and fisheries. In a similar manner, the Azov Sea has been increasingly salinized from reductions in the flow of the Don River (for the location of placenames referred to in the text, see Figure 3.1). In both cases, fish stocks have suffered greatly, with sizable losses to the economy.

The environmental wisdom of routinely opting for large reservoirs is now openly debated, and the dialogue concerns such resultant adverse effects as shoreline erosion, siltation, algae build-up, fish losses at dams, loss of wildlife habitat, and climatic changes.[5] Part of the reason was succinctly stated in *Izvestiia*:

> Nobody will build a dam 50 centimeters higher or lower than the design calls for. But if the area of the reservoir exceeds the figure in the design by tens or hundreds (or even thousands) of square kilometers, what institute or designer finds this disturbing or gives it precise considerations?
>
> Every project must have its own designing norms and norms of permissible error, of course, but . . . while these norms are inviolate for hydraulic-engineering structures, they are essentially nonexistent for reservoirs.
>
> It's difficult to name a reservoir where all parameters correspond to the design, and all the consequences of the reservoir's construction have been provided for. Who foresaw . . . at the Kakhovka hydroelectric station's reservoir the overgrowth, the water bloom, and all the undesirable conditions that were created there? . . . Who anticipated the sharp falloff in the rated output of the Novosibirsk hydroelectric station on the Ob', the losses to agriculture on the Don or the losses to fisheries on the Volga?[6]

As a result of problems such as these, over the past two decades, the probable environmental effects of major projects have been studied ever more in advance. The first highly publicized instance of this was the controversy over two new wood-processing plants along Lake Baikal, which began in the 1960s.[7] In certain cases involving extremely important resources, such as Lake Baikal and the Volga-Caspian region, special commissions or even new institutes (such as the Institute of the Ecology of the Volga Basin) have been established to help maintain the environmental vitality of the entire region.[8] Today, major projects generally receive considerable advance environmental study.

An example of a fairly broad Soviet environmental impact study (and one that uses that phrase in its title), is one carried out for the Kansk-Achinsk fuel and energy complex (KATEK) in East

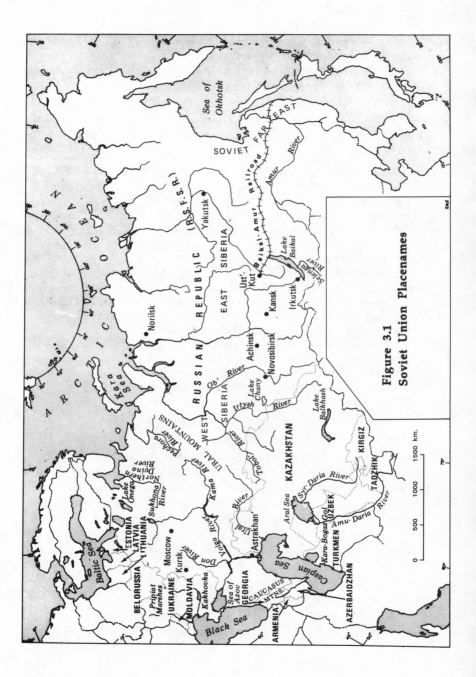

Figure 3.1
Soviet Union Placenames

Siberia.[9] KATEK is a vast coal mining-thermal power plant development that could ultimately involve extracting as much as one billion tons of coal.[10] The environmental study for this project, conducted under the supervision of the Institute for Applied Physics in Moscow, addressed the impact on hydrology, air quality, water quality, forests, and climate that could result from the project. The study suggested that it might be advisable, given the high potential for adverse impact, to limit the project to two strip mines and two power stations (instead of four of each). As further mitigation, it recommended enlarging the size of the cooling reservoirs, instituting a water recycling system, and reducing the volume of waste products.

Of all the reports listed in the bibliography and reviewed for the present chapter, the work done in connection with the Kansk-Achinsk project appeared to most resemble a comprehensive environmental impact statement of the type carried out under NEPA. On the basis of ongoing environmental studies, once the project is underway a subsequent decision could be made on design modifications for the second phase of the project. A number of these ongoing studies, involving soils, forests, groundwater, sulfur transport, and atmospheric studies, were published in summary form in 1984.[11] Despite all this, reports have appeared in the Soviet press noting severe air pollution from this operation.[12]

The question arises, however, whether other projects, not quite so large in scale, are receiving timely and comprehensive environmental analyses. Various articles in the Soviet press suggest that they are not. For example, construction was well underway on an apatite processing plant on the Selenga River, which drains into Lake Baikal, when it was discovered that it would probably pollute both underground and surface waters. Only after prolonged public complaints did the design institute for the plant propose that a special center be created to study the potential harmful environmental impact of the plant.[13]

Among large Soviet projects, the ones receiving the most intensive environmental study at present are, without question, the various large-scale water diversion proposals.

Assessing Water Transfers

The most significant of the environment-altering projects being considered in the Soviet Union today are the various proposals to transfer water from large northern rivers south into the Caspian and Aral Sea basins and Central Asia.

These proposals themselves are, in part, a form of mitigation for previous environmental transformations, such as building large reservoirs on the Volga River and diverting large volumes of water from the Volga, Ural, Amu Dar'ia, and Syr Dar'ia Rivers for irrigation. The adverse consequences of these diversions was inadequately studied or understood at the time; as a result, the shorelines of both the Caspian and Aral Seas have significantly receded, producing economic problems.[14] The Aral Sea in particular has been markedly reduced in area (see Figure 3.2). A variety of proposals has been offered to remedy the situation, including a suggestion to partition the sea into two separate water bodies.[15]

In addition, previous efforts to alleviate these problems have sometimes been environmentally questionable and, on occasion, even counterproductive. For example, the flow of water from the Caspian Sea into the Kara-Bogaz Gol (the latter acting as a large, shallow evaporation basin) was stopped in 1980 to reduce evaporative losses from the Caspian. But so many problems were

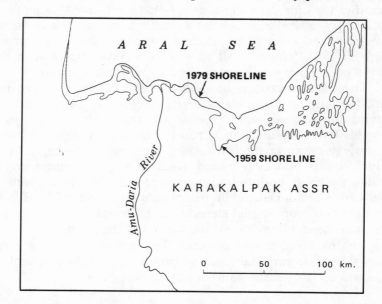

Figure 3.2 Decline in Aral Sea Shoreline

Source: Adapted from A. A. Rafikov, "Environmental Change in the Southern Aral Region in Connection with the Drop in the Aral Sea level," *Soviet Geography: Review and Translation*, vol. 22, no. 6 (June 1981), 353–360.

caused by the newly exposed salt pans on the bottom of the formerly inundated gol, and by the loss of replenishment salts from the Caspian to maintain the local chemical salt industry, that four years later it was decided it would be best to partially reflood it, and by early 1985 this had been done.[16]

To correct these problems, and to provide for additional irrigation in the southern European steppes, several schemes have been studied to divert water from northern European rivers, such as the Northern Dvina or the Pechora, into the Volga River system.[17] These European water transfers, when completed, would produce more hydroelectricity at the existing Volga River dams, and would also benefit the ecological balance at the important Astrakhan *zapovednik* (nature preserve) in the Volga estuary.

Simultaneously, other studies looked at even larger transfers from the Ob'-Irtysh River system into the Aral Sea basin via the Tobol' River (see Figure 3.3). The additional water supplies would permit increased irrigation in Kazakhstan and Central Asia, and also could be used to stabilize the surface level of the Aral Sea. These West Siberian transfer proposals represent huge engineering projects; one version would have involved a diversion canal 2,550 kilometers long capable of moving 27.2 cubic kilometers of water a year to Central Asia.[18] However, some of these proposed transfers themselves contain significant potential problems, some global in their possible impact. The most serious of these are potential changes in the amount of ice cover in the Kara Sea and Arctic Ocean that could be caused by reductions in the volume of Ob' River discharge, which if realized might have worldwide climatic repercussions.[19]

In the absence of a generic law mandating standardized environmental impact analyses, the Soviet Union relies on studies carried out by various scientific research institutes. For the water diversion projects, these include such organizations as the State Hydrometeorological Institute, the Arctic and Antarctic Institute, and the Institute of Geography and others associated with the Soviet Academy of Sciences. These institutes contribute to a coordinated environmental research program, in existence since 1976, which was created by the State Committee on Science and Technology. This research program is headed by G. V. Voropaev, Director of the Institute of Water Problems. With regard to the potential Arctic Ocean problems noted above, Voropaev has given assurances that "the plans take into account the possible environmental changes cited by the opponents of the canal. Studies conducted over a period of many years . . . show that

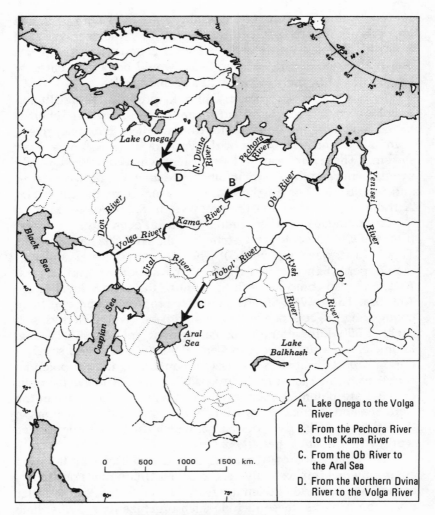

Figure 3.3 Proposed Soviet Water Diversions

global environmental changes will not occur with the planned volumes of diversion."[20]

The various environmental studies that are prepared for a project apparently are incorporated into, or at least accompany, the basic technical-economic studies for the project.[21] Although sometimes a single comprehensive report is prepared, it also happens that there might appear a number of studies by several authors on different aspects of the project. On occasion, these may embody varying conclusions or recommendations.[22] In the case of the proposed river diversions, a very large number of analytical studies have appeared in the geographic journals of the Academy of Sciences.[23]

These studies outline potential problem areas and suggest possible mitigation measures, but the more important question is whether such mitigation programs are actually carried out. In the case of the river diversions, the main effect has been lengthy delays to allow still more intensive engineering and environmental studies. One diversion proposal, from the Pechora to the Kama River ("B" on Figure 3.3), seemed imminent in the late 1960s but subsequently took on a lower priority. The West Siberian river diversions, long referred to by many as "essential," by 1985 had been placed in a secondary developmental priority to less costly diversions from smaller European rivers such as the Sukhona (tributary of the Northern Dvina), and from such lakes as Onega, Lacha, and Vozhe.[24] However, one Soviet source suggested the Sukhona might be so degraded from timber processing operations that its water, if diverted, could pollute the Rybinsk Reservoir.[25] While the debates go on, the scope and structural details of the projects continued to undergo modifications, which no doubt reflected as least some of the environmental considerations that the scientists have raised.[26] Finally, in August 1986, the CPSU Central Committee made the decision to terminate all diversion plans, for both economic and environmental reasons, and to focus on the more efficacious use of existing water supplies.[27]

Large-scale Baseline Monitoring

In addition to studies that relate to a specific project, Soviet researchers are also carrying out baseline investigations, and in some cases continuous monitoring, of large regions. "Baseline studies" attempt to assess the environmental condition of a region at a specific time, to which subsequent environmental changes, for better or worse, can be compared.

One example of this in the Soviet Union has been a set of comprehensive studies of the area surrounding the new Baikal-Amur Mainline (BAM) railroad in East Siberia.[28] This line represents a second trans-Siberian railroad north of the original line, extending from Ust' Kut to the Sea of Japan.[29] These studies have analyzed and mapped such features as the vegetation associations along the BAM route, on a relatively small scale.[30]

The purpose of these particular investigations is to provide baseline data for the expected economic development that will occur as a result of the new railroad. It should be noted that some of these studies were not commenced prior to the start of building the railroad itself, and thus they do not function precisely as an environmental impact report on that project. They do, however, provide background data and attempt to suggest some of the broad types of changes that the ensuing regional economic development might entail.[31]

The lack of adequate mitigation measures within the various environmental studies done on the BAM was noted in *Izvestiia*:

> We became acquainted with a project . . . known as the Territorial Comprehensive Plan for Environmental Protection Along the BAM. Its many volumes provide a comprehensive analysis of the territories and resource potential of the BAM zone and forecast potential pollution and environmental damage. But we failed to find in the plan specific proposals as to how to protect primary topographical features and basic ecosystems . . . and what kind of organizational measures are needed to protect the environment. Yet such proposals are essential.[32]

This concern would seem to be underscored by the writings of other experts, who warn of the many environmental pitfalls, such as little-studied biotic complexes and high air pollution potential, that await the unwary developer of Siberian resources.[33]

Another example of a generalized, region-wide study to identify potential problem areas was one done for the Pripiat Marsh region of Belorussia.[34] Although much effort has been spent to convert these marshes to productive agricultural use, the results have not always been as successful as hoped owing to inappropriate uses assigned to the reclaimed lands. The goal of this study was to generate planning maps of the specific landscape associations in the region, based on local physiography, soils, and vegetation, so as to identify optimal potential land uses once reclamation in a given area has been completed. This type of analysis is sometimes called a "land capability" study, and is advisable in any location prior to commencing economic development.

A second type of regional environmental study takes the form of an ongoing, comprehensive monitoring of environmental conditions in an already heavily developed area. The term commonly used in the Soviet Union to describe such efforts is "geosystems monitoring." A major example of this type of study is the one being carried out in Kursk oblast', known as the "Kursk Model Oblast'" project.[35] Kursk oblast' is a major black-earth agricultural region, but also includes the extensive open-pit iron ore mines of the Kursk Magnetic Anomaly (KMA), numerous raw material processing and other industrial enterprises, and a major complex of nuclear power plants whose thermal waters are being used for fish and food production (see Figure 3.4).

The Kursk Model Oblast' project will involve a number of interrelated studies on such topics as air pollution, soil fertility and erosion, water quantity and quality, the monitoring of pesticides and other toxics, and changes in flora and fauna.[36] The manner in which large-scale agriculture affects all of these factors, and is affected by them, is a central part of these investigations.[37] In a similar manner, the effects of the open-pit mining at the Kursk Magnetic Anomaly on the surrounding environment are also being studied.[38] It should be noted that much of this research involving the Kursk Magnetic Anomaly, like the BAM, was initiated after the mine had been put into operation, and hence does not fulfill the "in advance" requirement of environmental impact reports in the United States. It might also be noted that the units at the Kursk atomic power station are of the same RBMK graphite design as was the unit 4 at Chernobyl' which was involved in the tragic accident in 1986.

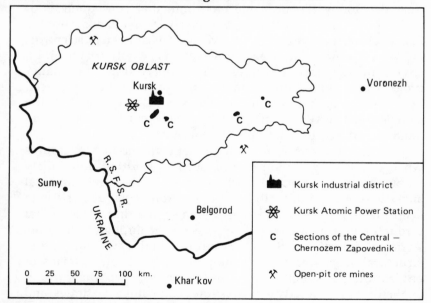

Figure 3.4 Key Features of Kursk Oblast

Much of this research in the Kursk region is being conducted by the Academy of Sciences' Institute of Geography at their research station at the Central Black Earth *zapovednik*; other research is being carried out by the geography faculty of Moscow State University.[39] One of the latter studies involves an evaluation of land uses and potential environmental problems in the KMA area in the year 2000.[40]

It is hoped that eventually this type of study can be conducted in all regions of the country, if the considerable amount of funding that would be required to do this can be made available. Such studies are already underway in a limited number of smaller regions.[41]

Summary and Analysis of the Soviet Approach

The Soviet experience in analyzing the environmental impact of economic development shows both similarities and differences as compared to practices in the United States. Although neither the Soviet Union nor the individual republics have any law precisely similar to the National Environmental Policy Act, the Soviet Union accomplishes many of the same goals through studies conducted by a variety of scientific research institutions. It is clear that today the probable environmental consequences of major projects such as the Siberian river diversions and the Baikal- Amur railroad are well reviewed by competent scientists.

What is not so clear, however, is whether thorough environmental impact studies are routinely done on smaller projects; for example, on the impact on regional air quality caused by opening up a new but relatively small factory. Yet the cumulative effects of a number of such smaller emission sources can often exceed that from a single large factory.

Soviet law provides for many strict compensatory measures when excessive pollution occurs, such as shutting down dirty plants, but this is not the main purpose of the environmental analysis process. Rather, the goal of environmental analysis is to keep major problems from happening in the first place, either through requiring alternative approaches or through mitigation. Articles describing Soviet environmental law emphasize structural measures to prevent pollution and other forms of environmental degradation, but specific laws that would explicitly mandate advance environmental impact studies and mandatory mitigation on *all* significant projects are still lacking.

For this reason, calls for a comprehensive national law on environmental protection are frequently made.[42]

Also unclear is the extent to which recommended mitigation measures that would reduce the adverse environmental impact of a project are actually carried out. Mitigation measures should not be confused with project redesign to reduce the scope of adverse effects. Mitigation measures refer to treating those *inevitable* adverse effects that will still occur, even after the best possible engineering design has been selected (for example, the downstream effects on riparian vegetation caused by the construction of a hydroelectric dam). Since the implementation of mitigation measures is a fairly new approach, little information is available on how expeditiously such measures are carried out in the Soviet Union. However, frequent commentaries in the Soviet press about delays in installing required pollution abatement equipment do not bode well for the success of the concept of mitigation measures.

A major reason for this latter concern involves the inevitable year-end rush to complete projects that have been programmed for construction during a given calendar year, so as to fulfill plan targets and possibly qualify for incentive bonuses. This rush is particularly noticeable at the end of the fifth year of each five-year plan. Under these circumstances, the temptation to circumvent, or at least delay, the simultaneous completion of pollution abatement facilities could be irresistible.

Nevertheless, the overall trend in the Soviet Union with regard to environmental studies appears to be moving in a favorable direction. Many new environmental agencies and research centers have been created over the past two decades.[43] Since the mid-1970s, the number of articles describing Soviet environmental impact studies has increased markedly. The number of researchers engaged in such studies has also gone up, as has the sophistication of the studies themselves. The decision not to divert northern rivers into the Caspian-Aral basins is perhaps the most significant result of the Soviet environmental impact review process.

As a result, there is reason to hope that the common perception, during the Stalin and Khrushchev eras, of nature as little more than a toy of the engineering profession (or worse, as a malevolent obstacle to be thoroughly defeated), is now being replaced by a solid understanding of the interrelationship and dependency of human activities on a diverse and healthy natural environment. The Soviet Union and the United States must both show by example that such an understanding is an integral part of their day-to-day economic planning and development. Both the future quantity and the future quality of the world's resource base depends on it.

Notes

1. P. S. Kolbasov, *Ecology: Political Institutions and Legislation* (Moscow, 1983), 111ff.

2. "Law of the U.S.S.R. on the Protection and Utilization of the Animal World," *Current Digest of the Soviet Press* (hereafter *CDSP*), vol. 32, no. 29 (20 August 1980), 10–14, 24.

3. *Constitution (Fundamental Law) of the Union of Soviet Socialist Republics* (Moscow, 1977).

4. Iu. A. Isakov, "The Protection of Nature in the U.S.S.R.: Scientific and Organizational Principles," *Geoforum*, vol. 15 (1984), no. 1, 93.

5. M. Podgorodnikov, "Man-made Seas—A Time for Summing Up," *Literaturnaia gazeta*, 24 October 1984, 11, as translated in *CDSP*, vol. 36, no. 46, 1–4.

6. S. Zalygin, "Moving Water, Standing Water," *Izvestiia*, 20 October 1984, 2, as translated in *CDSP*, vol. 36, no. 46, 4–5.

7. P. R. Pryde, *Conservation in the Soviet Union* (Cambridge: Cambridge University Press, 1972).

8. V. Shalgunov, "Keep the Volga Bountiful," *Pravda*, 29 April 1984, 6, as translated in *CDSP*, vol. 36, no. 17, 27.

9. This study is summarized in Iu. A. Izrael et al., "Basic Principles and Results of Environmental Impact Studies of the Kansk-Achinsk Lignite and Power Project," *Soviet Geography: Review and Translation* (hereafter *SGRT*), vol. 22, no. 6 (June 1981), 353–360.

10. V. V. Vorob'ev, "Problems of Protecting the Environment in Siberia," *Geoforum*, vol. 15 (1984), no. 1, 105–111.

11. See *Geografiia i prirodnye resursy* (1984), no. 1, 30–37 and 159–165; and no. 4, 69–97.

12. *Pravda*, 17 October 1984, 2.

13. V. Orlov, "Look Before You Leap," *Pravda*, 28 December 1984, as translated in *CDSP*, vol. 36, no. 52, 18.

14. O. K. Leont'ev, "Why Did the Forecasts of Water-level Changes in the Caspian Sea Turn Out to Be Wrong?" *Soviet Geography*, vol. 25, no. 5 (May 1984), 305–312.

15. M. I. L'vovich, and I. D. Tsigel'naia, "Management of the Water Balance of the Aral Sea," *SGRT*, vol. 20, no. 3 (March 1979), 140–153; V. M. Borovskii, "The Drying Out of the Aral Sea and Its Consequences," *SGRT*, vol. 21, no. 2 (February 1980), 63–77; A. A. Rafikov, "Environmental Change in the Southern Aral Region in Connection with the Drop in the Aral Sea Level," *SGRT*, vol. 24, no. 5 (May 1983), 344–353.

16. T. Shabad, "Soviet Plugs Caspian Leak, Then Restores It," *New*

York Times, 28 November 1984, A–15; M. Nurberdiev, "The Kara-Bogaz's Second Birth," Turkmenskaia iskra, 10 January 1985, as translated in CDSP, vol. 37, no. 14, 16.

17. M. I. L'vovich et al., "Territorial Redistribution of Streamflow Within the European USSR," SGRT, vol. 23, no. 6 (June 1982), 391–405.

18. Iu. Iudin, "A River Will Flow from Siberia," Sovetskaia Rossiia, 29 August 1984, 3, as translated in CDSP, vol. 36, no. 35, 8 and 19.

19. P. M. Kelly et al., "Large-scale Water Transfers in the USSR," GeoJournal, vol. 7 (1983), no. 3, 201–214.

20. Iu. Romanov, "The Sibaral is the Canal of the Century" (interview with G. V. Voropaev), Sovetskaia Kirgiziia, 5 April 1985, as translated in CDSP, vol. 37, no. 16, 21.

21. P. P. Micklin, personal communication, February 1985.

22. As an example, see R. Z. Gareishin et al., "Possible Environmental Changes and Environmental Protection in the Interbasin Transfer Zone of the European USSR," SGRT, vol. 23, no. 9 (November 1982), 646–653.

23. N. T. Kuznetsov et al., "Compilation of Alternative Predictive Maps of the National Environment and Reclamation Measures for the Plains of Central Asia," SGRT, vol. 22, no. 3 (March 1981), 162–174; M. E. Gorodetskaia, "Forecast of Possible Changes in the Natural Environment Along the Proposed Transfer Canal for West Siberian Streamflow," SGRT, vol. 23, no. 6 (June 1982), 406–413; L. A. Chubukov et al., "Predicting the Climatic Consequences of the Interbasin Transfer of Water in the Midlands Region of the USSR," SGRT, vol. 23, no. 6 (June 1982), 426–444; A. G. Voronov, S. M. Malkhazova, and L. V. Komarova, "Evaluation of the Medical-Geographic Setting in the Midland Region of the USSR and Possible Changes Resulting from the Proposed Interbasin Transfer of Water from Siberia to Central Asia," SGRT, vol. 24, no. 7 (September 1983), 503–515; G. V. Voropaev et al., "The Problem of Redistribution of Water Resources in the Midlands Region of the USSR (the Siberia-Central Asia Transfer Project)," SGRT, vol. 24, no. 10 (December 1983), 713–727.

24. V. Zakharko, "Northern Water for the South," Izvestiia, 22 June 1984, 2, as translated in CDSP, vol. 36, no. 25, 1–3; P. P. Micklin, "The Vast Diversion of Soviet Rivers," Environment, vol. 27, no. 2 (March 1985), 12–20 and 40–45.

25. N. Mel'nikov, "Important Problem: On Diverting Part of the Flow of Northern Rivers and Lakes to South," Ogonek, no. 28 (July 1982), 26–27, as translated in CDSP, vol. 34, no. 36, 14–15.

26. P. P. Micklin, "Water Diversion Proposals for the European USSR: Status and Trends," SGRT, vol. 24, no. 7 (September 1983), 479–502.

27. Pravda, 20 August 1986, 1.

28. I. V. Luchitski, V. V. Vorob'ev, and V. D. Iermikov, "The 'Siberia' Comprehensive Programme and Environmental Protection," in V. P. Maksakovskii, ed., The Rational Utilization of Natural Resources and the Protection of the Environment (Moscow, 1983).

29. The BAM project is thoroughly analyzed in T. Shabad and V. Mote, *Gateway to Siberian Resources (The BAM)* (New York: John Wiley & Sons, 1977). See also Chapter 7, 125–147 in this book.

30. A. V. Belov and V. M. Krotova, "Geobotanicheskoe raionirovanie Amurskoi oblasti," *Geografiia i prirodnye resursy* (1981), no. 4, 34–43.

31. A. V. Belov, "Ecological Problems in Economic Development of the BAM Zone" (paper presented at Soviet-American Meeting on the Social-Geographic Aspects of Environmental Change, Irkutsk, September 1983).

32. V. B. Sochava, "The BAM: Problems in Applied Geography," in Shabad and Mote, *Gateway*, 163–175; A. Druzenko et al., "The Law of Restitution," *Izvestiia*, 7 October 1984, 2, as translated in *CDSP*, vol. 36, no. 40, 23.

33. Vorob'ev, *Geoforum*, 105–111.

34. V. N. Kiselev, "Optimal Use of Land Resources in the Belorussian Part of the Poles'e Swamps," *SGRT*, vol. 23, no. 8 (October 1984), 572–584.

35. *Kurskaia model'naia oblast'* (Kursk Model Oblast'), (collection of papers prepared for the Commission on Environmental Problems of the International Geographical Union, Moscow: Academy of Sciences Institute of Geography, 1979); I. P. Gerasimov, *Geography and Ecology* (Moscow, 1983), 137–141.

36. A. M. Grin, ed., *Izuchenie i otsenka vozdeistviia cheloveka na prirodu* (Moscow, 1980); A. M. Grin, "The Monitoring of Geosystems: The Case of the Kursk Biosphere Nature Preserve," *Geoforum*, vol. 15 (1984), no. 1, 113–122.

37. T. G. Runova and A. D. Akhaminov, "The Impact of Agriculture on the National Environment," *Soviet Geography*, vol. 25, no. 10 (December 1984), 733–747.

38. T. V. Zvonkova, "Natural Environmental Potential of the Kursk Magnetic Anomaly: Trends and Aspects of Nature Conservation," *Geoforum*, vol. 15 (1984), no. 1, 101–104.

39. P. R. Pryde, "Biosphere Reserves in the Soviet Union," *Soviet Geography*, vol. 25, no. 6 (June 1984), 398–408.

40. V. V. Andreev et. al., "Problems of Environmental Protection in Connection with the Formation of the Industrial Complex of the Kursk Magnetic Anomaly," *SGRT*, vol. 20, no. 5 (May 1979), 291–296.

41. I. L. Gordenina, "Prirodookhrannoe kartografirovanie nizovogo administrativnogo raiona," *Vestnik Leningradskogo Universiteta: ser. geol.-geog.*, 1984, no. 6, 114–116.

42. Kolbasov, *Ecology*, 123ff.

43. For a general discussion of the organization of environmental research in the Soviet union, see B. A. Ruble, "The Emergence of Soviet Environmental Studies," *Environmental Review*, vol. 5, no. 1 (1980), 2–13.

KATHLEEN E. BRADEN

4

The Function of Nature Reserves in the Soviet Union

Covering one-sixth of the earth's land surface, the Soviet Union has the potential to serve as a major preserver of habitats and species. Estimates of the amount of preserved lands in the Soviet Union vary, but .5 percent to 1 percent of the total area of the country falls within the category of land withdrawn from economic utilization.[1] These lands are broken down into several classes, depending on their major purpose, and include two types that emphasize conservation and research goals: the biosphere and the *zapovednik*, or nature preserve. The Soviet geographer Krinitskii has stated that the term *zapovednik* has no direct equivalent outside the Russian language because the preserves focus on scientific work and serve as "outdoor laboratories of nature."[2] This chapter examines the functions of preserved lands in the Soviet Union, particularly the goal of creating *zapovedniki* as science centers.

Because data on research projects and personnel on Soviet preserves are not readily available, empirical evidence is cited to describe several aspects in which the scientific research record of the Soviet preserve system may be deficient. However, some trends are examined that indicate that the Soviets are attempting to address these deficiencies.

Overview of the Soviet Preserved Lands System

Three major factors in the Soviet preserved lands system may be noted as particularly affecting the success of scientific work on the national *zapovedniki* network:

1. Geographic skewness of lands selected for preservation: the reserves east of the Urals on average tend to be larger than those in the European regions of the country, and some biotypes are not represented at all;[3]
2. Alternating periods of growth and contraction in the preserved lands system, a factor that can negatively affect systematic observations in pristine habitat;[4]
3. Increasing diversity in the classification of preserved lands, beginning in the 1960s: in recent years the Soviet Union has added two classes—*biosphere* and *national park*—to the system in recognition of the variety of goals for land preservation; this trend has allowed greater separation of the science goal from, for example, that of recreation.

Four main types of preserved lands, totaling 11.4 million hectares, may be noted: *zapovedniki*, biosphere reserves, national parks, and game reserves.

Currently, approximately 140 *zapovedniki* are delineated in the Soviet Union, encompassing more than 10.8 million hectares.[5] By the year 2000, another twenty to thirty *zapovedniki* may be added, bringing in another 5 million hectares.[6] The largest are in the Asian USSR: Taimyr in north-central Siberia (1.35 million hectares), Kronotskii on Kamchatka (946,000 hectares), Altai (864,000 hectares), and Wrangel Island (796,000 hectares).[7]

Zapovedniki serve multiple functions: (1) preservation of endangered species and landforms; (2) propagation and sometimes reintroduction of rare and vanishing species of flora and fauna; and (3) scientific study of habitat, species, and ecological relationships. In addition, *zapovedniki* often play the role of education centers, tourist attractions (although not by design), and sources for breeding economically useful animals for transplant to other locations, such as sable on the Barguzin Reserve in Siberia.

Biosphere reserves are *zapovedniki* that have been accepted by UNESCO under the "Man and the Biosphere" program as representatives of major ecosystem types. As of 1984, eight *zapovedniki* had been accorded biosphere status, with another six planned to be nominated in the near future.[8] If these six achieve biosphere status, this category will encompass 10 percent of preserved lands in the Soviet Union.

National parks are lands that are under some degree of preservation, but in which tourism is allowed within prescribed areas. National park lands appear to total 500,000 hectares, but for more recent examples it is difficult to determine exactly *when* an area achieves national park status. For example, the Ala-Archa National Park in Kirgizia was thought by geographers at the Academy of Sciences in Moscow to exist in name only, although a director had recently been appointed.[9]

Seven national *game reserves*, as well as many smaller ones at the individual republic level, are designated to serve more than one million members of hunting organizations in the Soviet Union. GLAVOKHOTA, the Main Administration for Game Management and Nature Reserves of the RSFSR, administers Russian lands under this class.[10]

Other lesser categories of preserved lands exist, including monuments of nature (small zones drawn around geologic and botanical oddities) and *zakazniki*, short-term reserves designed to restore specific animal populations in an area. These totalled 25 million hectares of land in 1980.[11]

The Scientific Research Function of Preserved Lands

As a result of the emphasis on science in the *zapovednik*, a structure has been established to tie each reserve to larger scientific organizations. This network often proves very complex because administrative decision making overlaps several agencies. The Soviet Academy of Sciences and the republic-level Academies of Science, as well as local universities, special institutes, the Ministry of Agriculture research institutes, and the Hydrometeorological Service may vie for project approval on *zapovedniki*. For example, on the Central Black Earth Biosphere Reserve, up to twenty-six scientific organizations take part in research, representing groups as diverse as the Leningrad Forestry Academy and the Medicinal Institute of Kursk University.[12]

Zapovedniki are organized so that each has a science staff, but systematic data on numbers of employees are not published. However, one Soviet researcher has reported that a typical science staff for a *zapovednik* should have twenty to twenty-five specialists, with twenty to twenty-five assistants, divided by specialty and led by an ecologist.[13] Each *zapovednik* is also designed to have laboratory facilities, a library, and an on-site nature museum. Although references to these museums are plentiful in well-established reserves, such as the Central Black Earth, evidence is not cited for the establishment of museums on remote reserves.

A mainstay of scientific work on the *zapovedniki* is a document known as the *letopis' prirody,* or nature register.[14] The term was first used in 1937 on the Astrakhan *zapovednik,* and some of the registers are reported to provide a forty-year record of flora and fauna fluctuations. Each register is compiled by reserve workers, covers one calendar year, and includes maps, photographs, text, and data (see Table 4.1).[15]

Given this established framework for accomplishing scientific work, each *zapovednik* would appear to be not only functioning as a nature preserve, but also as a science center. In the absence of actual data on the scientific productivity of the *zapovedniki,* the success of the science function may be assessed by examining some cases of *zapovednik* research.

Evaluating the Status of Scientific Work on *Zapovedniki*

Anecdotal evidence suggests that the Soviet record of achievement with respect to science work on reserves is mixed. It could be argued that, while the concept of "outdoor laboratories" is laudable, actual use has been haphazard and poorly controlled. At the same time, trends are emerging that could lead to a much improved record in the future. The following six issues may be identified that indicate problems with scientific work on *zapovedniki.*

Uneven Scientific Work Among Reserves

Although some *zapovedniki* serve as models for the scientific work the system is designed to accomplish, many are less dynamic. Older, well-established reserves in more accessible areas appear to have stronger records of research. Many excellent examples of work based on data collected on *zapovedniki* exist for the Darwin Reserve (Rybinsk Reservoir, RSFSR), Astrakhan', Central Black Earth, Voronezh, Oka Terrace (near Moscow), Caucasus, Teberdin (Stavropol'skii krai), and Sikhote-Alinskii

Table 4.1 Sample Organization of a Zapovednik Nature Register, 1967

Importance of a nature register
Orientation
Introduction
Preservation and use

Contents

1. Territory
2. Landforms, relief, and soils
3. Climate
4. Water
5. Calendar of nature
6. Flora, plants
    changes, changes under human influence, station-test areas,
    interdependence of various plant groups, population dynamics,
    seasonal and long-term changes in plant cover
7. Fauna and animal world
    land animals, marine animals, tracks, new species, birds, unusual
    appearances of animals on reserve territory, insects
8. Scientific works

Source: A. A. Nasimovich and Iu. A. Isakov, eds., *Opyt paboty i zadachi zapovednikov SSSR* (Moscow, 1979), 42–43.

(Primorskii krai). Well-known individual studies of particular species of animals or plants have also been done on other reserves, such as on the polar bear and snow geese of Wrangel Island or the beaver of the Berezina *zapovednik*. However, Soviet scientists have been critical of the lack of research on many reserves. In the 1970s, the botanist L. S. Belousova examined almost 2,000 publications for evidence of *zapovednik*-based research. Twenty-four percent of the *zapovedniki* had no botanical research at all; more than 70 percent had no flora inventories, and 40 percent did no detailed work on the plants characteristic of their territory.[16] K. D. Zykov of the Institute of Ecology and Evolutionary Morphology of the Academy of Sciences has complained of the uneven nature of reserve work, the failure to use data previously collected on reserves, the lack of modern research tools in the field such as radio telemetry and aerial photography, and the lack of consistent quantitative techniques in data collection.[17]

Zapovednik workers are responsible for conducting baseline surveys of habitat in their territory when the reserve is first established, as well as yearly nature registers, and special projects. The Soviet Ministry of Agriculture has requested overall management goals and long-range plans for scientific work from *zapovedniki* but with a few exceptions, such as the Darwin and Astrakhan' reserves, few have apparently accomplished these objectives.[18]

Spatial Constraints

To avoid Diamond's island biogeographic trap, reserves must be large enough to represent accurately the biotype that serves as the focus for preservation.[19] F. R. Shtil'mark has determined optimum sizes for *zapovedniki* based on characteristics of natural zones, but in reality many *zapovedniki* are too small to represent biotypes with any precision; indeed twelve *zapovedniki* are less than 1,500 hectares.[20] Iu. A. Isakov has stated that each *zapovednik* should contain a major river system with tributaries and be surrounded by a buffer zone, particularly if human development is encroaching on the surrounding areas.[21] Buffer zones have been mandated under the RSFSR land code and by GLAVOKHOTA, but there appears to be no systematic way in which buffer zone size is determined. Buffer zones are noted in the literature for several *zapovedniki*, including Zhigulev, Oka, and Central Black Earth, but the author was told at the Ministry of Agriculture in Moscow that information on the size of buffer zones is not published regularly.[22]

The creation of both buffer zones and the reserves themselves is a process that begins with the Soviet scientific community and ends with final approval by the union republic and national Councils of Ministers, as well as the state economic planning agency, GOSPLAN. The determining norm for *zapovednik* size may be altered along this route, often by non-scientists.[23]

Uneven Representation of Disciplines

In the autumn of 1984, the Ministry of Agriculture reviewed plans for scientific research on *zapovedniki*. Isakov recommended that the first themes to be advanced should be those that help accomplish the primary goal of the *zapovednik*: preservation. Other Soviet scientists have been critical of the fact that work on the *zapovedniki* is often concentrated along the lines of basic disciplines, rather than being integrated research that would lead to better understanding of ecological relationships. On one *zapovednik*, conservation themes made up less than 5 percent of the work, while zoological surveys were the most prevalent type.[24]

Another emphasis of *zapovednik* research is a focus that will lead to commercial utilization of animal species. Examples include research on sable on the Barguzin Reserve and beaver on the Voronezh Reserve. In the case of the beaver, research on the Voronezh Reserve provided habitat data to allow the introduction of the beaver as an exotic species into the Soviet Far East for later use in the fur industry.[25]

Deficiencies in Nature Registers

A. M. Krasnitskii notes that approximately 1,000 nature registers have been created by Soviet *zapovedniki* staff, indicating uneven record keeping among the reserves. Each *zapovednik* is obligated to produce a yearly register, and given even a five-year time lag between establishment of the reserve and production of the first annual report, the total number of nature registers at present should be twice that number.[26] In addition, only three or four copies of each are produced, and they are intended for use at the *zapovednik*, rather than for wider dissemination. Some *zapovedniki*, such as the Central Black Earth Biosphere Reserve, do publish proceedings, but reports of scientific work on the reserves are apparently not collected with any regularity.

Time Lags and Changing Ecosystems Conditions

Zykov has recommended that some uniform system be established to allow continuity among data collection on *zapovedniki*. The fact that differing time bases are used may cause problems for correlation with other studies. Also, the time lag, often of many years, between initiation and completion of inventories may lead to shifts in populations and relationships.[27]

Overuse by the Scientific and Educational Community

Scientists are supposed to conduct work on *zapovedniki* only within specified zones, and are instructed not to disturb the ecological balance of the reserve. Student use of the reserves is supervised by staff people, and the students and schoolchildren who use reserves for educational purposes are limited to the visitor center, the museum, or particular footpaths. However, some of the statistics for visits are surprising: in the past twenty years, more than 18,000 university students have visited the Central Black Earth Reserve, usually for fieldwork in the basic disciplines of botany, zoology, and geomorphology. Approximately 33,000 schoolchildren visited the reserve over a similar period. The Berezina *zapovednik*, until 1975, still permitted plant collecting, including some species listed as rare in the Soviet *Red Book*.[28]

The visitor burden would appear to fall more heavily on the accessible *zapovedniki* with well-established ties to universities and institutes—the same *zapovedniki* that apparently have the greatest research output.

To sum up some of these drawbacks, one could make a case for *zapovedniki* that are differentiated by "popularity" with respect to attention from the science research and education communities. An example of a popular reserve would be the Central Black Earth Biosphere Reserve, which keeps a prominent profile, is accessible to domestic and foreign visitors alike, has a lengthy record of data keeping, lists many scientific research projects, and maintains close contacts with university departments and Academy of Science institutes. The reserve is also fairly small (4,800 hectares) and close to developed industrial areas. Philip Pryde has visited the reserve and reported that while a portion has been set aside for experimentation on the impact of agricultural use, a portion is also left in an undisturbed state.[29] At the other end of the spectrum would be newer, larger,and more remote reserves, particularly in the northern and Asian Soviet Union, for which one finds few citations in the Soviet literature of activities other than preservation.

There is also evidence that the noted deficiencies in the functioning of *zapovedniki* for scientific work are being addressed. The reserve abolition period seems to have ended, and the Soviets are in a period of building up their preserved lands. While a shift toward more integrated ecological studies is being called for by Soviet scientists, the basic research disciplines of botany and zoology continue strong and often are vital to the goal of preservation. In studies of endangered species such as the kulan, snow leopard, gazelle, Siberian tiger, and European bison, as well as many bird species, the Soviet achievement is deservedly recognized as having contributed to the rescue of many threatened types of fauna.[30]

In 1975, a national conference on "Theoretical Questions of Zapovednik Affairs in the USSR" recommended accelerating basic inventories on many reserves and noted:

> All the insufficiencies in *zapovednik* work may be explained by the absence of a scientific research strategy, concomitant with the traditionally complex fragmentation of departments in the nation's *zapovedniki* within a single national structure of *zapovednik* management.[31]

To remedy the disconnected situation of scientific work on the reserves, a commission was created in 1981 within the Academy of Sciences: The Interagency Commission to Oversee Scientific Work on Zapovedniki. Headed by V. E. Sokolov of the Institute of Ecology and Evolutionary Morphology, the commission's fifty-six members include representatives from the sciences, the *zapovedniki* themselves, and administrative agencies. Although the commission does not engage in research, it does coordinate research and education at the graduate and postgraduate levels.[32]

Some of the problems in the scientific work base of the *zapovedniki* may be explained by the conflict between preserving and utilizing land, and the dilemma of *how* to preserve land. The Soviets are examining the choices between complete nonintervention in natural processes and selective manipulation. Even when the manipulation is for laudable ends—such as supplemental feeding of endangered species, forest fire amelioration, or scientific research—there is a price to pay from the point of view of ecological purity. However, this dilemma for science is not unique to the Soviet Union. Professor Isakov has noted that, thanks to externalities such as air pollution, there are few, if any, pristine natural systems remaining on earth.[33] The *zapovednik* network, with an improved structure for scientific research, may provide important future contributions to understanding such management choices.

Notes

The author acknowledges the support of the International Research and Exchanges Board.

1. For estimates of amount of preserved lands, see Dora Fischer, "Nature Reserves of the Soviet Union: An Inventory," *Soviet Geography:*

Review and Translation, vol. 22, no. 8 (October 1981), 510–522; Philip Pryde, "Recent Trends in Preserved Natural Areas in the U.S.S.R.," *Environmental Conservation*, vol. 4, no. 3 (Autumn 1977), 173–177; A. M. Krasnitskii, *Problemy zapovednogo dela* (Moscow, 1983). If green belts are included in the estimate, the total may reach 24 million hectares, and further increments may be derived from buffer zones around preserved lands and republic-level hunting reserves, as noted in B. Lopyrev, B. Ivashchenko, F. Shtil'mark, K. Zykov, and I. Shurupov, "Okhraniaemye territorii i okhotnich'e khoziaistvo RSFSR," *Okhota i okhotnich'e khoziaistvo*, no. 3 (1979), 12–15.

2. Iu. A. Isakov and V. V. Krinitskii, "Sistema osobo okhraniaemykh prirodnykh territorii v Sovetskom Soiuze, ee struktura i perspektivy razvitiia," *Izvestiia AN SSSR, seriia geograficheskaia*, no. 3 (1980), 46–52.

3. Tundra, taiga, and subtropical zones have yet to be represented under the biosphere designation, and the steppe zone is considered underrepresented among the *zapovedniki*.

4. This fluctuation in size and numbers of preserves has been well documented by Pryde, *Environmental Conservation*, and Krasnitskii, *Problemy*, ch. 1. Krasnitskii notes that in 1950 there were 12.5 million hectares of preserved lands in the Soviet Union, but by 1953 there were less than 1.4 million hectares, after eighty-nine *zapovedniki* were abolished.

5. Krasnitskii (p. 3) claims there are 142 *zapovedniki*.

6. Fischer, *Soviet Geography*; Isakov and Krinitskii write that the total land on *zapovedniki* by the end of 1985 will be 16.9 million hectares. Iu. A. Isakov, ed., *Okhraniaemye prirodnye territorii Sovetskogo Soiuza, ikh zadachi i nekotorye itogi issledovaniia* (Moscow, 1983).

7. N. K. Noskova, ed., *Geograficheskoe razmeshchenie zapovednikov v RSFSR i organizatsiia ikh deiatel'nosti* (Moscow, 1981), 89–90.

8. For information on Soviet participation in the program, see D. M. Gvishiani and V. E. Sokolov, eds., *Prikladnye aspekty programmy "Chelovek i biosfera"* (Moscow, 1983). The number of current biosphere reserves was determined by interviews with Iu. A. Isakov at the Institute of Geography, Moscow, AN SSSR, 12 October 1984, and with Iu. A. Starikov, Scientific Council on Biosphere Problems, AN SSSR, Moscow, 24 October 1984.

9. Isakov interview, 12 October, 1984.

10. Lopyrev writes that a total of 909 million hectares of land in the RSFSR is accessible for hunting!

11. Fischer, *Soviet Geography*.

12. Krasnitskii, *Problemy*, 85.

13. Krasnitskii, *Problemy*, 158.

14. For more details on the nature registers, see the article by Isakov in Isakov, ed., *Okhraniaemye prirodnye territorii*, 140–148.

15. See K. P. Filonov in A. A. Nasimovich and Iu. A. Isakov, eds., *Opty raboty i zadachi zapovednikov SSSR* (Moscow, 1979), 43.

16. Cited in Krasnitskii, *Problemy*, 79.

17. K. D. Zykov in Noskova, *Geograficheskoe razmeshchenie*, 78. A. F. Kovshar' of the Institute of Zoology, Kazakh Academy of Science, reported in an October 1984 interview with this author that aerial photography was being employed for ungulate surveys in western Kazakhstan.

18. Iu. A. Isakov reported that the Darwin Reserve now has a fifteen-year plan. See also Nasimovich and Isakov, *Opyt raboty*, 37–38.

19. Jared M. Diamond, "The Island Dilemma: Lessons of Modern Biogeographic Studies for the Design of Natural Reserves," *Biological Conservation* (1975), 129–146.

20. Shtil'mark recommends that reserves in the Arctic be not smaller than 500,000 hectares; in the mountain taiga of Asia, at least 200,000 hectares; south Siberian mountains and Far East, 100,000; Urals, Siberia, European North, and the Caucasus, 50,000; central Europe, 10,000. Cited in Nasimovich and Isakov, *Opyt raboty*, 187.

21. Interview with Iu. A. Isakov, Moscow, 12, October 1984.

22. Interview with A. G. Bannikov at the Ministry of Agriculture, Moscow, 22 October 1984. See also Krasnitskii, *Problemy*, 160.

23. Interview with A. F. Kovshar', Alma-Ata, 15 October 1984.

24. See Krasnitskii, *Problemy*, 78.

25. Krasnitskii, *Problemy*, 86–87.

26. Krasnitskii (p. 157) states that five years should be allowed as a setting-up period for the reserve.

27. K. D. Zykov in Noskova, *Geograficheskaia razmeshchenie*, 76–87; Krasnitskii, *Problemy*, 156–157. Another problem is the fact that nature registers are taken by the calendar year, while seasonal measures for wildlife and plant cycles overlap calendar years.

28. Krasnitskii, *Problemy*, 162–163.

29. Philip Pryde, "Biosphere Reserves in the Soviet Union," *Soviet Geography*, vol. 25, no. 6 (1984), 398–408.

30. Pryde has noted some of these studies in "Strategies and Problems of Wildlife Preservation in the USSR," *Biological Conservation* vol. 36 (1986), 351–374. Some studies have been carried out with unusual dedication. Bannikov has noted the research in the 1940s of K. D. Kaplanov on the Sikhote–Alin Reserve. Kaplanov tracked and studied tigers during the winter, living and working continually in rugged terrain in the nighttime temperatures that often reached –40° C. His work was published posthumously the year after he completed his study.

31. Krasnitskii, *Problemy*, 79.

32. Interviews with Iu. A. Isakov (Moscow) and commission members Iu. A. Starikov (Moscow) and A. F. Kovshar' (Alma-Ata), October 1984.

33. Interview with the author, October 1984.

5

IHOR STEBELSKY

Agricultural Development and Soil Degradation in the Soviet Union: Policies, Patterns, and Trends

The relationship between agricultural development and soil degradation is an established environmentalist concern.[1] As land is plowed repeatedly for growing crops and as domestic animals overgraze and trample pastures, the soil is exposed to water and wind erosion and, in arid regions, is subjected to desertification. Irrigation often brings about increased soil salinity, whereas drainage of marshes dries the land, exposes organic soil to oxidation and compaction, and makes sandy soil susceptible to wind erosion. But the relationship between changing land uses and soil degradation is far from simple. Soil degradation depends in part on the way in which agricultural land is managed, and the latter depends on the technical, economic, social, and political factors that influence farming.

Soil degradation and land management are interactive. Physical processes of soil degradation may be triggered by the activities of those who use the land and those who influence the users. Conversely, losses resulting from soil degradation lead to some response among the users and policy makers. The nature of their response depends on their perception of the problem, their knowledge, ability and willingness to undertake ameliorative measures, and the support available to the farmers from their superiors and government institutions.

The purpose of this chapter is (1) to identify those aspects of

71

land management, including the technical, economic, social, and political factors that contributed to soil degradation in the Soviet Union; and (2) to examine Soviet response to soil degradation. Since soil erosion is, in part, an outgrowth of agricultural development, and since there is considerable delay from the time degradation begins to the time it is recognized and, finally, to the time response occurs, the subject will be treated in a historical perspective.

Agricultural Expansion and Soil Degradation Before the Revolution

The Russian Empire entered the twentieth century as a major exporter of grain. It was able to attain this position by expanding its cropland to grow increasing quantities of wheat and barley for export in the recently colonized steppes and by constructing railways that would bring the grain to ports for shipment abroad. Food for the Russian cities, however, was supplied from the old agricultural lands that released some of their rural population to colonize the steppes and man the growing industries, but were still considered overpopulated. And so, while the new granaries of the empire were showing early signs of stress with the giant dust storm of 1892, the old lands experienced advanced environmental degradation involving severe soil erosion.

Most severely water-eroded soils were on the densely peopled uplands and slopes of the forest-steppe zone. These extended from the deeply incised Bessarabian Plateau in the southwest through Podolia and the Dnepr Upland in Ukraine, the Central Russian Upland south of Moscow, and the Volga Upland in the east. Here, the degraded chernozems (black earth) formed on the fragile loess deposits, had been the object of cultivation since the Neolithic Age. The removal of protective natural vegetation exposed the soil to water erosion.

Soil erosion in the East European Plain is not new. In antiquity, Herodotus observed the silt-laden rivers of Scythia—indirect evidence that the wheatfields of the Ukrainian forest-steppe and steppe, which provided grain exports to Greece, were suffering from soil erosion.[2] Although nomadic incursions from the east disrupted farming in subsequent centuries, pushing the farmers north into the forest zone, the damage to soil resumed at an even faster pace when the forest-steppe zone was recolonized in the seventeenth and eighteenth centuries, and reached an unprecedented magnitude by the end of the nineteenth century.

It was not only the return of the farming peasantry who cleared the natural vegetation for growing crops that was responsible for increased soil erosion, but a number of other new developments were also involved. New technology facilitated the clearing of the forest and the plowing of the tough sod in the forest-steppe zone. Row crops, especially the commercial cultivation of sugar beets in the Ukraine, increased the exposure of soil to rain. Land-owning gentry, after the emancipation in 1861, forced redemption payments on the peasantry, causing them to plow every available plot of land in order to feed themselves. Even the peasant concern for equity was damaging. Communal fields were divided into strips laid down the slope to allow each peasant to have various soil types, but the furrows served as conduits for runoff and were soon transformed into gullies that removed valuable soil and moisture, intensified floods, silted up ponds and rivers, and contributed to typhus and cholera epidemics.[3]

To the south, in the steppe zone, commercial grain farming displaced natural grasslands. Already in 1837, a major dust storm foretold of tragedies to come.[4] Powerful winter storms of 1848, 1876–1877, 1885–1886, 1890–1891, and 1892–1893 removed snow cover, blew away topsoil, and destroyed young sprouts of winter wheat and newly planted orchards and vineyards. The dust storm of 1892 encompassed all of the southern Ukraine and extended eastward across the lower Don and the northern part of the Kuban lowland. Dry strong easterly winds, blowing intermittently from 18 April to 12 May, removed deep layers of topsoil, destroyed crops, caused enormous drifts that obstructed communications, and carried dust as far as the Baltic Sea. Removal of the protective grassland cover and repeated cultivation, as well as the preceding drought desiccated the soil plowed the previous fall. But the prevalent techniques of moldboard plowing and the desire of commercial grain growers to make a quick profit and plow large tracts of land pulverized the soil and enabled the wind to pick up and blow away the fine particles of humus and silt.

In the foothills of the Caucasus, the traditional cropping methods involved the construction of terraces in order to conserve the moisture from runoff and reduce water erosion. By the end of the nineteenth century, however, the growth of population, overgrazing, and deforestation of mountain slopes, and the revival of commercial agriculture with emphasis on corn and tobacco accelerated soil erosion.[5]

Asiatic Russia experienced a massive infusion of Slavic settlers at the beginning of the twentieth century. Some of the best grasslands of Siberia and the Steppe krai (now known as Kazakhstan) were plowed for grain. In the dry foothills of central Asia, Slavic settlers practiced spring season plowing, or *bogara*, exposing the soil to water and some wind erosion.[6] In the oases of central Asia, the Russian government inaugurated an expansion of cotton and large-scale irrigation. Modern technology, applied to dam the Murgab River and to irrigate the Hungry Steppe, allowed increased waterlogging and salinization.[7]

The build-up of salinity resulting from desert irrigation is not new. In central Asia, where irrigation had been practiced for over 3,000 years, the natives had devised some methods to cope with salinization. In Fergana and the Amu Dar'ia delta they used shallow drainage for washing out salts during fall and winter; the use of moderate amounts of water conserved the resource, minimized runoff, and reduced salinization. Along canals, poplars were planted to draw down excess water and thus avoid the build-up of salts and waterlogging. Alfalfa grown in rotation meliorated the soil. In Khorezm and Bukhara, saline soil was scraped off and replaced with sand and manure. In Fergana a small tile drainage system was employed.[8]

Modern Russian irrigation in the Hungry Steppe provided large quantities of water for cotton, raising the groundwater and aggravating salinization. In the absence of proper drainage, attempts were made to wash out the salts by flood irrigation of rice cultivation and the heavier application of water, but this simply passed more salt onto lower terraces and led to the abandonment of the land.[9]

Scientific recognition of soil degradation was limited in the nineteenth century mainly to the European portion of the Russian Empire, where conditions were clearly the worst and the most highly visible to Russian scientists. As early as the eighteenth century, scientists on field expeditions (M. V. Lomonosov, P. S. Pallas, V. Zuev, and others) described active gullies, wind-blown sands, and soils suffering from water erosion. The first Russian professor of agronomy, M. I. Afonin, recommended (1771) the use of contour trenches to intercept runoff; C. Drukovtsev (1773) condemned downslope plowing and recommended tillage perpendicular to the slope; A. T. Bolotov recommended (1779) the protection of stream banks with ivy, and advanced (1781) methods of combatting gully erosion. By the early nineteenth century, a few leading conservationists (gentry landowners, Mennonite colonists) were already planting forests to control wind-blown sand, combat dust storms, and improve soil moisture availability. Subsequently the effort was encouraged by the newly organized (1838) Ministry of State Domains, which also sponsored cadastral surveys and the preparation of the first soil maps of European Russia. Soil scientists (G. Andrievskii, A. Grossul-Tolstoi) studied the nature of soil erosion, noted its locational characteristics, and made the first efforts to map its extent. They even voiced their opinion in the Ministry of State Domains journal that soil erosion led to poor yields.[10] The ministry, however, did little to promote good farming practices, let alone soil conservation.

In the postemancipation period, Russian soil scientists (V. V. Dokuchaev, N. M. Sibertsev, P. A. Kostychev, I. Levakovskii, N. A. Sokolov, A. P. Pavlov, V. R. Vil'iams, G. N. Vysotskii, and others) contributed much new knowledge to the understanding of soil erosion. They conceptualized the environmental transformation and ecological degradation that resulted from clearing the land of its natural vegetation.[11] Moreover, Dokuchaev headed the Forestry Department expedition to develop and test, on experimental plots, a number of measures to conserve the soil; in the steppe zone, he proposed measures to conserve soil and water. In 1893, M. N. Annenkov headed a major expedition into southeastern Russia, encompassing twenty-one provinces, to combat gullies and drought that were considered responsible for the famine of 1891. Subsequently, other soil scientists (P. V. Iankovskii, A. A. Gel'fer, V. M. Bortkevich, and others) proposed and tested practical measures to retain snow in the fields, hold back the meltwater, deflect and store runoff, stop gully erosion, and regulate stream flow. The proposed land use reorganization, agronomic methods, and hydrological structures have not lost their validity to this day.[12]

Salinization of irrigated land was also noted by Russian scientists. The agronomist N. A. Dimo observed (1906–1908) the rise of groundwater in the Hungry Steppe since 1891, measured its mineral content, mapped the results, and found that it was associated with the flood irrigation of rice. M. M. Bushuev and V. S. Malygin experimented with and recommended tile drainage for the irrigation of cotton (1912). A conference of agronomists (Taskhent, 1915) recommended drainage to solve the salinization problem that, by the end of 1915, developed into a health crisis as malaria swept the Hungry Steppe.[13]

By contrast, the government record concerning soil conservation was, initially, abysmal. Russian government policy was aimed at industrialization at the expense of agricultural development. Gentry exploited the peasants for sharecropping the estates, and the government used the peasant communes to assure the collection of taxes. Farming was neglected and, until 1894, there was no Ministry of Agriculture. In the whole empire, until the end of the nineteenth century, there were only three agricultural colleges, and government extension services were lacking. "Almost until the end of the past century," as V. V. Morachevskii put it, "the population had not received agronomic aid to any serious extent, either from the government or from the organs of local self-government, and was left in this respect entirely to its own devices."[14] It required pleading from the learned professionals, a famine, and peasant upheavals for the government to respond. In 1890, the Eighth Congress of Russian Naturalists and Physicians, appalled by soil erosion, poverty, and cholera epidemics, appealed to the Ministry of State Domains to study the gullies and take measures against them. As a result, the ministry conducted a survey (1891 and 1893) and commissioned Prince Masal'skii to analyze the results.[15]

The famines of 1891 and 1892 prompted the Russian government to replace the Ministry of State Domains with the Ministry of Agriculture and State Domains, and the recurrence of such famines (1897, 1898, and 1901) convinced the authorities that more had to be done for agriculture. One Russian government commission, after an exhaustive study, established that the peasantry of the severely gullied Central Russian Black Earth Region had suffered the greatest impoverishment since the emancipation.[16] An even broader study, involving committees in forty-nine provinces, focused on the needs of agriculture, including problems of land ownership and land tenure. It put in doubt the value of the traditional peasant commune and repartition of the strips of cultivated land.[17]

Only the peasant revolts of 1905 shocked the Russian autocracy into land reform. The Stolypin reforms (1906, 1910) aimed to preserve the estates whose lands the peasants wanted, to convert the Russian peasant communal land tenure into private land ownership, and to provide for consolidation of the tiny strips of plowland. In order to diffuse the political pressure for the partition of the estates, the government encouraged peasants to sell their plots and migrate from their severely eroded lands to the steppe frontier in Asiatic Russia. Peasants who remained were encouraged to purchase the abandoned holdings. Credit was expanded and cooperatives of all kinds were encouraged. Much more effort was placed on the education of the peasantry and on agronomic service to them, but government insistence on the Russian publications for non-Russian peasantry created barriers to the flow of information. More favorable prices during this period made commercial farming lucrative, increased the use of machinery, and led to agricultural intensification and improved agronomic practices. These favorable policies toward agriculture, however, did not last a decade as they were interrupted by World War I, the Revolution, and civil war.

Agricultural Expansion and Soil Degradation During the Stalin Era

Following the communist victory, a period of transition ensued: land was nationalized, but the New Economic Policy (NEP) allowed for peasant farming to continue in whatever form the peasants preferred. The communist government favored the establishment of collective and state farms, and gave priority to land consolidation of "socialized" holdings, but the peasantry sometimes set up bogus collectives to get their land surveyed. The government also viewed the Central Black Earth Region and Ukraine as overpopulated, and advocated continued migration to Asiatic Russia. In effect, migration and land consolidation, begun with the Stolypin reforms, revived during NEP. Commodity price structures also changed in favor of animal products rather than food grains, and land uses underwent slow adjustment to more feed crops. Schooling and agronomic services in native languages also helped improve the spread of information.

During NEP, little change occurred in the agricultural systems to alter the processes of soil degradation. In the European forest-steppe zone, the shift to more livestock production and less grain was counterbalanced by more row crops, including corn and sugar beets. Expansion of grain farming into the steppe resumed its earlier course. In the deserts of central Asia, overgrazing and cutting of the *saksaul* for firewood continued as before the Revolution, promoting desertification.[18] Irrigation of cotton resumed soon after the civil war ended, and the accumulation of salt demanded immediate attention for melioration. A delegation of agronomists was dispatched to the United States, studies were conducted, and drainage was initiated. Even so, careless or improper irrigation resulted in massive salinization.[19]

Stalin's program of collectivization, however, brought dramatic changes to the countryside. Liquidation of the kulaks divested the farming population of its best talent. Compulsory collectivization, combined with fear that all private livestock would be lost, caused peasants to slaughter their animals and thus reduce the livestock number dramatically. Increasing quotas set by the government so deprived some grain-growing regions of food that a man-made famine, killing millions, caused the reluctant peasants to submit to the system. The government allowed peasants to raise a few animals privately (to rebuild the stocks) and to grow fruit and vegetables on personal plots (for domestic consumption and sale to the cities), but the major herds were to remain in the socialized sector, and field crops were to grow on collective lands. Surveying of collective property ensued, and the individual strips were merged into large collective fields.

According to Soviet soil scientists, socialist agriculture created favorable conditions for combatting soil erosion, and, allegedly, the capitalist incentive to chase profits by destroying soil was eliminated.[20] The pre-collectivization peasant strips, often plowed downhill for reasons of equity, were merged into large, rectangular collective fields, while the use of tractors allowed for deeper plowing, made fuller use of the soil, and increased its percolation ratio. Rural overpopulation, once the cause of overplowing, overgrazing, and rural poverty, was dissipated through migration to the cities and industrial regions, as well as rural projects in Siberia, Kazakhstan, and central Asia, (not to mention the loss of life during collectivization). Centralized management provided for the diffusion of new techniques. New crops were introduced, and multifield crop rotation replaced traditional systems.[21] Furthermore, with the reduction of livestock numbers and inadequate supply of fertilizer to meet the agronomic needs, V. R. Vil'iams, the Russian soil scientist who enjoyed great influence under Stalin, claimed that soil must first be improved structurally before it can be enriched chemically, discouraged chemical fertilizers in favor of manure, and promoted the soil-conserving grass-field rotation. In central Asia, this meant increased importance for alfalfa in rotation with cotton, and in the desert a program of *saksaul* afforestation was encouraged. The most spectacular drive in the Soviet Union, however, was the widespread planting of shelterbelts and construction of ponds in the steppe and forest-steppe zones of the European region, which climaxed in a decree that became known as "Stalin's Plan for the Transformation of Nature."[22]

Given the political climate of the day and in light of the changes described above, Soviet scientists asserted victory over soil erosion. In 1949, V. S. Dmitriev emphasized that the agricultural decline suffered before the Revolution was reversed by progress made under the Soviet rule, and S. I. Silvestrov claimed that the erosion evident in the country was directly caused by poor agricultural management before the Revolution. Indeed, so confident was the government that it was widely accepted that a land cadastre was unnecessary.[23]

Since Stalin's death, however, Soviet scientists have admitted to the mismanagement of soil in that period.[24] Perhaps a more open political environment and new empirical evidence gathered by the soil scientists contributed to this change. During Stalin's rule, soil erosion was observed by researchers of the V. V. Dokuchaev Soils Institute of the Soviet Academy of Sciences. Studies of the process, methods of its measurement and classification of eroded soils was conducted, conferences were held, and the intensity of soil erosion processes was recorded for the first time on a map of the European region. Measures for combatting water and wind erosion were also devised and tested on six typical collective and state farms representing various parts of that region.[25] But the disillusionment came several years after the Academy of Sciences dispatched an expedition in 1951 to study the progress made against soil erosion in the regions encompassed by Stalin's shelterbelt afforestation program. The findings of this expedition were published in 1954, at a time when Stalin's successors, in maneuvering for political advantage, opened agricultural policy to criticism.[26]

In a revealing article, D. L. Armand noted a number of practices that nullified the effectiveness of shelterbelts and had harmful effects on the soil. Downslope layout of shelterbelts and their poor management promoted, rather than curtailed, gully erosion. Plantings along the edges of existing gullies failed to absorb the runoff from the fields above and accumulated snow in the winter for an even greater runoff in the spring, thus rejuvenating gully erosion. Pastures, instead of being placed along the more eroded edges of the fields, were concentrated in one massive block, their value for soil conservation wasted. Furthermore, the collective farm management, Armand observed, overextended its plowland beyond safe limits and onto slopes generally considered too steep for plowing. This disregard of slopes, and the eroded soils on them, stemmed from a blind observance of outdated local land cadastres and a rigid adherence to the recommendation that fields of no less than 100 hectares were to be delineated for the sake of economic plowing. As a result, many fields were broken by ravines and included all kinds of slopes, each of which should have warranted a different program of management. Fields were not laid out in accordance with contours, and with only huge, unmaneuverable tractors available, differences in topography were ignored. Cases were reported in which fields were cultivated downslope in order that the tractor brigades of the Machine Tractor Stations (MTS) could save money on gasoline.[27] This was not uncommon, despite a 1941 law that specifically prohibited plowing down the slope.[28]

Soil erosion in the Stalin era was not restricted to the European forest-steppe zone. Expansion of cultivated land in the steppe exposed more land to the wind and, were it not for the grass-field crop rotation, would have increased the occurrence and extent of dust storms.[29] Moreover, the Soviet program for self-sufficiency in cotton, combined with the influx of evacuees from the war zone in 1942, meant that more grain for central Asian consumption had to be grown in the foothills on *bogara*, a practice that increased wind and water erosion on the slopes.[30] The expansion of irrigation onto excessive slopes of the Kirgiz SSR for growing grain and sugar beets led to deep gullying.[31]

Irrigation under Stalin experienced considerable expansion. Canals were reconstructed to allow for the large, rectangular fields of collective and state farms. New projects expanded irrigation to make the Soviet Union self-sufficient in cotton, but low yields reflected continued problems of salinization. Various agronomic measures were applied to reduce salinity, including reduced dosages of water, afforestation, and the use of alfalfa in the grass-field rotation. But the imperative to meet the planned targets of irrigated land displaced drain construction to lesser priority and prompted some scientists, such as V. M. Shaumian, to promote the "theory" that irrigation could be developed without drainage.[32] Mainline canals in Fergana and elsewhere were built without cement lining, resulting in a great deal of seepage, waterlogging, and accumulation of salt. Not until 1950 was furrow irrigation made mandatory, and a new emphasis placed on drainage.

Agricultural Expansion and Soil Degradation
During the Khrushchev Years

Khrushchev's agricultural policies aimed at inexpensive and rapid increase in agricultural production by means of expanding the sown area, and eliminating fallow and grass-field crop rotation. Between 1953 and 1963, the sown area was increased by 61.3 million hectares, of which 44.8 million hectares were added in the "virgin lands."[33] In the European region, crops such as winter wheat, oats, and grasses were replaced with corn. Although the program produced, in the short run, the desired result of more grain, milk, and meat, in the long run it had a devastating effect on soils.

In the European forest-steppe zone, attempts to intensify agriculture boosted both the area and the percentage composition of industrial crops (potatoes, sugar beets, and sunflowers) and especially corn [maize], and raised the total area under crops. The long maturing period for corn, however, made it impossible to follow corn with winter grain. Thus, small grains and especially winter grain, which offers some protection for the soil during the spring runoff, declined, whereas corn, which offers no ground cover in the spring and readily exhausts the soil, increased. This combination resulted in accelerated soil erosion.[34]

In the steppe zone, where drought is frequent and the *sukhovei* (a dry wind) always a threat, increased plowland exposed more soil to the wind. Repeated plowing pulverized the soil, desiccated it, and made it all the more susceptible to wind erosion. The frequency and ares of dust storms increased. In Kustanai oblast' of Kazakhstan, for example, after the plowing of the lighter chernozem or chestnut soils (1954–1957), the wind removed humus and the fine-textured fractions of clay and silt, converting nearly one-third of the plowland into infertile blowing sand.[35] In Pavlodar oblast' alone, more than 3 million hectares of cultivated land, or two-thirds of the cultivated land of the oblast', were threatened by deflation, as entire administrative areas became engulfed in dust storms, their crops destroyed, and pastures damaged.[36] Yields dropped dramatically.

In the desert oases, the demise of the grass-field crop rotation led to the increase of cotton at the expense of alfalfa.[37] As a result, despite increased application of fertilizers, the yields of cotton stagnated and progress in the reduction of soil salinity came to a halt.

Soil scientists and agronomists recognized the pitfalls of

planting row crops in large fields down the slope, the dangers of repeated moldboard cultivation in dry steppes, or the sharp reduction of alfalfa from rotation with cotton. On the farm, however, their scientific judgment had to yield to the immediate need of satisfying the ambitious quotas and often shifting targets for sown areas, especially row crops, that were conveyed from above and then modified by the oblast' party officials in order to meet the plans. The soil scientist, S. S. Sobolev, criticized the direct application of techniques, developed on flat lowlands (where the experimental stations were located), to collective farms in the uplands, where erosion was severe. He knew the advantages of contour strip cropping and its successful application in the United States, advocated its use in the hilly, gully-prone areas, and argued its economic adaptability.[38] Yet his lucid arguments could not overcome the inertia of Soviet large-scale mechanized farming with huge, unwieldy caterpillar tractors on criss-crossed, enormous rectangular fields. Contour strip cropping, recommended even before the Revolution by A. I. Voeikov,[39] was dismissed by other Soviet experts as not applicable[40] or wasteful, because on complex slopes it would leave wedges of uncultivated land.[41]

Similarly, Soviet soil scientists (K. I. Andrianova in 1958, A. I. Baraev in 1958, T. F. Iakubov in 1960) recommended various agronomic measures in the dry steppe to prevent dust storms and crop losses. They proposed alternating strips of grasses, aligned perpendicular to the prevailing direction of the wind, to shelter the bare ground. For the cultivation of soil, especially of light or sandy texture, they discouraged the use of the traditional moldboard plow, condemned the use of disk cultivators, and recommended a special set of equipment designed for dry farming: a deep, chisel-like plow, a shallow blade cultivator, and a cutter-seeder. They also recommended the acquisition of pneumatic wide-wheeled vehicles that would reduce soil compaction. To conserve moisture for the spring, they advocated planting shelterbelts, and on the fields the use of curtains, stubble mulching, and snow plowing in winter. Where practicable, they also advocated the use of winter feed crops in rotation. Few of these recommendations were implemented, however. The fields were aligned along interfarm roads and hastily established during the virgin lands campaigns; dry farming equipment and rubber-wheeled machinery were lacking; most winter crops were not hardy enough to survive in northern Kazakhstan; and the natural copses of birch, aspen, and pine were being depleted with the construction of new state farms in the virgin lands more rapidly than the shelter belts could be planted.[42] More important, the campaigning style of government "planning" (or interference) in agricultural production made it impossible to implement soil conservation measures on the farms. Both farm management and agricultural workers showed little interest in soil conservation and no responsibility for the condition of the land.[43]

Deteriorating soil conditions, along with successive dust storms and decreasing grain yields in the virgin lands, were in part responsible for the demise of Khrushchev, and led to the changes in the agricultural policies of his successor, Brezhnev.

Agricultural Changes and Soil Conditions During the Brezhnev Period

Brezhnev's agricultural policies alleviated those farming practices that led to soil degradation. Recognizing the futility of forced, low-cost crop expansion into climatically marginal lands, Brezhnev made a number of significant changes. He eliminated "campaigning," allowed the return of fallow ground, grass, and oats, and emphasized farm autonomy within the limits of the quota. He set a flat quota on grain for six years in advance at a level below the needs of the economy, and raised the prices so that additional grain would be sold to the state voluntarily. By increasing the farm commodity prices, raising pay, and improving benefits to the peasantry, and by directing more investments into the agricultural sector, Brezhnev allowed for the replacement of aging and chronically deficient machinery and equipment on the farms. In particular, he rushed the production of blade cultivators for the virgin lands. *Selkhoztekhnika* was established to improve maintenance and repair facilities, and *Selkhozkhimiia* to enhance the conditioning of soils. He also committed the government to an even greater effort in expanding irrigation and drainage. In conjunction with land improvement, the non-chernozem zone of the European Soviet Union was selected as a target area for massive investment to enhance the production of animal products and vegetables for the cities.[44]

Brezhnev's program of agricultural intensification, however, raised some new concerns. In the non-chernozem zone of the European Soviet Union, agricultural expansion was to be accomplished by means of mechanization, application of chemicals, drainage, liming of acidic soils, and some irrigation.[45] Since the best agricultural lands, mainly in the southern part, have long been farmed and exposed to erosion, and the uplands had severely fragmented plowland with stony soils that reduced yields and wore out implements, the possibilities for expansion were limited primarily to the relatively flat and stone-free marshlands, which, when drained, were conducive to mechanized farming.[46] When these marshes (Pripiat, Meshchera, and Unzha- Vetluga) were drained, however, their sandy or organic soils appeared susceptible to drought and wind erosion.[47] Open drainage, in particular (characteristic of Belorussia, the Ukraine, and the RSFSR), proved to be wasteful of land because it fragmented fields and inefficiently removed water, yet contributed most to soil desiccation and erosion. Closed drainage, long used in East Prussia and the Baltic countries, was expensive, but it provided greater efficiency for mechanization and land use, and for this reason was being expanded in Belorussia, the Ukraine, and the RSFSR. Recent experiments with closed two-way drainage systems in the Ukraine promised not only better drainage, but also the reversal of water in dry periods so as to maintain soil moisture and good yields.[48] Whether this technique, if implemented widely, would also prevent wind erosion has not been established, but the fear of overexpanding drainage beyond ecologically safe levels has been expressed.[49]

In the forest-steppe and steppe zones, the problem of frequent droughts was attacked with a vigorous expansion of irrigation. Construction of the irrigation schemes in the North Caucasus, along the Volga, in the Ukraine, and in Moldavia, begun since 1951 and expanded in the last years of Khrushchev's leadership, received particular impetus under Brezhnev.[50] In addition to surface irrigation, applied on flat terrain for paddy rice and on gentle slopes along furrows for row crops, the irrigation of vegetables, grain crops, and grasses, especially on soils with a high percolation capacity and on rolling terrain, was by means of the sprinkler. Whereas surface irrigation prevailed in central Asia and the Transcaucasus, sprinkler irrigation assumed dominance in the European steppe and forest-steppe zones, where the largest increase in irrigation agriculture took place. In 1974, in the RSFSR sprinkler irrigation accounted for 59 percent of all land under irrigation, in Ukraine 88 percent, and in Moldavia 93 percent.[51] Thus, while the expansion of irrigation increased the threat of salinization of the soil in the steppe as well as in the desert oases, irrigation on slopes has augmented the danger of water erosion. Fears have been expressed that, as sprinkler irrigation is expanded (and it can expand only onto steeper slopes and heavier soils), the danger of water erosion may dramatically increase.[52]

At the root of the problem of controlling soil erosion is the question of who bears the personal responsibility of misuse of the land that is farmed collectively. Each collective and state farm comprises hundreds of collective farmers or employees who perform tasks according to incentives designed specifically to maximize some aspect of performance of each task. But the ultimate and sometimes conflicting goals of satisfying the food needs of the society and retaining soil fertility are lost as each worker strives to maximize the performance of his task, sometimes at cross-purposes with another. Since the farms and the brigades are rather large units, requiring formalized administration, several Soviet authors have suggested that the link, or *zveno*, the smallest grouping of farm labor, should be given the responsibility for both food production and stewardship over the land. In so doing, they precipitated a discussion concerning the merits of establishing an autonomous link or *beznariadnoe zveno*.[53] Such an autonomous link would be attached to a specific area of land, have the necessary equipment, and perform the tasks as it sees fit, with its income depending on the results. Moreover, argued I. Kopysov in his *Literaturnaia gazeta* article, the autonomous link would recover that "love of the land" that had been lost within the large impersonal units.[54]

This brief discussion involving possible decentralization in Soviet agriculture, however, came to naught. The collective and state farms, rather than undergoing fragmentation, were being integrated horizontally and vertically through the establishment of interfarm cooperation and agroindustrial complexes. Various measures designed to deal with soil conservation also began to assume, over time, a more centralized approach. Thus, while in the mid-1960s the increasing complexity of the Soviet economy had made centralized management appear increasingly unfeasible, the subsequent emergence of a new appreciation of information sciences and integrated systems theory made a return to centralization seem possible once again.[55]

Impetus to the soil conservation efforts was provided by government decrees (16 June 1966) on land melioration,[56] and (20

March 1967) "on urgent steps to protect soils against wind and water erosion."[57] The latter outlined a comprehensive program aimed at preventing and checking erosion through the use of a variety of agricultural practices that were to be applied with due regard for local conditions. To put the decree into action, large appropriations, supplies, and machinery were allocated, and the scientific community responded with appropriate research.[58] The land legislation (ratified by the Supreme Soviet on 13 December 1968) specified the land users and individuals who were responsible for maintaining land quality, and fines were set for violations.[59] The land cadastre was to provide a benchmark against which degradation of soils could be established, but it took nine years before the government could issue specific instructions as to how a state land cadastre should be carried out throughout the Soviet Union.[60] And it was the Ministry of Agriculture that was made responsible for the conduct of the cadastre and prosecution of those who were responsible for soil degradation—the same governmental body that was also responsible for establishing production plans.

A major contribution to the preparation of a tool that would enable central planners to take into consideration regional needs in soil conservation was also in the making. Begun in 1958 this project, directed by S. I. Silvestrov of the Institute of Geography of the Soviet Academy of Sciences, published its first volume in 1965, which presented the measurements and maps of the major factors of erosion, notably climate, relief, and agricultural land use. These factors of erosion were used to regionalize the territory of the Soviet Union according to three main categories: (1) those not threatened by erosion, (2) those potentially threatened by erosion, and (3) those suffering from erosion.[61]

The second volume, published in 1972, recommended regional systems of antierosion measures. This pioneering effort was seen as a guide to help overcome the ineffective application of individual soil conservation measures worked out by various branch institutes, when implemented without proper specified or spatial differentiation. Recommendations were specified for 72 regions and 123 subregions with the intent that these soil conservation practices would become part of the regional agricultural systems. It was also recognized that soil conservation measures should vary, as conditions required, on each farm and on every field. Such detail, it was recommended, should be left to the oblast' and raion organizations and the farms themselves to work out.[62]

Given this broad overview, plus a good deal of research at

various institutes, considerable progress was made in the Brezhnev period, especially in the virgin lands that had suffered from
wind erosion. Already by 1968, mainly in Kazakhstan and
Siberia, some 14.2 million hectares of land was worked with
blade cultivators that left a protective surface of stubble mulch,
crops were planted in strips on 2.3 million hectares, and curtains
of high-stemmed plants were employed on some 1.4 million
hectares.[63] By 1974, this had increased to 26.7, 5.0, and 2.4 million hectares respectively, resulting in a significant increase in
yields.[64] The success has spurred the spread of moldboardless
plowing, with appropriate modifications in equipment and
methods, to suit the crops and environment of the Ukraine. By
1983, plowless low-till farming in the Ukraine expanded to more
than 7 million hectares.[65] Other modifications of plowless cultivation were developed in the North Caucasus.[66] Although many
years have passed since the major dust storm of 1969, soil scientists have cautioned that the weather conditions have not been
severe enough to put the new agronomic practices to the test.[67]

Measures to combat water erosion were also implemented, but
proved less effective. General plowing perpendicular to the main
slope, pitting, furrowing, and other agronomic techniques
received wider usage, increasing from 2.5 million hectares in 1967
to 9 million hectares in 1969, but little contour strip cropping was
employed. The rate of afforestation of ravines and gullies
doubled from 1967 to 1968. Some 8,500 hectares of slopes were
terraced, and an inventory of shelterbelts was completed in 1968.
Some 1,500 farm projects were completed, reorganizing the land
uses to combat erosion. Yet much more could have been
accomplished with the available equipment had it been
available on the farms in proper combinations. Terracing and
other hydrotechnical work achieved scarcely more than half of
its objectives because the service agencies did not find such
projects attractive enough to enhance their own success indicators.
Pastures were overgrazed and subjected to greater erosion, and the
soil conservation techniques were not applied in proper
combinations to maximize the effect. Intrafarm land reorganization proceeded much too slowly. Moreover, complained V. V.
Matskevich, the Minister of Agriculture, many republics had not
yet established a soil conservation service. No one knew the
condition of the land at any given time, or of anyone being
apprehended for contributing to soil erosion; and, he stressed, it
was time to establish responsibility for land.[68]

Since 1970, more effort has been expended to combat water

erosion. Differentiated zonal systems of soil conservation practices were being developed and introduced.[69] Some prosecutions of agronomists and collective farm chairpersons for neglecting afforestation or terracing were noted.[70] With the availability of more earth-moving machinery, more ravines and gullies have been filled and their wastelands reclaimed.[71] Calls were made to devote more attention to territorial reorganization and to introduce contour strip farming, including grassed spillways.[72] Indeed, a comprehensive study was published that summarized the theoretical foundations, zonal systems, machine complements, economic effectiveness, and leading domestic and foreign practices of soil conservation techniques on slopes. It indicated that, in the Soviet Union, 54 percent of the agricultural land and 67 percent of the cultivated land was threatened by water erosion.[73] If contour strip cropping were introduced on 50 million hectares of cultivated land, for example, it would yield a net benefit of 20 million tons of grain equivalents.[74]

Although contour strip cropping admittedly had great meliorative qualities, there were difficulties encountered in introducing the system: the surveyors had no practice in eliminating the many lenses that would appear among the strips on complex slopes, and would cause some land to be withdrawn from cultivation.[75] The farms, too, lacked the small, maneuverable tractors and proper implements to work the curvilinear strips effectively.[76] Without proper machinery little progress could be made in contour strip cropping. The answer to this problem was sought not only through a better response from the agricultural machine-building industry to the farming needs through the agroindustrial complex, but also by means of special studies that would match the machines to the farming regions.[77]

Irrigation areas susceptible to water erosion and salinization have also received more attention. Recommendations have been made to reduce the dosage of water application and to adjust the methods of sprinkling in order to reduce water erosion, such as along the right bank of the Volga.[78] Particular attention has been given to surface application of irrigation water and to drainage associated with irrigation in order to reduce the build-up of salt. Both horizontal closed drainage and vertical drainage, using pumping wells, have been expanded in the oases of central Asia.[79] In the non-chernozem zone of the RSFSR, closed drainage has increased at the expense of open drainage, attesting to the progress being made in land improvement, including pastures. Yet, despite the increased fertility of tile drained land in

Transcarpathian Ukraine, productivity has remained low because of poor labor incentive.[80]

Since the end of the Brezhnev period and the rise of Gorbachev, a roundtable discussion by soil scientists in the literary monthly of the RSFSR, *Nash sovremennik*, once again revealed the growing problem of soil degradation. V. A. Kovda, the chair of the Soviet Academy of Sciences Council on the Problems of Soil Management and Melioration and president of the Soviet Society of Soil Scientists, led the discussion. He pointed to the loss of humus in the chernozem, which has accelerated in the last fifty years because of mechanized farming and— especially in the last twenty years—because of chemical fertilization. While the displacement of draft animals has reduced the manure input into soils, and the use of heavy machines has increased soil compaction, it was the use of chemical fertilizers that caused soil acidification, the leaching of humus, calcium, and magnesium, the accumulation of clay, and the petrifaction of the plowed horizon. Chernozem degradation was aggravated by monoculture and, except for a few outstanding examples, the lack of soil conservation practices resulted in continued intensive gullying.[81]

Even more damaging, in Kovda's assessment, was the irrigation of the chernozem. This inappropriate transfer of desert irrigation technology into the steppe environment, with its horrendous seepage (40 to 60 percent) from open canals, the use of mineralized water, overwatering, and use of heavy machinery has caused waterlogging, salinization, formation of surface hard crust, loss of humus and water erosion, and thus the reduction of yields below the expected levels obtainable on experimental farms. Partly to blame was the former leadership that perceived irrigation as a panacea for improving yields; also partly at fault were the Ministry of Melioration and Water Management, which developed its schemes to suit its own interests without consulting the soil scientists and without serving the best needs of agriculture, and the incentive structure, in which the pay of the irrigators was based on the frequency and the amount of water dispensed on the fields regardless of agronomic requirements.[82]

What is needed, according to Kovda, is the end of *shablon* (the carbon copy approach) that is so common on collective and state farms. Each soil type should be given individual attention, care, monitoring, and management. To achieve this, according to Kovda, it is necessary to establish, within the Ministry of Agriculture, a Soil Conservation Service. This service would account for and monitor soil fertility, and help select and implement proper soil conservation and improvement measures. It would also need air photography and satellite imagery for proper land inventory and evaluation. Finally, the Ministry of Melioration and Water Economy should be reorganized into a branch subordinate to the Ministry of Agriculture so that drainage and irrigation projects would be developed only if they are cost-effective and ecologically sound.[83]

Conclusion

In the course of agricultural expansion in Russia and the Soviet Union, the problem of soil erosion has grown in magnitude. Before the Revolution the main impediment, at first, was the government's lack of recognition of the problem, and then its unwillingness to act until forced by a crisis. Although Russian scientists pioneered soil research and provided valuable recommendations, the ossified agrarian structure was not receptive to change until the Stolypin reforms, and the latter only initiated change that was interrupted by the Revolution.

Following NEP, the institutional structure provided for the infusion of science into agriculture, but Stalin's leadership stifled independent or objective inquiry. Although "Stalin's Plan for the Transformation of Nature" was to provide for soil conservation, subsequent research found the scheme poorly executed and ineffective. Khrushchev's expansion of sown areas, especially under row crops, and the reduction of grass-fallow rotation accelerated soil erosion. Although soil scientists and agronomists were painfully aware of the consequences, the farms lacked the necessary machinery and skills for soil conservation, and had to yield to ambitious production plans dictated from above. Brezhnev's reaction to farming by decree brought stability to agricultural planning, more generous funding, and soil-conserving legislation. However, the centralized socialist farming system, with its interorganizational conflicts, remained intact.

Although the Soviet farming system may be superior in its ability to impose innovations from above, it harbors contradictory incentive structures at various levels and areas of operations, and allows for little decentralized decision making. Indeed, the individuals who work the soil continue to lack a vested interest in the land and fail to bear personal responsibility for soil erosion.

Notes

1. For a pioneering inquiry into the relationship between man and his environment, with considerable attention devoted to soil, see George P. Marsh, *Man and Nature; or Physical Geography as Modified by Human Action* (New York: Charles Scribner, 1865; Cambridge, Mass.: Harvard University Press, 1965). A review of the concept of soil conservation, especially as it evolved in the United States, is summarized in R. B. Held and M. Clawson, *Soil Conservation in Perspective* (Baltimore: Johns Hopkins University Press, 1965). A recent expression of global concern is Lester R. Brown, "Conserving Soils," in *State of the World 1984*, ed., L. R. Brown (New York: Norton, 1984), 53–73.

2. S. S. Sobolev, *Razvitie erozionnykh protsessov na territorii Evropeiskoi chasti SSSR i bor'ba s nimi* (Moscow, 1948), vol. 1, 9.

3. I. Stebelsky, "Rural Poverty and Environmental Deterioration in the Central Russian Black Earth Region Before the Revolution," *International Geography 1972*, eds., W. P. Adams and F. M. Helleiner (Toronto: University of Toronto Press, 1972), vol. 1, 450–452.

4. A. G. Doskach and A. A. Trushkovskii, "Pyl'nye buri na iuge Russkoi ravniny," in *Pyl'nye buri i ikh predotvrashchenie*, ed., D. L. Armand (Moscow, 1963), 5–10.

5. B. A. Kaloev, *Zemledelie narodov Severnogo Kavkaza* (Moscow, 1981), 34–36; E. P. Maslov and K. N. Kerefov, *Ekonomiko-geograficheskii ocherk Kabardino-Balkarii* (Moscow, 1957), 52–57.

6. E. A. Stradomskii, "Bogarnoe zemledelie," in *Sredniaia Aziia: ekonomiko-geograficheskaia kharakteristika i problemy razvitiia khoziaistva*, ed., A. A. Mints (Moscow, 1969), 163.

7. I. M. Matley, "The Murgab Oasis: The Modernization of an Ancient Irrigation System," *Canadian Slavonic Papers*, vol. 17, no. 2–3 (Summer and Fall 1975), 417–435; I. M. Matley, "The Golodnaya Steppe: A Russian Irrigation Venture in Central Asia," *Geographical Review*, vol. 60, no. 3 (July 1970), 328–346.

8. R. S. Igamberdyev and A. A. Razzakov, *Istoriia melioratsii v Uzbekistane* (Tashkent, 1978), 28–29.

9. Ibid., 22.

10. Sobolev, *Razvitie erozionnykh protsessov*, 14–24.

11. See, for example, V. V. Dokuchaev, *Nashi stepi prezhde i teper'* (St. Petersburg, 1892); A. A. Izmail'skii, *Kak vysokhla nasha step'* (Poltava, 1893).

12. Sobolev, *Razvitie erozionnykh protsessov*, 27–52.

13. Igamberdyev and Razzakov, *Istoriia melioratsii*, 23–24, 32–35.

14. V. V. Morachevskii, ed., *Agronomicheskaia pomoshch v Rossii* (Petrograd, 1914), 34, as quoted in Lazar Volin, *A Century of Russian Agriculture* (Cambridge, Mass.: Harvard University Press, 1970), 66.

15. V. Masal'skii, *Ovragi chernozemnoi polosy Rossii, ikh rasprostraneniia, razvitie i deiatel'nost'* (St. Petersburg, 1897).

16. *Materialy vysochaishe utverzhdennoi 16 noiabria 1901 g.*

Komissii po issledovaniiu voprosa o dvizhenii s 1861 po 1900 gg. blagosostoianiia sel'skogo naseleniia srednezemledel'cheskikh gubernii (St. Petersburg, 1903).

17. Osoboe soveshchanie o nuzhdakh sel'skokhoziaistvennoi promyshlennosti, *Printsipial'nye voprosy po krestianskomu delu s otvetami mestnykh sel'skokhoziaistvennykh komitetov* (St. Petersburg, 1904); *Svod trudov mestnykh komitetov po 49 guberniiam Evropeiskoi Rossii. Krestianskii pravoporiadok* (St. Petersburg, 1904); *Svod trudov mestnykh komitetov po 49 guberniiam Evropeiskoi Rossii. Krestianskoe zemlepol'zovanie* (St. Petersburg, 1903); *Svod trudov mestnykh komitetov po 49 guberniiam Evropeiskoi Rossii. Zemlevladenie* (St. Petersburg, 1904).

18. I. S. Zonn, V. N. Nikolaev, N. S. Orlovskii, and I. P. Svintsov, *Opyt bor'by s opustynivaniem v SSSR* (Moscow, 1981), 39. Saksaul is a desert tree with twisted branches.

19. Igamberdyev and Rezzakov, *Istoriia melioratsii,* 44–46.

20. *Sel'skokhoziaistvennaia eroziia i bor'ba s nei,* ed., G. D. Rikhter and A. E. D'iachenko (Moscow, 1956), 3.

21. In the Central Russian Black Earth region, for example, multifield crop rotations that included some new technical crops replaced the three-field system, and clean follow was virtually eliminated. *Razmeshchenie i spetsializatsiia zemledeliia i zhivotnovodstva v Tsentral'nochernozemnoi zone,* ed., N. P. Aleksandrov (Moscow, 1968), 20.

22. Postanovlenie Soveta Ministrov Soiuza SSR i Tsentral'nogo komiteta VKP(b) ot 20 oktiabria 1948 goda, "O plane polezashchitnykh lesonasazhdenii vnedreniia travopol'nykh sevooborotov, stroitel'stva prudov vodoemov dlia obespecheniia vysokikh i ustoichivykh urozhaev v stepnykh i lesostepnykh raionakh evropeiskoi chasti SSSR," appended in *O travopol'noi sisteme zemledeliia,* ed., V. S. Dmitriev (Moscow, 1949), 335–372, map.

23. *O travopol'noi sisteme zemledeliia,* 5, 10; S. I. Sil'vestrov, *Eroziia i sevooboroty* (Moscow, 1949), 16; K. V. Zvorykin, "Mesto geografov v rabotakh po zemel'nomu kadastru i sel'skokhoziaistvennoi otsenke zemel'," *Geografiia i zemel'nyi kadastr,* vol. 67 of *Voprosy geografii* (Moscow, 1965), 11.

24. *Sel'skokhoziastvennaia eroziia i bor'ba s nei,* 3–4; S. I. Sil'vestrov, "Efforts to Combat the Process of Erosion and Deflation of Agricultural Land," in *Natural Resources of the Soviet Union: Their Use and Renewal,* ed., I. P. Gerasimov, D. L. Armand, and K. M. Yefrom, trans. by J. I. Romanowski, English ed. by W. A. D. Jackson (San Francisco: Freeman, 1971), 161.

25. Sobolev, *Razvitie erozionnykh protsessov,* 55–71.

26. S. Ploss, *Conflict and Decision-Making in Soviet Russia: A Case Study of Agricultural Policy, 1953–1963* (Princeton: Princeton University Press, 1965), 67–97.

27. D. L. Armand, "Izuchenie erozii v lesostepnykh i stepnykh

raionakh SSSR i sostoianie protivoerozionnykh meropriiatii," *Izvestiia AN SSSR, seriia geograficheskaia*, vol. 4, no. 2 (March–April 1954), 3–14.

28. S. S. Sobolev, *Bor'ba s eroziei pochv* (Moscow, 1958), 17.

29. In the southern Ukraine the dust storms of 1928, although less damaging than those of 1892, were of the same magnitude, and were not followed again by major dust storms until 1960. Doskach and Trushkovskii, in *Pyl'nye buri i ikh predotvrashchenie*, 10–11. In northern Kazakhstan, the dust storms during the Stalin era were of a local nature because of the smaller areas of plowland and grass-field crop rotation. A. V. Tikhonov, "Vzaimosviaz' sel'skogo khoziaistva s protsessami deflatsii v vostochnykh raionakh osvoennoi tseliny," in *Pyl'nye buri i ikh predotvrashchenie*, 134.

30. E. A. Stradomskii, "Bogarnoe zemledelie," in *Sredniaia Aziia*, ed., A. A. Mints (Moscow, 1969), 163; G. Solianko, "Mery bor'by s eroziei na bogare," *Zemledelie*, vol. 18, no. 8 (August 1970), 24–26.

31. See, for example, a detailed study conducted on the south shore of Lake Issyk-Kul': E. N. Lisichek, "Eroziia pochv na polivnykh zemliakh Priissykkul'skoi ravniny," *Trudy Instituta Geografii*, vyp. 60 (Moscow, 1950), 55–75.

32. A. N. Askochenskii, *Voprosy irrigatsii* (Tashkent, 1969), 94, as cited in Igamberdyev and Razzakov, *Istoriia melioratsii*, 9, 60, 137. Also see G. F. Raskin, *Ekonomika oroshaemogo zemledeliia* (Moscow, 1967), 39.

33. *Narodnoe khoziaistvo SSSR v 1963 g.: statisticheskii ezhegodnik* (Moscow, 1965), 294. Also see W. A. Douglas Jackson, "The Virgin and Idle Lands Program Reappraised," *Annals of the Association of American Geographers*, vol. 52, no. 1 (March 1962), 69–79.

34. I. Stebelsky, "Environmental Deterioration in the Central Russian Black Earth Region: The Case of Soil Erosion," *Canadian Geographer*, vol. 18, no. 3 (Fall 1974), 224.

35. A. G. Gael and L. F. Smirnova, "O vetrovoi erozii legkikh pochv v Severnom Kazakhstane," in *Pyl'nye buri i ikh predotvrashchenie*, 122.

36. Tikhonov, in *Pyl'nye buri i ikh predotvrashchenie*, 134–135.

37. Z. G. Freikin, "Polivnoe zemledelie," in *Sredniaia Aziia*, 153.

38. Sobolev, *Bor'ba s eroziei pochv*, 16–17.

39. A. I. Voeikov, "Zemel'nye uluchsheniia i ikh sootnoshenie s klimatom i drugimi estestvennymi usloviiami," *Ezhegodnik otdela zemel'nykh uluchshenii*, vol. 1; reprinted in A. I. Voeikov, *Vozdeistvie cheloveka na prirodu*, ed., E. M. Murzaev (Moscow, 1963), 98.

40. T. F. Antropov and D. L. Armand, "Organizatsiia territorii i sevooboroty v kolkhozakh erodirovannykh raionov Sredne-Russkoi vozvyshennosti," in *Sel'skokhoziaistvennaia eroziia i bor'ba s nei*, 247.

41. I. D. Braude, *Eroziia pochv, zasukha i bor'ba s nimi v TsChO* (Moscow, 1965), 68.

42. Tikhonov, in *Pyl'nye buri i ikh predotvrashchenie*, 145–153.

43. Sobolev, *Bor'ba s eroziei pochv*, 10, 13.

44. Summarized in Alec Nove, "Soviet Agriculture Under Brezhnev,"

Slavic Review, vol. 29, no. 3 (September 1970), 386–388.

45. TsK KPSS and Sovet Ministrov SSSR, *O merakh po dal'neishemu razvitiiu sel'skogo khoziaistva nechernozemnoi zony RSFSR* (Decree of the Central Committee of the CPSU and Council of Ministers, Moscow, 1975), esp. 8–12.

46. A. D. Panadiadi, *Problemy meliorativnogo ustroistva nechernozemnoi zony* (Moscow, 1974), 14–23; B. B. Shumakov, "Problemy melioratsii v Nechernozem'e," in *Intensifikatsiia sel'skogo khoziaistva nechernozemnoi zony RSFSR*, ed., L. K. Ernst et al. (Moscow, 1976), 27.

47. S. V. Zonn, "Pochvy," in *Sredniaia polosa Evropeiskoi chasti SSSR*, ed., S. V. Zonn and A. A. Mints (Moscow, 1967), 187.

48. S. M. Alpat'ev, "Dosiahnennia nauky v haluzi hidrotekhniky i melioratsii na Ukraini," *Visnyk sil's'kohospodars'koi nauky*, vol. 14, no. 4 (April 1970), 91; M. A. Harkusha, "Stan i perspektyvy rozvytku melioratsii na Ukraini," *Visnyk sil's'kohospodars'koi nauky*, vol. 14, no. 4 (April 1970), 82; T. A. Kozlova, *Ispol'zovanie meliorirovannykh zemel' Poles'ia USSR* (Kiev, 1982), 176–193.

49. *Ukraina: obshchii obzor*, ed., A. M. Marinich (Moscow,1969), 409.

50. B. G. Shtepa et al., *Melioratsiia zemel' v SSSR* (Moscow, 1975), 22, 28–30.

51. Ibid., 102, 107.

52. I. I. Borodavchenko, "Voprosy zashchity pochv ot irrigatsionnoi erozii," in *Zashchita pochv ot erozii*, ed., V. D. Pannikov et al. (Moscow, 1971), 61.

53. Nove, *Slavic Review*, 391–392; Roy D. Laird, "New Trends and Old Remedies," *Problems of Communism*, vol. 15, no. 2 (March–April 1966), 21–28.

54. A. Kopysov, *Literaturnaia gazeta* (1968), no. 6, 10, as cited in Nove, *Slavic Review*, 392.

55. Robert F. Miller, "The Future of the Soviet Kolkhoz," *Problems of Communism*, vol. 25, no. 2 (March–April 1976), 35.

56. TsK KPSS and Sovet Ministrov SSSR, "O shirokom razvitii melioratsii zemel' dlia polucheniia vysokikh i ustoichivykh urozhaev zernovykh i drugikh sel'skokhoziaistvennykh kul'tur," as cited in D. V. Iarmizin et al., *Meliorativnoe zemledelie* (Moscow, 1966), 5.

57. As translated in V. P. Sotnikov, "Control of Soil Erosion," *Soviet Soil Science*, vol. 10, no. 10, (October 1967), 1288. The original is: TsK KPSS and Sovet Ministrov SSSR, "O neotlozhnykh merakh po zashchite pochv ot vetrovoi i vodnoi erozii," as cited in P. S. Zakharov, *Eroziia pochv i mery bor'by s nei* (Moscow, 1971), 3.

58. Indicative of this subsequent flurry of research is the bibliography T. I. Novikova and N. K Shikula, *Bibliograficheskii ukazatel' po zashchite pochv ot erozii* (Moscow, 1970), to be followed by a serial bibliography, issued by VASKhNIL, Tsentral'naia Nauchnaia Sel'skokhoziaistvennaia Biblioteka, *Eroziia pochv i bor'ba s nei* (Moscow, 1972).

59. *Okhrana prirody: sbornik normativnykh aktov*, ed., V. M. Blinov (Moscow, 1971), 8, 34–53; A. A. Riabov, *Otvetstvennost' za narushenie zakonodatel'stva o zemlepol'zovanii* (Moscow, 1981), 20–23; *Pravovoi rezhim zemel' v SSSR*, ed., G. A. Aksenenok, N. I. Krasnov, and I. A. Ikonitskaia (Moscow, 1984), 77–78.

60. Postanovlenie Soveta Ministrov SSSR, no. 501, "O poriadke vedeniia gosudarstvennogo zemel'nogo kadastra," 10 June 1977, as cited in T. P. Magazinshchikov, *Zemel'nyi kadastr* (Lvov, 1980), 4–6. Preparation for the land cadastre was long in coming; geographers, agricultural economists, and others suggested to the government the value of land cadastre for agricultural planning in 1955; this request was approved in 1962 and a flurry of activity on the land cadastre was unleashed. See a collection of articles in *Geografiia i zemel'nyi kadastr*, vol. 67 of *Voprosy geografii* (Moscow, 1965).

61. *Raionirovanie territorii SSSR po osnovnym faktoram erozii* (Moscow, 1965).

62. *Regional'nye sistemy protivoerozionnykh meropriiatii* (Moscow, 1972), 3–4.

63. V. V. Matskevich, "O vypolnenii postanovleniia TsK KPSS i Soveta Ministrov SSSR 'O neotlozhnykh merakh po zashchite pochv ot vetrovoi i vodnoi erozii i zadachakh sel'skokhoziaistvennoi nauki'," in *Zashchita pochv ot erozii* (Moscow, 1971), 15–16.

64. *Vetrovaia eroziia i plodorodie pochv*, ed., A.A. Baraev et al. (Moscow, 1976), 3–4.

65. F. T.Morgun and N. K. Shikula, *Pochvozashchitnoe bezpluzhnoe zemledelie* (Moscow, 1984), 6–7.

66. A. S. Tereshchenko, "Razrabotka tekhnologii i sredstv mekhanizatsii dlia zashchity pochv ot vetrovoi erozii na Severnom Kavkaze," in *Vetrovaia eroziia i plodorodie pochv*, 283–291.

67. L. N. Gavrilenko, D. S. Bulgakov, and V. S. Rodionov, "Pyl'nye buri 1969 g. v Stavropol'e," *Biulleten' Pochvennogo Instituta imeni V. V. Dokuchaeva*, vyp. 24 (Moscow, 1982), 26.

68. Matskevich in *Zashchita pochv ot erozii*, 16.

69. A. N. Kashtanov, "Usilit' bor'bu s vodnoi eroziei pochv," *Zemledelie*, vol. 25, no. 10 (October 1977), 34–36.

70. V. P. Kuznetsov, "Zashchita pochv ot erozii i otvetstvennost' zemlepol'zovatelei," *Zemledelie*, vol. 26, no. 12 (December 1978), 42–46.

71. V. V. Kolomeichenko, "Osvoenie sklonov pod senokosy i pastbishcha," *Zemledelie*, vol. 27, no. 4 (April 1979), 27–30.

72. V. S. Fedotov, "Sovershenstvovat' bor'bu s vodnoi eroziei pochv," *Zemledelie*, vol. 28, no. 11 (November 1980), 29; V. G. Tkachenko, "Konturno-meliorativnoe zemledelie," *Zemledelie*, vol. 30, no. 4 (April 1982), 17–21; K. S. Ragimov and V. L. Korobov, "Bor'ba s eroziei v Azerbaidzhane," *Zemledelie*, vol. 30, no. 6 (June 1982), 20–22; V. A. Dzhamal', N. M. Sheliakin, and N. V. Medvedev, "Konturnoe zemledelie na sklonakh Ukrainy," *Zemledelie*, vol. 32, no. 2 (February 1984), 22–23.

73. E. I. Gaidamaka and S. I. Nosov, "Osobennosti proektirovaniia i vnedreniia kompleksov protivoerozionnykh meropriiatii v usloviiakh proiavleniia vodnoi i vetrovoi erozii zemel'," in *Pochvozashchitnoe zemledelie na sklonakh*, ed., A. N. Kashtanov (Moscow, 1983), 38–39.

74. M. N. Zaslavaskii, "Zashchita pochv ot erozii i povyshenie plodorodiia smytykh pochv," in *Pochvozashchitnoe zemledelie na sklonakh*, 58.

75. M. I. Lopyrev, "Povysit' kachestvo proektirovaniia," *Zemledelie*, vol. 32, no. 3 (March 1984), 20–23.

76. A. N. Kashtanov, "Prodovol'stvennaia programma i zadachi nauchnogo zemledeliia," in *Aktual'nye problemy zemledeliia*, ed., A. N. Kashtanov et al. (Moscow, 1984), 6–7.

77. L. L. Shishov, I. I. Karmanov, D. S. Bulgakov, and N. N. Vadkovskaia, "Skhema spetsializirovannogo raionirovaniia territorii SSSR dlia sovershenstvovaniia zonal'nykh sistem mashin i zonal'no-regional'nykh sistem zemledeliia," in *Aktual'nye problemy zemledeliia*, 90–97.

78. A. M. Gavrilov, "Meliorativnoe zemledelie i povyshenie plodorodiia pochv," in *Aktual'nye problemy zemledeliia*, 256–257.

79. Shtepa et al., *Melioratsiia zemel' v SSSR*, 116–119.

80. A. K. Beskrovnyi, "Sovremennye problemy zemledeliia na osushennykh zemliakh Ukrainskoi SSR," in *Aktual'nye problemy zemledeliia*, 259.

81. V. A. Kovda, "Kak pomoch' nashim chernozemam," *Nash sovremennik*, vol. 53, no. 7 (July 1985), 122–124.

82. Ibid., 124–127. Similar disincentives were documented for soil conditioning, for which *Selkhozkhimiia* is responsible. Unfortunately, this organization, which has its own fleet of equipment and operators, performs the tasks according to its own incentive structure, and not according to the needs of individual fields, and the end result is not beneficial for agriculture. N. V. Usol'tsev, "Vremia vozvrashchat' dolgi," *Nash sovremennik*, vol. 53, no. 7 (July 1985), 152.

83. Kovda, *Nash sovremennik*, 128.

BRENTON M. BARR

6

Regional Alternatives in Soviet Timber Management

Utilization of timber in the Soviet Union is commonly approached through an examination of physical demand for roundwood and wood products rather than through economic evaluations of timber resources and the volumes of growing stock of individual species.[1] The growing stock is so large and extensively distributed that it tends to be taken as given in discussions of regional development or analyses of such industries as pulp, paper, paperboard, lumber, plywood, etc. (see Figures 6.1 and 6.2). Despite general world concern with problems of resource degradation and deforestation, and the regeneration backlog of nearly 130 million hectares in the Soviet Union (approximately 11.5 million of this are in the European-Uralian zone), the Soviet timber resource still is not viewed by Soviet or Western analysts within a coherent context of deforestation and environmental degradation.[2]

The literature on Soviet forests, however, contains numerous divergent schools of thought on the efficacious use of timber; selection of any one approach leads to conclusions quite different from those obtained through consideration of other formulations of the subject. This chapter, consequently, examines the commercial significance of Soviet regional forests by reviewing the findings of the 1983 forest inventory in relation to the drive for more intensive (rather than extensive) utilization of raw materials.[3] Soviet regional timber reserves are overwhelmingly

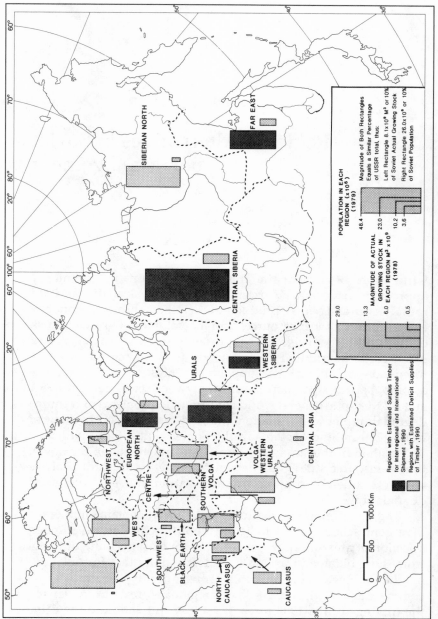

Figure 6.1   USSR: Distribution   of   Forest   Resources   and   Population

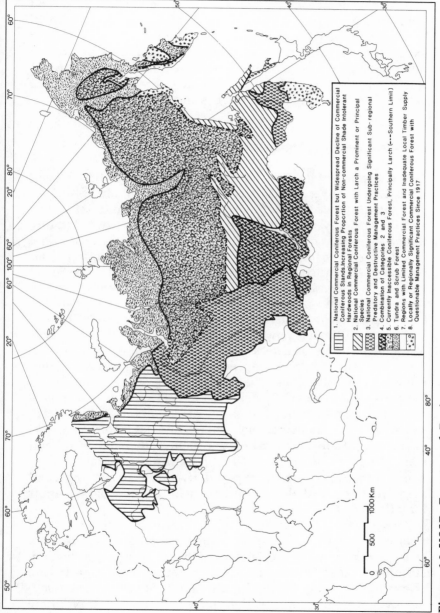

1. National Commercial Coniferous Forest but Widespread Decline of Commercial Coniferous Stands.Increasing Proportion of Non-commercial Shade Intolerant Hardwoods in Regional Forests
2. National Commercial Coniferous Forest with Larch a Prominent or Principal Species
3. National Commercial Coniferous Forest Undergoing Significant Sub-regional Predatory and Destructive Management Pracices
4. Combination of Categories 2 and 3
5. Currently Inaccessible Coniferous Forest, Principally Larch (--Southern Limit)
6. Tundra and Scrub Forest
7. Regions with Limited Commercial Forest and Inadequate Local Timber Supply
8. Locally or Regionally Significant Commercial Coniferous Forest with Questionable Management Practices Since 1917

Figure 6.2 USSR: Forests and Regions

conditioned by spatial variations in the qualitative and locational (including distance) characteristics of the forest itself, and by the degree of willingness among central forestry and industrial agencies to view forest exploitation as a form of harvesting rather than an exercise in high-grade mining. The extent to which forests in existing areas of infrastructure are utilized and regenerated, and the degree of recovery of wood waste from logging and processing sites directly influence the need to develop increasingly remote stands of virgin timber.[4]

Divergent Regional Arguments

The enormity of the resource and of the subject, however, necessitate stringent disclaimers and careful delimitation of the approach followed here. Soviet forestry literature is extensive and increasingly research-based. During the past two decades, the measurement of the forest resource has become scientific and increasingly accurate. Descriptions of the resource and evaluations of the commercial uses of timber abound in the Soviet and Western literature; they have been extensively utilized and referenced in previous works by the author and in recent studies by two prominent Western scholars, K. E. Braden and J. Eronen.[5] Utilization of timber, however, is dictated by the planning goals of the Soviet state as directed to the Soviet Ministry of Timber, Pulp and Paper, and Woodprocessing, and to numerous other ministries and agencies. These goals are essentially related to the current fulfillment of production targets and not to relatively long-term considerations such as preservation of the forest, sustained-yield management, environmental protection, etc. Forest utilization is subordinate to many other industrial and state priorities associated with high-profile mineral, energy, and manufacturing sectors, export-derived foreign exchange, and associated regional developments including the Baikal-Amur Mainline (BAM).

Assessment in the West of the regional utilization and relative utility of Soviet forests cannot proceed on the basis of reliable estimates of spatial variations in cost of production, stumpage fees, labor costs, etc., because these figures are unavailable. Analyses published in the Soviet Union itself, however, are not based on rigorous evaluations of appropriate logging, transportation, processing, and marketing costs. Recent Soviet attempts at optimization contain extensive lacunae and suggest that coherent regional management strategies have yet to be formulated.

The major problem in Soviet industrial analyses seems to lie in the very size and visibility of the forest resource. Many Soviet analysts wax eloquent on the vast reserves of timber in the European North, Siberia, and the Soviet Far East. They note the relatively large share of mature and overmature timber in these forests, the proportions of juvenile stands in European-Uralian forests, and the prevalence of deciduous species in forests closer to the industrial heartland of the country (approximately the western two-thirds of the population triangle). Furthermore, in all major Soviet primary industries except iron ore, the prevailing wisdom and calculations of the so-called "economic effect" of utilizing various deposits appear to favor the exploitation of "spectacular" eastern deposits to offset declining reserves in the European-Uralian zone. The apparent negative economic characteristics of associated higher exploitation and transportation costs are of necessity overlooked in oil, gas, coal, hydroelectric, and other sectors, given the lack of choice in selecting alternative supplies, although the hardships and penalties are commonly acknowledged throughout Soviet industry and society. A general momentum seems to extend this enthusiasm for development of eastern resources uncritically to the area's forests, although the annual increase in the cost of producing a cubic meter of roundwood varied between .7 percent and 3.6 percent from 1971 to 1978.[6]

In forestry, as in agriculture and nuclear power, however, European alternatives exist. This chapter argues that effective utilization of forestry land in the European-Uralian zone could offset the need for exploitation of peripheral forests by providing lower cost supplies of timber and related products.

The Soviet forestry literature and the forestry program adopted by the twenty-sixth Party Congress in 1981 envisage sustained-yield management, comprehensive utilization of wood material, and improvement of the quality of the growing stock. Specific attention is paid to European-Uralian forest utilization, including the development of special timber plantations to support that region's pulp and paper industry.[7] Much of the literature related to wood processing or espousing a partisan approach to eastern development, however, pays little attention to non-Siberian or Far Eastern alternatives. Thus, the Soviet forester, S. V. Belov, demonstrates unequivocally that effective management and utilization of timber can obviate depredation of the country's forests.[8] At the same time, analysts of wood processing, such as S. V. Kazakov (although accepting that the Soviet Union does not fully utilize low-quality wood and wood waste), state, with no discussion, that in the future the country will need "to process wood comprehensively and to utilize waste through integrated processing...and to transfer the center of gravity of logging and processing to eastern regions of the country."[9]

N. I. Kozhukhov, however, while noting that major future increments to the supply of basic wood products will originate from integrated production complexes in heavily forested Siberian and Far Eastern regions, states also that the cost structure of using these forests should be evaluated. According to Kozhukhov, while these forests effectively represent free goods in that they have been created without capital investment, their climatic environments are far less favorable than those in the European region, their productivity is low (less than 100 cubic meters per hectare), their site quality is low, and their average tree trunk diameter does not exceed 24 centimeters.[10] Furthermore, argues Kozhukhov, regeneration of timber in these regions will be more expensive than in other regions because all aspects of their utilization will occur in undeveloped circumstances— development of infrastructure and construction organizations cost 2 to 2.5 times more than those in European regions. Because regeneration cycles are much longer than farther west, the process of regeneration will take too long to ensure sustained yield forest management and a continuous supply of timber to the region's mills. To use eastern timber to supply European processors, on the other hand, means average hauls of at least 3,000 kilometers. Consequently, other solutions are needed: intensification of regeneration and production and utilization of European-Uralian timber.[11] Kozhukhov, however, cannot resist adding that Siberian and Far Eastern timber should be utilized more comprehensively in regional complexes so that raw, semifinished and finished products can be delivered to all customers as efficiently as possible.

The reluctance of Soviet analysts to subject eastern forest projects to deeper scrutiny suggests that, on the one hand, their criticism would fly in the face of official development policy. On the other hand, utilization of eastern forests without due regard for their effective regeneration would buy time for the Soviet economy to organize an effective sustained-yield forest system in the European-Uralian zone over the next thirty to fifty years, which would compensate for the mining or depletion of the extensive eastern peripheral forests. Much of the following analysis is devoted to an elaboration of the extent to which such a strategy could be undertaken.

Although having little apparent influence in determining the regional distribution of wood processing, many of these forest analysts are publishing cogent analyses of the relative merits of sustained utilization of accessible forests (including those in south-central Siberia). Underlying their arguments is the often overlooked fact that timber resources are a spatially extensive phenomenon whereas minerals, hydroelectricity, and coal—even oil and gas—are reasonable punctiform, or capable of relatively constrained primary gathering networks, and concentrated, or of high-volume bulk movement to market. They worry about the ever increasing length of hauling timber to market. They note the problems of accessibility to northern, Siberian, and Far Eastern forests, the harsh environmental conditions for labor and equipment, the seasonality of harvesting and movement of timber, and the physical remoteness of logging sites from settlements, infrastructure, and domestic markets. They imply that investment capital could be more effectively utilized not only in reforestation in the European-Uralian zone, but also in renovating existing processing plants in that zone. In many cases, established mills, settlements, and transportation links in western regions are in jeopardy because the forests have been ruthlessly exploited in the past and appropriate reforestation has not been undertaken.

In light of these considerations and the imputed advantages of effective European-Uralian forest management over unconstrained growth of logging east of the Urals, the incomplete but nevertheless compelling evidence presented by the major thinkers in Soviet forestry must be evaluated for the support it lends to our understanding of the regional alternatives that users of this resource may seek to adopt in the future.

Resource Inventory

Western analysts, such as Eronen and T. G. Honer et al., have noted the improved accuracy of forest mensuration and greater reliability in the manner of establishing permissible cutting limits that have occurred during the past two decades.[12] Inventories taken in 1961, 1966, 1973, 1978, and 1983 are considered methodologically reliable by Soviet foresters, especially in evaluation of remote or peripheral forests in the European north, Siberia, and the Far East.[13] The data published after each of the last four inventories are consistent with previous publications; improvements in survey methods, mensuration technology including use of satellite imagery, and electronic data processing suggest that these inventories reflect a state-of-the-art approach to resource measurement. Many decisions associated with utilization of Soviet forests made prior to the mid-1960s, therefore, probably reflect a methodologically and technically inadequate data base and may have promoted expediency in the utilization of all forests.

The growing scientific approach to forest mensuration and a more profound understanding of biophysical constraints on silviculture evident in the Soviet forestry literature have produced, by the 1980s, a body of thought that seems to be more reliable and less dogmatic or ideologically constrained than at any previous period of Soviet development.[14] Thus, although we still do not have detailed economic analyses of spatial alternatives in timber utilization, we now seem to have reliable physical or technical evaluations of developmental alternatives. Increasing costs and myriad other developmental constraints cited in numerous evaluations of peripheral regions also may prompt Soviet investment administrators to pay more attention to the possibilities for effective management of renewable resources in more propitious regions such as the European-Uralian forests. The growing Soviet reluctance to publish data, especially detailed regional information, is all the more regrettable now in view of the improved quality of information which could be made available.

The 1983 Forest Inventory

The report on the 1983 inventory notes that 19 percent of the forest land is found in the European-Uralian zone.[15] In comparison with 1978, the volume of total Soviet forest land increased by 2.1 million hectares to 1,259.4 million hectares, although that in the European-Uralian zone decreased by .7 million hectares to 239.5 million hectares. These are relatively minor changes compared to those reported between the 1973 and 1978 inventories and seem to suggest that major changes in survey accuracy no longer occur between inventories and that the rate of change in alienation of forest land in the European region may have diminished. The size of the area administered by central state forestry agencies, however, diminished after 1978 as more land was transferred to nonforestry ministries and agencies. The area of *kolkhoz* forests declined slightly due to the transfer of control over some forests to forestry agencies and the transformation of some *kolkhozy* into *sovkhozy*.

Area and Volume

Three-quarters of the Soviet population lives in the European-Uralian region, an area comprising 25.5 percent of the forested area, 27.3 percent of the total growing stock, and 18.3 percent of the nation's mature timber. Central state forestry organs administer 745 million of the 811 million hectares of the forested land; approximately 566 million hectares comprise coniferous stands. Mature and overmature stands make up 52 billion of the 86 billion cubic meters of the total growing stock; 43 billion cubic meters of the mature and overmature stands comprise conifers. Of the forested land administered by central state forestry organs, 689 million hectares represent principal stands; 539 million hectares (78.2 percent) of these are conifers. The total area of principal stands includes 40.5 percent larch, 17.5 percent pine, 11.9 percent spruce, 6 percent Siberian stone pine, 2.3 percent fir, 13 percent birch, 2.7 percent aspen, .4 percent alder, and .4 percent basswood; shade-tolerant species (oak, beech, ash, maple, etc.) comprise most of the remaining 5.3 percent. Environmental constraints limit most of the shade-tolerant species to the European-Uralian zone, and most of the Siberian stone pine and larch stands to eastern Siberia or the Far East.

Soviet authors note that because of its widespread distribution in eastern regions, larch will become the basic raw material for wood processing in the twelfth five-year plan (presumably for industries deriving their raw material from eastern forests). Furthermore, "future development of Siberia is related to the utilization of larch for local needs, needs of other Soviet regions, and for forest-product exports."[16] Most Soviet larch is found in eastern Siberia (77 percent of national total volume) and in the Far East (21 percent of national total volume).[17] Larch comprises approximately half of the coniferous forest volume of eastern Siberia and almost three-quarters of that of the Far East. Iu. R. Bokshchanin predicts that by the 1991–1995 period, larch will comprise 40 percent of the harvest in eastern Siberia and 60 percent of that in the Far East; he reports that the annual harvest of larch in the early 1980s had already reached 2 million cubic meters in Irkutsk oblast' and made up 40 percent of the export volume from the Far East.[18] If the last official figures on all roundwood harvested in Irkutsk oblast' (1975) are taken as a base, then the annual harvest of larch comprises only 6 percent of the timber harvest[19] (official figures likely do not include that cut by "nomadic" loggers, which is a major problem in eastern Siberia).[20] The species composition of all Soviet forests is highly problematic, however. We cannot assume that domestic or foreign customers will adjust willingly or rapidly to larger volumes of larch in their timber consumption mix although foreign experience with utilization of larch and numerous deciduous species, and Soviet shortfalls of accessible coniferous timber, seem to be stimulating greater awareness of their commercial properties in the Soviet Union.[21]

Limitations of space restrict subsequent discussion of this topic to considerations of regional variation in deciduous and coniferous forests undifferentiated by species. Nearly 21 percent (155.5 million hectares) of the forested area administered by central state forestry organs is situated in the European-Uralian zone. Coniferous species comprise 63.6 percent, shade-tolerant species 7.2 percent, and shade-intolerant species 28.5 percent. The remainder is composed of various shrubs, willows, and other species. The traditional overcutting of conifers in this zone, plus the poor performance of natural regeneration and the insufficient investment in silviculture, have adversely affected the age composition of stands in these forests; in particular, the prevalence of immature stands of conifers and the proportion of deciduous trees, especially shade-intolerant species, have increased.

Forest Groups

The importance of the European-Uralian forests, however, is often masked by the tripartite division of Soviet forests into three groups: (1) protection forests, (2) restricted industrial forests, and (3) general industrial forests.[22] The European-Uralian zone contains 33 percent of the group 1 forested area, 74 percent of group 2, but 12 percent of group 3. Because most commercial harvesting occurs in group 3 forests, and because four-fifths of their area lies outside the European-Uralian zone, the conclusion is frequently drawn both in the Soviet Union and abroad that logging must be based in these forests. This expectation is compounded by the fact that most Soviet mature and overmature timber is found in group 3 forests and that, because the growing stock is biologically in jeopardy in such stands, removal of these stands would provide the basis for future regeneration and general improvement in land productivity. These expectations, however, ignore the spatial or geographical realities of many group 3 forests, particularly their remoteness, harsh climate, topography, species composition, and slow regeneration.

Mature and Overmature Stands

In the last interinventory period, for example, the national area of mature and overmature stands decreased by 13.1 million hectares, including 2.4 million hectares in the European-Uralian zone. This decrease occurred chiefly in coniferous forests. Nevertheless, as in previous periods, the relative share of mature and overmature species remains significant in the Soviet Union at 53 percent of total forested area. Even in the European-Uralian zone, however, mature and overmature species make up 37 percent of the forested area. Their share of forested area in the European north, Urals, and Volga-Viatka—the regions of chief timber reserve in the European-Uralian area—comprises 82 percent of the coniferous forested area. Inappropriate harvesting practices in these regions are particularly harmful if they lead to destruction or premature cutting of the relatively small share of the stands composed of the age group "approaching maturity."

In the European lightly forested regions, however, the opposite age structure prevails; juvenile stands are predominant (46 percent of the forested area in the Ukraine, 51 percent in Belorussia, 39 percent in the Black Earth region, for example). Depletion of the forests in previous periods and the small present proportion of mature timber thus precludes intensive timber harvesting in the near future.

Species Composition

Despite the increase in area of coniferous forest in Asiatic and heavily forested European-Uralian regions, a large share of the stands regenerated after conifer logging contains deciduous species, an undesirable process in terms of sustained-yield management. In European regions such as the Ukraine, Belorussia, the Baltic republics, the Northwest, the Center, the Volga littoral, and traditional forest-deficit regions of the RSFSR, this process reportedly has been halted, although much remains to be done to improve the species composition of the forest. Analysts of the 1983 inventory claim that the basic reason the species composition adversely changed in the heavily forested regions is related to inadequate silviculture in relation to the felling of mature stands, an imbalance caused by insufficient equipment and shortages of labor.[23] Furthermore, the introduction of forest-harvesting machinery has increased the incidence of destruction of new growth (the understory of new trees) and juvenile stands, thereby retarding the rate of forest regeneration. Until this problem is overcome, Soviet foresters recommend that available equipment be limited to forests without significant understories.

In forests administered by central state forestry organs, 82 percent of the growing stock comprises coniferous forest, but 67 percent of the coniferous forest is classified as mature or overmature. Shade-tolerant and intolerant species make up only 18 percent of the growing stock and only half of their area is mature or overmature forest. Of the increase in growing stock in the interinventory period, 47 percent occurred in coniferous stands. The dilemma facing Soviet foresters is thus related to the need to reduce, in the interests of sustained-yield management, the excessive share of mature and overmature stands without adversely changing the species composition of the forest. In theory, this could be facilitated by effective regeneration and silvicultural practices; in practice, natural and human regeneration are inadequate, and undesirable deciduous species are increasingly occupying prime forest regions.

In the European-uralian zone, for example, with one-quarter of the centrally administered volume of growing stock, conifers comprise 65 percent, but their share of growth in the last interinventory period was only 52 percent. The problem associated with this imbalance is particularly associated with shade-intolerant species (in some cases a larger regeneration of shade-tolerant species like oak would be desirable), which comprise 27 percent of the volume of growing stock but accounted for 36 percent of the interinventory growth in volume. As yet, these species are inadequately utilized by Soviet wood processors, although calls for improvement in this matter have been registered for decades.

Commercial Forest

When conservation and accessibility are taken into consideration, 385 million hectares or 55.1 percent of the Soviet forested area is available for commercial timber harvesting. In the European-Uralian zone, however, the commercial timber harvesting area is 128 million hectares or 85 percent of the regional forested area. The area commercially available outside this region is almost entirely located in Siberia and the Soviet Far East and represents approximately 257 million hectares or almost exactly twice that located in the European-Uralian zone, In addition, a very large area—184 million hectares mainly found east of the Urals—is classified as reserve forest largely because of its remoteness and adverse physical environment. Great geographical variation in environmental adversity may be gauged from inventory figures released on the distribution of forest land in *gornyi les* (mountain/alpine/montane forest). Approximately 40 percent (474 million hectares) of Soviet forest land comprises *gornyi les*; half of this forest is composed of forested land. Two-thirds of the 26 billion cubic meters of growing stock reported from the 1978 inventory is listed as mature or overmature.[24] Of the total *gornyi les*, 65 percent of the area is found in the Far East, 25 percent in eastern Siberia, but only 5 percent in the European-Uralian zone and 5 percent throughout the remainder of the country. Given that 90 percent of this forest area is found in eastern Siberia and the Far East (*gornyi les* comprises 39 percent of the forested land area in eastern Siberia, 56 percent of that in the Far East, but only 28 percent of that in the Urals and 2 percent of that in the Northwest), then some of the adverse topographical limitations on forests of those peripheral regions are immediately apparent.[25] Of the total national growing stock in the *gornyi les*, 56 percent of the volume is situated on slopes over 20 degrees, and 30 percent is found on slopes of 20 to 30 degrees.[26] Approximately 50 million cubic meters are harvested annually (agencies are not specified) from *gornyi les* forests, although the volume from slopes in excess of 15 to 20 degrees is only 4 million cubic meters.[27]

The volume of national commercial forest is set at 28.6 billion cubic meters or 58 percent of the volume of mature and overmature stands. In the European-Uralian zone, however, the commercial forest comprises 88 percent of such stands. Despite increases in the overall volume of growing stock throughout Soviet forests, the volume of commercial stands declined in the European-Uralian zone during the interinventory period by 3 percent (260 million cubic meters). Nevertheless, more precise mensuration and the extension of regulated utilization in various categories of European protected forest in the 1978-1983 period increased the volume of forest available for commercial exploitation by 3 percent. This increase apparently offset some of the impact of the decline in commercial forest during this period. In addition, some 1.25 billion cubic meters (70 percent of which is conifer) of mature and overmature timber in group 1 forests are proposed for utilization in the near future. At present, the annual allowable cut of 38 million cubic meters in these forests is only half utilized. Over 40 million cubic meters of timber was being harvested annually by 1975 from intermediate cutting, largely from group 1 forests.[28] This cutting, important in the overall supply of wood although not included as part of the annual allowable cut, is particularly important in the European-Uralian zone where most group 1 forests are situated. When conducted throughout all groups of Soviet forests, intermediate cutting as a form of improvement cut could account for 50 percent of the annual Soviet timber supply.[29] Proponents of sustained-yield forestry now frequently refer to the guidelines for economic and social development of the Soviet Union from 1981 to 1990 that require foresters to undertake the gradual transition toward a forest industry based on sustained and coherent utilization of its resource, including improvement in the quality composition of the forest. This transformation is to be accomplished on the basis of effective improvement felling.[30]

Secure supplies of timber depend on the commercial forests, particularly those in the north and Urals economic regions of the European-Uralian zone having large proportions of mature and overmature stands.[31] Their volumes of growing stock, however, are continually diminishing partly in relation to the objective of reducing the proportion of older timber, but partly because appropriate measures are not being undertaken to guarantee replenishment of the resource. Observers of this process fear that a large discrepancy between rates of harvesting and regeneration will lead to extensive fluctuations in logging and exhaustion of the resource.[32] Thus, the allowable principal cut exceeds the mean annual increment by 86 percent in Arkhangel'sk, 69 percent in Murmansk, 56 percent in Komi, 45 percent in Vologda, and 29 percent in Karelia, and by 22 percent in Kirov and Perm' areas. Although the volume of growing stock is still great in the European-Uralian regions, the reserves of mature and overmature timber that constitute the basis for designation of commercial forests have a life expectancy (at existing levels of utilization) of thirteen years in Kostroma, twenty years in Kirov and Vologda, thirty years in Karelia, and fifty years in Arkhangel'sk and Komi. The extent of current middle-age forests and those approaching maturity in these regions is too small to ensure future replacement of their mature timber now being harvested or to sustain their present levels of logging. Hence, one of the major conclusions from an analysis of the 1983 inventory is that measures should be incorporated into the twelfth five-year plan to reconcile the gross discrepancies between utilization and regeneration of timber in European-Uralian forests.[33]

In the optimistic and data-rich 1960s, figures of overcutting were regularly published for logging regions, many of which today are described as having extremely undesirable forests. Although permissible levels of principal harvesting are lower than the annual increment, actual harvesting practices suggest that the commercial forests will be exhausted within four years in Belorussia, nine years in the Ukraine, eight to ten years in the Baltic republics, and ten years in the Central Black Earth region. The levels of allowable principal cut are meant to reflect continual increases in the maturing of growing stock, and to permit achievement of rotation cutting within fifteen to twenty years.[34]

Quality of Growing Stock

Differences in physical environment among major forest regions are reflected in the quality of the resource. Nationally, 11 percent of the Soviet Union is classified as high-yield forest, 49 percent as average-yield, and 40 percent as low-yield. In the European-Uralian forests, however, the proportions of forest distributed among these groups are almost equal. With steady improvements in the age structure, increases in forested area, and increases in silviculture, the annual increment in growing stock is now rated at 931 million cubic meters which represents an increase of 25 million cubic meters over previous estimates. Approximately one-third of the annual increment accrues to European-Uralian forests, which register a mean annual increment per hectare of 2.2 cubic meters compared to the national average of 1.35 cubic meters. The annual increment of this region is nearly 310 million cubic meters, which represents approximately three-fourths of the total timber harvest from all sources, 97.5 percent of the total volume of timber harvested nationally by central state forestry organs or 113 percent of commercial roundwood removals.[35] Although obviously an oversimplification because of omission of any consideration of timber size, species composition, etc., these estimates clearly demonstrate what could be achieved in the European-Uralian zone with effective forest management.

One of the major factors detracting from full utilization of the potential of Soviet forested land is the imbalance between planned timber harvesting and the "trade" mix of timber designated in the allowable cut. To "fulfill the excessive planned harvesting volumes of commercial roundwood," the best, high-yielding stands have been cut first with the result that the composition of commercial forests has continually diminished.[36] The present mature and overmature forests of the north and the Urals have lower than average yields, which are close to those expected from forests approaching maturity. In Arkhangel'sk (141 cubic meters per hectare) and in Kirov (212 cubic meters per hectare) the two forests are equal, but in other regions forests approaching maturity exceed the mature forests in average volume of growing stock per hectare: by 12 cubic meters in Vologda, by 27 cubic meters in Karelia, and by 31 cubic meters in Komi. To overcome the depletion of quality timber within mature forests, analysts of the 1983 inventory recommend that timber harvesting be related to the wood product mix that given commercial stands can support.

Regeneration

In addition to better matching of product plans and growing stock profiles, effective silvicultural practices including all forms of reforestation have great importance for improvements in the regional efficacy of Soviet timber management. The Soviet regeneration backlog of approximately 130 million hectares (including all forest lands) appears to be growing, not declining as implied by Soviet sources.[37] If we estimate that annual harvesting occurs on between 3.5 and 4 million hectares, then the levels of reforestation are inadequate by 1 to 1.5 million hectares.[38] The quality of reforestation, particularly in terms of levels and success rates of seeding and planting, also is subject to debate among Soviet foresters. Unknown additional areas suffering annual depredations from fire, disease, and insects obviously raise the real annual need for reforestation still further.

Areas listed as reforested, however, belie low prevailing

levels of stocking density and the unsatisfied need for improvement felling in many forest stands.[39] Some thirty-one million hectares of forest stands, of which nineteen million are in the European-Uralian zone, apparently are overstocked and need improvement felling; an additional twenty-four million hectares require "sanitary" felling. Other areas of endeavor for improving forest productivity, particularly in the European-Uralian zone, include greater use of intermediate cut, improved road access to stands in the major forested regions, greater use of normally less desirable species, and extended rehabilitation of the national state-designated forested wetlands (80 percent of their seventy-one million hectares are concentrated in this zone).[40]

Discussion

Regional alternatives in Soviet timber utilization appear to fall within the broad category of debate so effectively assessed by Leslie Dienes: pro-Siberian development versus strengthening of the European economic core.[41] The arguments presented in this chapter confirm that development of eastern forests need not occur because of an inevitable or irreversable depletion of growing stock in the European-Uralian zone, although many Soviet analysts, especially in relation to the wood-processing industries, accept eastern resource utilization as being axiomatic. Most foresters, however, demonstrate, in physical or biological terms, that effective management and regeneration of the resource could lead to a much greater utilization of European-Uralian forests and could alleviate the need to extend development into the harsh environments of the eastern forests. At the same time, however, cutting practices in all regions are deemed unsatisfactory from the standpoint of environmental protection or rotation cut. Furthermore, industrial consumption in the east should be satisfied by regional production of major wood products and structural timber. Levels of production in eastern Siberia and the Far East, however, exceed those necessary to meet regional unprocessed and processed timber needs in the majority of products. European-Uralian regional timber supplies and consumption of wood products are supplemented by the output from eastern regions, although this is uneconomical in many cases, especially in roundwood and low-value timber commodities. Although boldly suggesting that the logging industry should be relocated to eastern regions or forests should be more effectively managed and utilized in the west to alleviate pressure on the European environment, I. N. Voevoda notes that the Soviet Union pursues both policies simultaneously in order to refurbish the European-Uralian resources and eventually to increase their utility to the national economy.[42]

Some regional diversity in Soviet timber development strategy[43] has been pursued in recent decades, although the impact of the natural environment on forest regeneration has been insufficiently understood.[44] Furthermore, the full implications of improvement felling are not known. This is a labor-intensive process, an uneconomical activity in many cases that needs to be avoided. In addition, greater extraction of minerals from the forest soil by the remaining trees is alleged to encourage its degradation unless supplemented by mineral fertilizers. Given that the outcome of improvement felling is not sufficiently predictable, Voevoda argues that foresters need to have at their disposal a reliable reserve supply, a process which is being met by greater reliance on heavily forested regions, particularly those of Siberia.[45] Such possible losses in the western heavily populated regions mean that expenditures on development in the east are not as expensive as otherwise expected. This argument, however, seems to confirm that eastern developments are not evaluated in terms of the cost of regenerating their associated forests, and that eastern timber utilization is essentially viewed as a mining operation with little long-term consideration for the environment or for sustained management of the resource.

Some analysts take a completely didactic approach to eastern forests and reduce all obstacles or supposed disadvantages to banalities subordinated to current national political policy. Some of their statements and prognoses are reminders that the Soviet academic and scientific establishments in which informed planning opinion is formulated still have proponents of regional development somewhat removed from spatial and economic reality.

> Despite the harsh climate, difficult terrain, and heavy demands for capital investment, the development of the forest sector of Siberia and the Far East has many economic advantages over other regions of the country. Moreover, production of commercial roundwood, lumber, chemical pulp and other processed wood products rightly does not have today competitors in other regions of the country. This is primarily explained by the impossibility of achieving similar large scales of production elsewhere in the USSR.[46]

Although unable to offer comprehensive cost estimates of regional development alternatives between forests of the west and the east, most rigorous analysts cite negative eastern cost influences that supposedly place the exploitation of those forests at a great disadvantage. Voevoda, for example, cites the harsh climate, low population density, and distance from the economic heartland as factors that even the system of regional coefficients, allowances, and longer annual vacations cannot overcome. Furthermore, the higher priority accorded other primary sectors in the east means that they can outcompete forestry for limited supplies of labor and that they have better records of labor turnover and higher productivity. In addition, myriad well-known environmental factors act adversely on eastern populations. Other exercises in deriving optimal values for regional utilization of roundwood also are unable to provide unequivocal evidence that development of Siberian forests offers greater utility to the Soviet economy than that which can be obtained from forests in the European-Uralian zone.[47] Part of the problem in interpreting such studies is related to the lack of detail provided on the assumptions and constraints built into the models and the extent to which the location and product mix of existing processing units is considered immutable.

In their extensive review of mathematical programming models used in Novosibirsk to derive and validate recommendations for Siberian development, M. H. Soule and R. N. Taaffe note that: "most of the quantitative approaches used in Soviet regional analysis in general, and Siberian development specifically, are still in the experimental stages and are used in preplanning and long-term projections rather than in operational planning" and that rigorous analytical approaches are

> constrained by the complexity of regional problems in general and by the specific difficulties of inadequate information, including the existing price system, unresolved methodological issues, limitations on computer capacities, and the intricacies of incorporating important noneconomic variables.[48]

With perhaps unusual candor, Voevoda notes that the inclusion of specific factors in regional comparisons can greatly affect the relative merits of eastern or western regions.[49] In one set of examples, he demonstrates that harvesting timber in Krasnoiarsk Krai is 19 percent more effective than in Komi ASSR, although this advantage changes greatly as variables are added or subtracted, and that many unknown relationships cannot be evaluated because of the simultaneous interaction of specific variables. Furthermore, the problem of deriving models of regional preference is compounded by the absence of an effective theoretical base for systematic sector analysis.[50] Thus, in an example drawn from Kemerovo oblast', Voevoda shows how one section of the RSFSR GOSPLAN determined that logging Kemerovo was between 2.3 to 3.7 rubles more expensive per cubic meter than bringing timber from the Krasnoyarsk, Irkutsk, or Tomsk regions. Analysts in another agency, Sibgiprolesprom, however, ascertained that 3 to 3.5 rubles could be saved per cubic meter by logging in the Kuzbas instead of bringing timber from the Tomsk or Krasnoiarsk regions.[51]

Modeling by Voevoda and associates in the 1970s on sectoral and regional development of the forest industry, despite many methodological problems including those identified above gives us some idea of possible future patterns of logging in the Soviet Union. Their optimization seems to have made few allowances for changes in the intensity of wood processing or for advances in silviculture, although they did include allowance for improvement felling and for greater utilization of deciduous species. They concluded that, in the near future (1976–1990), logging related to principal cut and improvement felling could expand in the European-Uralian zone, although levels of possible increase are smaller than those in eastern regions.

The figures in Table 6.1 serve to illustrate how the future appeared to analysts in Novosibirsk in the mid-1970s. Although not the specific subject of investigation here, their projection serves to reinforce the arguments made throughout the present analysis that greater use of European-Uralian forests is possible, assuming the political will to force substitution of deciduous species, the utilization of low quality timber, and the full adoption of effective silviculture. This same political will must ensure greater use of deciduous species in Siberia as well, a point often overlooked in analysis of the Soviet forest because of our customary preoccupation with the size of the eastern larch forest. Furthermore, the estimates of Voevoda rest on many assumptions that are not fully known; these estimates of possible increases during the 1976–1990 period predate the growth in desire for intensive utilization of resources apparently affecting investment decisions now. The estimates also probably include levels of subsidization of eastern projects, including those associated with the BAM, which reflect political and social priorities rather than strict economic considerations. Finally, the Novosibirsk

Table 6.1 Estimated Total Possible Regional Increases in Logging
Volumes, 1976–1990 (cubic meters X 10)

Region	Conifers	Deciduous	Total[a]
Baltic Republics, Belorussia			
Kaliningrad	–3.5	+6.8	+3.3
European RSFSR	+4.8	+26.3	+31.1
Urals	–4.6	+5.8	+1.2
Ukraine and Moldavia	+1.8	+4.3	+6.1
Volga Littoral	+0.7	+7.5	+8.2
West Siberia	+8.7	+14.5	+23.2
East Siberia	+34.2	+14.4	+48.6
Far East	+21.5	+8.0	+29.5

Source: Compiled from material in N. Voevoda, Lesnaia i lesoperab-
atyvaiushchaia promyshlennnost' Sibiri (Novosibirsk, 1980), 272.
[a]"Total" is used here to designate the total increase in levels of annual
output over the fifteen-year period; each figure includes wood derived from
principal cut and from improvement felling.

estimates and much of their accompanying discussion indicate
that evaluation of European-Uralian alternatives versus those of
Siberia and the Far East likely will become even more analytical
in the future as the Soviet scientific and planning organizations
incorporate more of the key variables affecting regional physical
planning of the distribution of resource industries, even if strictly
economic criteria do not improve in reliability.

Conclusion

The likely or possible future logging patterns are beyond the
scope of this chapter, which focuses on the 1983 forest inventory
and the physical distribution of the resource. Previous studies,
however, have demonstrated that regional supplies of wood and
fiber accessible in major wood-processing regions are extensive,
especially when logging and mill residues are included.[52] Many
Soviet studies have demonstrated over the past two decades how
the recovery of wood waste can assist in the fiber supply for
wood-processing industries in accessible regions. The present
chapter suggests that the increasing rigor of the forestry
literature has now provided another avenue for achieving
regional economies in resource utilization and improvements in
the stability of supply within existing European-Uralian wood-

processing regions. By implication, economies within the wood-processing sector and within the forestry sector also pertain to the accessible areas of western and south-central Siberia.

The present discussion is obviously only a small part of the breadth of material that should be assessed in comprehensive discussion of Soviet forests, wood processing, exports, and regional development.[53] Greater investigation is needed of regional variations in silviculture, improvements in technology for effective utilization of roundwood (including deciduous species and larch), and the impact that shortages of capital and labor will have on forestry and wood-processing investment in eastern peripheral regions, including the service area of the BAM and the Amur-Yakutsk railway.[54] It seems obvious that eastern forests will be utilized, especially to fulfill regional demand for unprocessed roundwood and some export obligations of roundwood, chips, and lumber to Pacific markets.[55] Areas accessible to the Soviet rail network will likely continue to ship roundwood to the European-Uralian zone for consumption in unprocessed or processed form. The key factor warranting investigation in these and associated spatial developments, however, is the rate of growth of logging and wood processing in various regions, and the extent to which substitutions can be made in the supply of raw material to existing consumers from greater efficiency in the utilization of accessible forests, especially those in the European-Uralian zone. The evidence presented here suggests that mining of the eastern resource in the near future may be undertaken as part of an effort to buy time while major areas of the European-Uralian forest are regenerated to sustain rotation cutting. On the other hand, problems in silviculture and delays in the introduction of rigorous planning in wood processing, plus the chaotic actions of numerous nonforestry ministries and agencies, are serving to delay and/or offset the adoption of alternatives needed for more effective regional management and utilization of Soviet forests.[56]

Notes

1. Basic descriptions of forests, timber utilization, and many associated issued are provided in *Lesnoe khoziaistvo SSSR* (Moscow, 1977); V. A. Nikolaiuk et al., *Razmeshchenie lesokhoziaistvennogo proizvodstva* (Moscow, 1982); I. S. Prokhorchuk et al., *Ekonomika lesoobrabatyvaiushchei promyshlennosti* (Moscow, 1981); N. V.

Timofeev, ed., *Lesnaia industriia SSSR* (Moscow, 1980); G. I. Vorob'ev, *Effektivnost' lesnogo khoziaistva SSSR* (Moscow, 1982); and G. I. Vorob'ev et al., *Ekonomicheskaia geografiia lesnykh resursov SSSR* (Moscow, 1979). The work by V. V. Stepin stands out as a major attempt to provide economic analyses of the spatial economy of Soviet forests: V. V. Stepin, *Ekonomicheskie osnovy prirodopol'zovaniia* (Moscow, 1982). A comprehensive economic evaluation of eastern development, including many sectors of the economy, is provided by P. de Souza, "On the 'Price' of a Siberian Development" (Gothenburg, Sweden: University of Gothenburg, Department of Human and Economic Geography, draft for research paper, 1985, provided in personal communication to the author). The present chapter, constrained by space, focuses on the 1983 inventory results; all of the foregoing references rely on previous inventories.

2. See V. M. Ivaniuta et al., *Ekonomika lesnogo khoziaistva* (Moscow, 1983), 30–31. A recent English-language assessment of this topic and related inventory matters is provided by T. G. Honer, F. Hegyi, and G. M. Bonnor, *Forest Inventory in the USSR, 1982: A Report on the Visit of Canadian Forest Inventory Specialists to the Soviet Union* (Ottawa: Government of Canada, Canadian Forestry Service, Forestry Technical Report 34, 1985), 2.

3. M. M. Drozhalov, "Lesnaia niva," *Lesnoe khoziaistvo*, no. 10 (1984), 59–63.

4. Space does not permit investigation here of the extensive literature on the substitution of wood waste or rejected timber for commercial roundwood. An estimated 110 million cubic meters of such material is available annually from the activities of all timber harvesting agencies although only two-fifths are deemed economically recoverable (three-fifths of the 62 million cubic meters available to the major ministry are deemed economically recoverable). The respective volumes actually available, however, are even smaller—33 percent and 47 percent. This subject is carefully discussed in A. P. Livanov, et al., *Perevozka shchepy* (Moscow, 1980), 3–9.

5. B. M. Barr, "Soviet Forest Resources: A Review and Summary," *Soviet Geography: Review and Translation*, vol. 22, no. 6 (June 1982), 452–462; B. M. Barr, "Regional Dilemmas and International Prospects in the Soviet Timber Industry," in *Soviet Natural Resources in the World Economy*, ed., R. G. Jensen, T. Shabad, and A. W. Wright (Chicago: The University of Chicago Press, 1983), 411–441; B. M. Barr, "The Soviet Forest in the 1980s: Changing Geographical Perspectives," in *Geographical Studies on the Soviet Union: Essays in Honor of Chauncy D. Harris*, ed., G. J. Demko and R. J. Fuchs (Chicago: The University of Chicago, Department of Geography, Research Paper, no. 211, 1984), 235–255; B. M. Barr, "Perspectives on Deforestation in the USSR," in *World Forests and the Global Economy in the Twentieth Century*, ed., J. F. Richards and R. P. Tucker (Durham, N.C.: Duke University Press, forthcoming); K. Braden, "The Role of Imported Technology in the Export Potential of

Soviet Forest Products," in *Soviet Natural Resources in the World Economy*, ed., R. G. Jensen, T. Shabad, and A. W. Wright (Chicago: The University of Chicago Pres, 1983), 442–463; J. Eronen, *Neuvostoliiton massa—Ja paperiteollisuuden alueellinen ekspansio* (Helsinki: Helsingin Kauppakorkeakoulun Julkaisuja B 50, 1981); J. Eronen, "Soviet Pulp and Paper Industry: Factors Explaining Its Areal Expansion," *Silva fennica*, vol. 16, no. 3 (1982), 267–285; J. Eronen, "Routes of Soviet Timber to World Markets," *Geoforum*, vol. 14, no. 2 (1983), 205–210; and J. Eronen, *Location, Strategy and Patterns: An Empirical Investigation of the Soviet Pulp and Paper Industry* (Helsinki: The Helsinki School of Economics, Acta Academiae Oeconomicae Helsingies, Series A:42, 1984).

6. Reports on the visit of M. S. Gorbachev to western Siberia in September 1985 attest to the role of national production goals in forcing the eastern development of high- profile sectors such as fuel and energy. These primary industries then become important to some related regional processors (e.g., petrochemicals) in the name of "intensification" and to other sectors, such as pulp and paper, which are energy-intensive or which consume large amounts of energy in aggregate. "Uskorennoe razvitie ekonomiki Sibiri i Dal'nego Vostoka," *Ekonomicheskaia Gazeta*, no. 37 (September 1985), 1. Increasing costs of production are stated to be chiefly due to increasing length of hauling roundwood, rising costs of building logging roads, corrections to pay schedules between 1973 and 1975, introduction of new depreciation allowances in 1975, etc. N. A. Burdin et al., *Spravochnik ekonomista lesnoi promyshlennosti* (Moscow, 1980), 241.

7. See L. E. Mikhailov and A. B. Bronina, *Sbornik normativnykh materialov po lesnomu khoziaistvu* (Moscow, 1984), particularly 5.

8. S. V. Belov, *Lesovodstvo* (Moscow, 1983), note comments on 225.

9. S. V. Kazakov, *Lesopererabatyvaiushchie kompleksy* (Moscow, 1984), 12. As noted elsewhere in this paper, the Soviet Union does utilize low-quality wood, deciduous species, and wood waste extensively in its processing industries. Stabilization of the annual harvest of industrial timber while continuing to boost the output of processed items is usually attributed by the principal Soviet wood-processing ministry to its increasing substitution of wood waste for roundwood. In the production of sulphate pulp, for example, 37 percent of the 1980 output comprised low-quality wood, wood chips, and deciduous species. The volume of these three fiber sources in the sulphate pulp industry is envisaged to reach 20 million cubic meters at some unspecified future date. V. S. Liublin et al., *Ekonomika tselliulozno-bumazhnykh proizvodstv* (Moscow, 1980), 24.

10. N. I. Kozhukhov, *Osnovy upravleniia v lesnom khoziaistve i lesnoi promyshlennosti*, (Moscow, 1984) 63.

11. Kozhukhov, *Osnovy upravleniia*, 63.

12. Honer, Hegyi, and Bonnor, *Forest Inventory in the USSR*; and Eronen, *Silva Fennica*, 267–285.

13. The evolution of Soviet forest mensuration and survey is described in N. N. Gusev, et at., *Lesoustroistvo v SSSR* (Moscow, 1981), 4–17. The first reliable data on the entire forest were obtained in 1957, 10.

14. In this context, two important evaluations of regional problems in the Soviet forest resource are those by I. V. Shutov et al., eds., *Lesnye plantatsii [uskorennoe vyrashchivanie eli i sosny]* (Moscow, 1984), particularly 5–13; A. P. Petrov and F. N. Morozov, *Ekonomika lesnoi promyshlennosti: uchebnik dlia vuzov* (Moscow, 1984), particularly 314–321.

15. Drozhalov, "Lesnoe khoziaistvo," 59–63.

16. Iu. R. Bokshchanin, *Obrabotka i primenenie drevesiny listvennitsy* (Moscow, 1982), 3.

17. Ibid., 8.

18. Ibid., 9.

19. *Narodnoe khoziaistvo RSFSR v 1975 g.* (Moscow, 1976), 89.

20. Discussed at length in Barr, "Perspectives on Deforestation in the USSR."

21. A. I. Bobrov et al., *Proizvodstvo voloknistykh polufabrikatov iz listvennoi drevesiny* (Moscow, 1984); and V. F. Shcheglov et al., *Spravochnik mastera lesopil'nogo proizvodstva* (Moscow, 1984).

22. Forest terminology, administration, classification, and regions are discussed in Barr, *Soviet Geography: Review and Translation*, 452–462.

23. Drozhalov, "Lesnoe khoziaistvo," 61.

24. A. P. Livanov, *Ekspluatatsiya gornykh lesov* (Moscow, 1983), 4.

25. *Lesnoe khoziaistvo SSSR* (Moscow, 1977), 19.

26. Livanov, *Ekspluatatsiya gornykh lesov*, 4.

27. Ibid., 4.

28. M. V. Kolesnichenko, *Lesomelioratsiia s osnovami lesovodstva* (Moscow, 1981), 9.

29. Kolesnichenko, *Lesomelioratsiia s osnovami*, 9.

30. For example, S. N. Sennov, *Ukhod za lesom: ekologicheskie osnovy* (Moscow, 1984), 3.

31. Drozhalov, "Lesnoe khoziaistvo," 62.

32. Ibid.

33. Ibid.

34. Ibid.

35. *Narodnoe khoziaistvo SSSR v 1983 g.* (Moscow, 1984), 378. Most Soviet and Western descriptions of timber harvesting in the Soviet Union focus on the logging volumes associated with commercial roundwood (275 million cubic meters in 1983), or a larger figure associated with total removals (356 million cubic meters in 1983) as customarily reported in the *Narodnoe khoziaistvo* volumes. The same volumes, however, report under the section of natural resources and conservation, a logging figure that lies between these two amounts (318 million cubic meters in 1983) and seems to include commercial roundwood plus improvement fellings. The largest figure (356 million)

expresses removals ("principal cut") for some thirty-four ministries and departments, but excludes that comprising improvement fellings and other cutting (wood for undisclosed users harvested mainly in the northwest, Volga-Viatka, Urals, Siberia, and the Far East) (see Burdin et al., *Spravochnik ekonomista*, 64–65). A large share of the total annual cut, however, is consumed as fuel—approximately 100 million cubic meters (*Narodnoe khoziaistvo SSSR v 1983 g.*, 152). Hence, the foregoing categories presumably include portions of this fuelwood, although Dienes and Shabad note that the official figures do not include firewood gathered by the population for its own use (L. Dienes and T. Shabad, *The Soviet Energy System* (New York: John Wiley & Sons, 1979), 33. The total annual cut of approximately 410 million cubic meters cited by Burdin et al., *Spravochnik ekonomista*, 64 and by Belov, *Lesovodstvo*, 224, although itself considerably in excess of what the wood-processing and statistical literature would have us believe, still seems to understate the annual cut. This subject requires considerable further investigation. Belov states (p. 225) that the main wood-processing ministry takes 54 percent of the annual harvest of 410 million cubic meters, the forestry ministries of the RSFSR, Ukraine, Belorussia, the Baltic republics, and of unspecified other republics take 22 percent (half of which comprises improvement and "sanitation" fellings), and the ministries of the fuel industry, transportation, ferrous metallurgy, agriculture, and unspecified others—the so-called independent loggers—take 24 percent.

36. Drozhalov, "Lesnoe khoziaistvo," 62.

37. Ibid., 60.

38. This rough approximation is based on an annual cut of 410 million cubic meters and an average stocking of 106.3 cubic meters per hectare. On the other hand, Belov, (*Lesovodstvo*, 224) states that 2.5 million hectares are harvested annually for the principal cut, improvement felling occurs on 2.3 million, "forest sanitation" cutting on 1.7 million, and unspecified cutting on approximately 300,000 hectares. Thus, directly (2.5 million) or indirectly (4.4 million), some 6.9 million hectares are affected by annual cutting.

39. Drozhalov, "Lesnoe khoziaistvo," 62.

40. Ibid., 62–63.

41. The detailed assessments made by Leslie Dienes suggest overwhelmingly that much of the development of Siberia and the Far East cannot be explained in terms of coherent economic analysis except for the crash development and exploitation of some specific raw materials such as petroleum, coal, gold, or other material supplies deemed essential for economic and military development. See L. Dienes, "The Development of Siberian Regions: Economic Profiles, Income Flows and Strategies for Growth," *Soviet Geography: Review and Translation*, vol. 23, no. 4 (April 1982), 205–244; and L. Dienes, "Regional Economic Development," in *The Soviet Economy: Toward the Year 2000*, eds., A. Bergson and H. S. Levine (London: George Allen & Unwin, 1983), 218–268. Siberia and the Far East seem to the present author to offer an

overwhelming psychological imperative to Soviet developers and planners that carries a logic of its own. Perhaps the assault on new, undeveloped regions offers a greater psychopolitical challenge than the careful, rather tedious management and husbanding of accessible resources such as the forests of the European-Uralian zone.

42. I. N. Voevoda, *Lesnaia i lesopererabatyvaiushchaia promyshlennost' Sibiri* (Novosibirsk, 1980), 31.

43. One of the ways in which the development of wood processing has been accommodated in European-Uralian regions and in the east has been to expand and reequip existing plant and equipment in the former while developing major new investments in the latter. This is succinctly described in *Sovetskii Soiuz: politiko-ekonomicheskii spravochnik* (Moscow, 1975), 181–182.

44. Voevoda, *Lesnaia i lesopererabatyvaiushchaia promyshlennost' Sibiri*, 32.

45. Ibid., 32–33.

46. N. V. Timofeev, *Osvoenie lesnykh bogatstv* (Moscow, 1979), 141.

47. G. M. Mkrtchian and S. A. Suspitsyn, *Prirodnye resursy v modeliakh territorial'no-proizvodstvennykh sistem* (Novosibirsk, 1982), 142–149.

48. M. H. Soule and R. N. Taaffe, "Mathematical Programming Approaches to the Planning of Siberian Regional Economic Development: A Nonmathematical Survey," *Soviet Economy*, vol. 1, no. 1 (January/March 1985), 75–98.

49. Voevoda, *Lesnaia i lesopererabatyvaiushchaia promyshlennost' Sibiri*, 84–85.

50. Ibid., 84–85.

51. Ibid., 85.

52. This subject is discussed at length in B. M. Barr, "Soviet Timber: Regional Supply and Demand, 1970–1990," *Arctic*, vol. 32, no. 4 (December 1979), 308–328; and in J. Eronen, *Silva fennica*, 267–285.

53. These and other topics are extensively explored in K. E. Braden and B. M. Barr, *Forests and Wood-processing: The Soviet Union and World Timber Markets* (Totowa, N.J.: Rowman and Allenheld, forthcoming).

54. Soviet literature on economic developments associated with the BAM or associated railways in the Far East tends to be lacking in precision and detail, which suggests that detailed planning on resource utilization, including timber, is still incomplete. See, for example, T. G. Morozova, *Territorial'no-proizvodstvennye kompleksy SSSR* (Moscow, 1983), 129, 133, and 141; and E. B. Aizenberg and Iu. A. Sobolev, *Kompleksnye programmy razvitiia vostochnykh raionov SSSR* (Moscow, 1982), 17–18, and 116–120. A recent book on regional analysis and forecasting, which purports to illustrate its theoretical formulations with evidence from the Far East, is sadly lacking in the type of convincing evidence that should be forthcoming from a region supposedly undergoing significant expansion of its infrastructure. V. P. Chichkanov

and P. A. Minakur, *Analiz i prognozirovanie ekonomiki regiona* (Moscow, 1984). The most effective analyses of the BAM and associated developments are found in T. Shabad and V. L. Mote, eds., *Gateway to Siberian Resources (The BAM)*, (Washington: Scripta Publishing Co., 1977); and in many of the analyses contained in R. G. Jensen, T. Shabad, and A. W. Wright, *Soviet Natural Resources in the World Economy* (Chicago: University of Chicago Press, 1983), particularly chapters 7, 8, 9, and 10.

55. Discussed in Aizenberg and Sobolev, *Kompleksnye programmy*, 116–120.

56. The incursions by so-called "nomadic" loggers and other unplanned users of timber into the reserves set aside to sustain large wood-processing complexes in Siberia is seriously threatening the viability of many projects. See Barr, "The Soviet Forest in the 1980s," 248–255; and V. N. Kalinkin, *Gigant na Angare* (Moscow, 1984), 21–24 (concerning the Ust'-llimsk wood-processing complex).

MILKA BLIZNAKOV

The New Towns on the Baikal-Amur Mainline: A Study of Continuity and Contradiction in the Urbanization of Siberia

Siberia, the vast land of immense natural resources and austere, unspoiled beauty, has always triggered the imagination of explorers, poets, and artists, as well as of conquerors and politicians. Paradoxically, for the exiled, Siberia was a place of banishment and oppression; yet for many rebellious thinkers and artists it provided a refuge for creative work. The advent of Western civilization, however, contrasted sharply with native traditions and culture. Contradictions have marked the historic development of Siberia. They have also permeated each step of the design and construction of Baikal-Amur Mainline railway (BAM) and its towns. The discrepancies in official guidelines for the planning and design of these towns are discussed here, and the antipodes of imaginative design proposals and the adopted plans for construction are illustrated.

Soviet new towns in general, and the new BAM towns in particular, are visual manifestations of Soviet policies on population resettlement and long-range plans for industrialization and urbanization. Industrial development is not only a source of material wealth and political power, but also, most significantly, it is a means toward urbanization and the equal redistribution of the technological, cultural and economic benefits typical of urban life. This fundamental ideological commitment has been a continuous inspiration behind short-term economic plans even when the latter seem to differ from the ultimate goal. Therefore, Soviet new towns have to be studied not only within the ideological context of population resettlement theories and the socioeconomic context of planned industrialization, but, most important, as a continuous historic process whereby persistent trends could be distinguished from deviating temporary objectives.

This chapter attempts to summarize the major urbanization trends in Siberia as part of an ongoing process in which past and present are integral parts of a future; therefore, time has the historic dimension of centuries rather than the short span of human life. The social cost of this urbanization in terms of suffering and lost life, however, has not been calculated. Although Siberia has been studied by geographers and demographers, economists and planners, historians and architects, no information is available on the human cost of its economic and urban development outside of a few shocking descriptions of forced labor camps. Therefore, this study perforce reflects the questionable Soviet view that no sacrifice, material or human, is too great if it holds promise for a better future.

Industrialization and Urbanization of Siberia:
A Historic Survey of Continuous Trends

No real attempt was made to industrialize and urbanize the lands east of the Urals until the Soviet period, although Russian expansion in Asia began in the middle of the sixteenth century with Ivan the Terrible's conquest of Kazan', the Tatar stronghold, in 1552. Subsequent incursions of Cossack freebooters resulted in the construction of many military strongholds such as Tiumen' (1586), Tobol'sk (1587), and Tara (1594). Since these towns continued to be exposed to Tatar attacks from the south, the Russian expansion was diverted to the northeast, in the Khanty territory, with the foundation of Nosovoi Gorodok (1595, now Selekhard) and Surgut (1594) on the lower Ob' River. Tomsk (1604) and Kuznetsk (1618) in western Siberia remained the outposts of the Russian advance in the southeast for a century, while trading posts continued to be established further north and east in the Evenki and Iakut territories (Ilimsk in 1630, Iakutsk in 1632, etc.). By 1638, the Russians had reached the east coast and, by the end of the century, Kamchatka. Russian expansion in central Asia was also preceded by Cossack settlement and military strongholds on the Om River (Omsk in 1716) and Ural River (Orenburg in 1735, now Orsk). The control over the caravan roads from China and southeast Asia to northern and Western Europe finally came into Russian hands after the battle for Tashkent (1865) when the Russian frontier was set on a line from the Caspian Sea to the Ural Sea, along the Syr Dar'ia to Tashkent (annexed in 1866) and the new military post of Vernyi (today's Alma Ata).

The abundant resources of the vast Asian territories, although not fully realized until a decade ago, were already under considerable exploitation during the second half of the eighteenth century: not only timber and furs from the north, cotton and wool from the south, but also iron, lead, polymetallic ores, silver and gold. Accelerated industrial growth during the last quarter of the eighteenth century, although concentrated on the eastern slopes of the Ural Mountains (with over fifty iron producing factories in operation by the end of the eighteenth century), spread also into western Siberia. For example, the iron works in Tomsk and the lead works in Barnaul both began operation in 1771. During the nineteenth century, however, the Russian government decided to develop its industrial base in Europe, and Asia became primarily an agricultural hinterland, not only for wheat, meat and fish, but also for cotton, wool, leather, and timber.

The European Russians, who began settling in Siberia at the end of sixteenth century, were mostly peasants: landless Cossack clans settled by the government to garrison the frontiers,[1] runaway serfs (or resettled serfs working on government as well as on monastery lands), and, above all, millions of exiles.[2] Exiles constituted the majority of settlers in the north, while forced labor camps (*katorga*) were centered in southern Siberia (Nerchinsk, Chita, and later Sakhalin). "The uttermost place of exile...until 1917 was the lower Kolyma, over 7,000 kilometers and normally two years' travel from the capital."[3] With the abolition of serfdom in 1861, the movement of freed peasants to Asia increased, but only in the 1880s did the free settlers outnumber convicts among the arrivals in Siberia.[4] Around the turn of the century, with the completion of the Trans-Siberian Railroad (1904), Trans-Caspian Railroad (1898), and the Orenburg-Tashkent Line (1906), Asia was flooded with immigrating peasants helped by favorable government policies and financial aid.[5]

While the concentration of peasants in western Siberia and central Asia did not contribute to the urban and industrial development of the area, the exile of liberal intellectuals and politicians to eastern Siberia and the Far East benefited the intellectual, cultural, and economic development of the region.[6] Not only did most of the exiles opt to stay in Siberia after being pardoned, but the avant-garde ideas, liberal thinking, and pioneering spirit they brought have become a continuous tradition in the development of local culture. Furthermore, many political exiles (Lenin, Stalin, and Molotov, to name a few) later became the decision makers who did not neglect to give Siberia its share of the economic resources.

The significance of the economic development of Asia and especially of Siberia was immediately realized by Lenin who wrote in 1918, "The development of these natural resources by the methods of modern technology will provide the basis of an unprecedented progress. . . ."[7] Addressing the Eighth All-Russian Congress of Soviets (December 1920), he warned about the length of time such a development would take. "Siberia's mineral wealth is literally boundless and we cannot exploit even a hundredth part of it for many years inspite of [technological] progress. The minerals are to be found in conditions that demand the best machinery. . . ."[8] The plan for state electrification of Russia (GOERLO),[9] which Lenin presented to this congress, also included regional power stations located in Siberia, such as the thermoelectric power plant in Novosibirsk.[10] Almost half of the appropriations in the GOERLO plan were for the development and improvement of rail transport. A new line was anticipated from Moscow into Siberia, running through "regions that are extraordinarily rich in natural resources and whose economic accessibility by means of an electrified mainline would create totally new conditions for the future structure of the economy not only in Russia but in world trade."[11] The actual realization of this ambitious goal, the construction of the Baikal-Amur Mainline (BAM), has taken over sixty years to fulfill.[12]

The foundations of a centrally planned economy were also laid out by Lenin with the establishment of the State Planning Commission in February 1921. The commission had to follow the directives of the Council of Labor and Defense of the Party Central Committee which, as the name indicates, combined economic and military interests. Ever since, military considerations have been on the top of the Soviet list of priorities. The military advantages of a dispersed and independently functioning economic base in Asia was fully realized during World War I and the ensuing Revolution. The first two five-year plans (1928–1932 and 1933–1937) devoted large resources to the development of a second industrial base in Siberia, the Ural-Kuznetsk Combine. While this project was widely publicized, the fact that approximately the same amount of capital investment was allocated in the second five-year plan to industrial developments in the Far East is little known. Military concerns were clearly defined by the Eighteenth Congress of the Communist Party (10–21 March 1939) and guided the development of the third five-year plan (1938–1942). The plan aimed at accelerating the development of the Far East and making the region self-sufficient in food, fuel, building materials, etc. Although these objectives have still not been achieved, the military significance of the Siberian industrial development was stressed even further after the end of World War II.[13]

The sociopolitical aspects of transforming the Asian peasantry into an industrial proletariat were recognized by the Party even before the Revolution. The lack of industrial development has made the organization of the proletarian movement in Asia next to impossible. In the years following the Revolution, obscure "workers" lacking intellectual and political awareness were sought to fill the membership in the Party. Forty ranking Communists, for example, had to be sent to southern central Asia in 1920 to staff the Party.[14] By building new industrial towns, the government hoped to diminish, and eventually completely erase, the role of national traditions and cultural variations, although on the surface it encouraged (especially in the 1920s) the formation of ethnic republics.[15] Invariably, new industrial towns drew together workers of diverse backgrounds and ethnicity, thus promoting desegregation, cultural exchanges, mixed marriages, and eventual racial balance. How important this last goal is for the Soviet Government is evident from the fact that immigration of Slavs from Europe to Asia has been continuously encouraged in the hope that the relocated population from the European territory would balance the much faster natural population increase of the Asian ethnic groups.[16] Futhermore, an accelerated industrialization of Asia would prevent farmers from migrating to overcrowded European cities.[17] Economic incentives, such as two to four times higher wages and longer vacations (often at national resorts with all expenses paid), are some of the recent government policies directing migration to Siberia. In addition, political rhetoric and patriotic calls to the Komsomol youth organization for volunteer labor in Siberia, and the forced relocation (temporary or permanent) to selected Siberian construction sites have maintained the flow of migrants.

Actually, very few new towns were founded during the 1920s, since the limited available capital was invested into restoring and enlarging existing industries, transforming old houses into multifamily units or workers' clubs, and erecting new governmental centers.[18] Within these economic limitations, avant-garde architects designed several significant buildings in Siberia such as, for example, the Novosibirsk Theater-Planetarium by Aleksandr Grinberg (1879–1938). Unrecognizable today behind the later additions of heavy neoclassic colonnades, this building was hailed as an achievement of the modern movement. The master plan for Novosibirsk was designed by the constructivist group of GIProGor (The State Institute for Urban Planning formed in 1930), and the State House (Dom Pravitel'stva) of Kazakhstan was entrusted to the constructivist leader Moisei Ginsburg (1892–1946).[19]

Most significant, however, were the theoretical debates of the 1920s on the form and character of the socialist city and the ardent formulation of urban planning principles. Formal classic urban schemes, garden city ideals, and social phalansteries were among the inspirations behind the theories of urbanization.[20] The antithesis of urbanization was provided by the de-urbanist camp lead by Moisei Ginsburg. The group formulated the so-called "socialist population resettlement" whereby linear urban development followed continuously the development of infrastructure networks. The basic premises of this concept were revived in Soviet planning theories of the 1960s.[21] A clear focus for the debate between urbanists and de-urbanists was provided by the 1930 national competition for the plan of Magnitogorsk, the new industrial town on the eastern slopes of the Urals. Highly imaginative de-urbanist entries treated Magnitogorsk as the beginning of a well-developed transportation, communication, and power supply network that would eventually cross Siberia and reach the Far East. While the de-urbanists' schemes were neglected and later severely criticized, a similar theoretical approach generated the contemporary development of Territorial-Production Complexes. The urbanist model of building small towns for 30,000 to 50,000 people became the norm during the next four decades.

Magnitogorsk was actually planned as part of the second economic base, that is, a self-sustaining economic unit in Asia independent of the industrial development in the European territories of the Soviet Union. The heart of this second economic base was the Ural-Kuznetsk Combine. Furthermore, a third economic base located in the Far East was already discussed by the Fourteenth Party Congress in December 1925. The first five-year plan (hereafter FYP) began implementing both the second and third economic bases. The new town of Komsomol'sk on the Amur River was located in conjunction with a proposed new east-west railroad line crossing Siberia north of the Trans-Siberian Railroad. Begun in 1932, Komsomol'sk's population had already reached 71,000 by January 1939[22] and 209,000 by 1967[23] because of its multi-industrial base (from iron, steel, cement, cellulose, and paper to oil refineries and ship building, the last already operating by the end of the 1930s). The second (1933–1937) and third (1937–1942) FYP led, according to statistics, to the construction of more new towns during the decade of 1930s than in any subsequent period.[24] The number of new towns, around 200, almost half of which were located in Asia, reflects the large dislocation of peasants from the collectivized farm lands to new industrial towns, the transformation of villages to towns through the introduction of food-processing industries, but above all the military concerns of locating these towns in Asia as far as possible from future European war fronts. And, not to be forgotten, an estimated ten million prisoners and forced labor camp inmates were sent east of the Urals during the 1930s and early 1940s.[25]

World War II had a positive impact on the urbanization and industrialization of Asia. Of an estimated 1,523 industrial plants dismantled during the second half of 1941, some 244 were moved to western Siberia, 78 to eastern Siberia, and a larger number reassembled in the Urals, Kazakhstan, central Asia, and the Volga basin.[26] Not only evacuated industries, but also cultural institutions, skilled workers, and scores of refugees relocating in Asia accelerated the process of modernization, especially in central Asia, Kazakhstan, western Siberia, and the southern regions of East Siberia.[27] The Pacific coast, the major trade route for U. S. military assistance, gained new ports such as Nakhodka and Sovetskaia Gavan'. "Shipments from the west coast of the United States of grain, oil, and machines have enabled the young industries and farming districts centered at Komsomol'sk and along the Trans-Siberian to concentrate on strengthening the Soviet Far Eastern frontier and its active armies in Europe."[28] Thus, Lenin's third industrial base grew during the war years and continued to expand during the decades thereafter.

The postwar fourth FYP (1946–1950), and the fifth (1951–1955), provided more funds for the restoration of the towns and industries in the European territories than for any other activities. Still, industrialization and urbanization in Asia continued to grow because Asian industries were the suppliers of goods for the country and for the reconstruction of the European industrial base. Most of the industries relocated to Asia, therefore, were not returned to Europe. Although these decisions led to duplications of the industrial base, the strategic need for backup plants safe behind the Urals was not questioned after the war. To sustain local industries and to supply European territories with cheap energy, a series of new electric power plants were planned on the upper reaches of the Ob', Enisei, and Angara rivers, in addition to those built during the war.[29] Therefore, most of this development continued to concentrate in the warmer climatic zones of central Asia and the southern part of Siberia. Two new towns, Angarsk and Bratsk, both in the Irkutsk region, demonstrated Soviet commitment to develop the economic potential of eastern Siberia before and immediately after Stalin's death.

Angarsk, begun (1947 or 1949) on virgin soil at the junction of the rivers Angara and Kitoi, lies approximately 50 kilometers northwest from Irkutsk.[30] The possibilities of using the power of the Angara River were already investigated by the GOERLO Commission during the early 1920s. The town, a major project of the fourth FYP (1946–1950), was originally planned for only 30,000 people around a single industry—the production of energy—and followed the model of the GOERLO towns. But realizing the potential of its cheap energy production (hydroelectric power from the Angara River and thermoelectric power from the coal mining in the area), the town was replanned in the early 1950s as a large industrial center of the Irkutsk economic region. Its growth was spectacular: 135,000 by 1959 and 204,000 by 1970. The town of Bratsk (begun in 1954) owes its existence to one of the world's largest hydroelectric plants envisaged in the fifth FYP (1951–1955).[31] It lies northwest of Irkutsk on the Angara River. By 1959 its population grew to 51,000, by 1967 to 122,000, and by 1976 to 195,000. Among its industries are aluminum metallurgical works, chemicals, and other energy-intensive industries. The new Baikal-Amur Mainline now connects it with Komsomol'sk-na-Amure.[32]

Bratsk was not originally planned as a large industrial center either. It owed its growth, as did many towns in Siberia of the late 1950s, to Khrushchev's eastward drive. His "virgin lands" scheme, as originally conceived in 1954, aimed at exploring the agricultural potentials of southern Siberia and northwest Kazakhstan. Extensive surveys conducted all over Soviet Asia resulted in the discovery of the territory's abundant mineral resources and sustained Khrushchev's shift of capital investments to Siberia in the sixth FYP (1956–1960) and, in the subsequent modifications of this plan in 1959, to a seven-year plan (1959–1965). Even after Khrushchev's fall in 1964 and the attempts to balance east-west development reflected in the eighth FYP (1966–1970), the discovery of the new gas and oil fields in western Siberia and Iakutia, the enormous coke reserves in southern Iakutia, and the large hydroelectric dams in central Asia, in northeast Kazakhstan, and in eastern Siberia, led to the decision to locate energy-consuming industries in these regions. This was reflected in the ninth (1971–1975) and tenth FYPs (1976–1980).[33]

The concerns with the speedy development of Siberia's natural resources and with the increase of population densities by attracting Europeans to Asia led to the relocation, in 1957, of part of the Soviet Academy of Science to Novosibirsk, and the formation of the Siberian section of the Academy. This marked the beginning of the development of a large research and education center in Siberia equal to those in Leningrad and Moscow. To accommodate such a center, a new town, Akademgorodok, some 25 kilometers from Novosibirsk, was begun in 1958 according to designs by M. Belyi and A. Mikhailov. In addition to its sixteen research institutes, a university with forty-four departments, a botanical garden, and a computer center, the Siberian section of the Academy of Sciences coordinates the work of some fifty-one science institutions located from Krasnoiarsk in the Far East, Irkutsk, Ulan Ude, and Iakutsk in eastern Siberia, to Alma Ata in Kazakhstan.[34] The development of educational and cultural institutions, consumers industries and better services, higher wages and quality living accommodations are some of the incentives intended to draw workers to Siberia.[35]

Planning and Designing the BAM Settlements: Contrasts Between Ideals and Realities

Detailed geological surveys during the 1960s indicated that the northern regions had enormous unexplored resources of oil and gas, nonferrous metal ores and minerals, while urban growth was concentrating in central Asia and the southern regions of Siberia. Special attention, therefore, was paid to the exploitation and urbanization of the northern regions of the Soviet Union during the 1970s. Two deterrents to northern development —transportation and harsh climatic conditions—had first to be overcome. The new BAM line has become part of the solution to the transportation problem (this is so especially after its branch north to Iakutsk and eventually east to Magadan is completed). Research on higher mechanization of industry and on construction methods in permafrost conditions, as well as on the relationship between building forms and microclimatic conditions led to new and imaginative proposals for new towns in the northern regions of Siberia.[36] The enormous capital investment required for building large permanent towns in the north (five to eight times higher than construction in moderate climates) was justified through studies, during the late 1960s and early 1970s, into integrated methods of industrialization, urbanization, and population resettlement—so-called "territorially coordinated economic development."[37] These studies, involving urban and economic geographers, ecologists and sociologists, as well as transportation planners and urban designers, were largely based on the past fifty years of experience in new town planning. The theoretical works on systems of territorial distribution of industrial production and on unified transportation networks culminated in the theories of unified population distribution systems, regional urbanization, and the formation of urban constellations.[38]

Applied to the northern regions, this theory led to the identification of sites for the development of fairly large industrial towns to serve as anchors for constellations of smaller towns with specific, often single, purposes. These small towns were to be the urban bases for temporary settlements or for moving units exploiting particular natural resources. The interdependence between permanent large and small towns, on one hand, and temporary settlements on the other was, ideally, to render each economic region fairly independent, overcome transportation problems, and prevent population migration to larger southern towns.[39] The gap between life in large cities and small provincial towns had been widening rather than closing; thus, it was finally realized that the urbanists' scheme of resettlement into small towns did not necessarily lead to the equal redistribution of technological, cultural, and economic benefits.

In order to gain a better perspective on long-range future development, a fifteen-year plan (1976–1990) was outlined while the tenth FYP (1976–1980) was still in progress. Accordingly, the industrial belt along the Trans-Siberian and the new BAM lines were strengthened to provide the springboard for further development of the northern regions. The industrial belt now divided into "Territorial-Production Complexes," each having a northern leg. In western Siberia, the Kuzbas-Novosibirsk Territorial-Production Complex will continue to expand in order to support the development of the Middle Ob' Territorial-Production Complex. In eastern Siberia, the Krasnoiarsk Territorial-Production Complex will be the basis for the development of the middle Enisei region.[40] This regional development includes, on the south, the Saian Territorial-Production Complex with Abakan, the administrative center of the Khakass Autonomous Region, and Saianogorsk, a new town begun during the ninth FYP (projected population of 200,000), as the centers of industrial development.[41] East of the Saian Territorial-Production Complex lies the Irkutsk-Cheremkhovo Territorial-Production Complex encompassing Shelekhov, Angarsk, and Cheremkhovo on the south, Bratsk, Zheleznogorsk, Ust' Ilimsk, and Ust' Kut on the west, and reaching north to the Lena-Vitim gold fields and Vilini-Udachnyi diamond mines. Ust' Kut (pop. 38,000), a new town since 1954 (the year the railroad connection to Taishet was finally completed after its start in 1938), is becoming a major transportation center connecting the new BAM line with the regular boat traffic on the Lena River.

The Far East is divided on two territorial-production complexes, the West Amur and the Lower Amur. The first includes the Zeia-Bureia Plain in the south with two hydroelectric stations, one on the Zeia River (designed capacity of 1,300 megawatts) and the other on the Bureia River (2,000 megawatts). The towns of Zeisk (pop. 18,000) and Tynda (pop. 30,000, with planned expansion to 70,000), at the west end of this territorial-production complex, will develop as metal and machine production centers in addition to their present saw milling and gold mining. With the extension of the little BAM line from Neriungri (pop. 11,000, planned expansion up to 100,000) northward, the economic influence of this complex will expand to Iakutsk and beyond. The Lower Amur territorial-production complex includes Khabarovsk (pop. 462,000) on the south, Komsomol'sk (pop. 250,000), its satellite town Amursk (pop.

25,000), Sol'nechnyi, and Pivan' on the north, and Sovetskaia Gavan' (pop. 31,000) and Vanino (pop. 16,000) as eastern ports on the Pacific. The large and diversified industrial base of the complex could support future expansion in the north in Khabarovsk krai and the Magadan oblast'.

The six territorial-production complexes (Kuzbas-Novosibirsk and Middle Ob' in west Siberia, Krasnoiarsk and Saian in east Siberia, west Amur and lower Amur in the Far east) are incorporating many aspects of the de-urbanist theories into a practical network. The basic idea of interconnected urban networks, rather than independent urban units, was first launched by the de-urbanists.[42] Although present urban constellation theories do not include continuous connections between major towns, many large cities have already developed linear suburban or satellite growth.[43] Provided that present trends continue, one could foresee "linear" cities of the types developed in the 1920s connecting the industrial centers of the territorial-production complexes. The most explicit common ground for the de-urbanists, as well as the present planners of systems of population resettlement, however, is the complete reliance on unified transportation networks for urban and economic growth.

The studies and planning of unified population distribution systems gave architects the possibility of initiating theoretical propositions for new, imaginative designs of urban agglomerations. The first group to concentrate on the problem since 1960 named itself NER (New Elements of Resettlement). The members of the group were mostly young architects: Aleksei Gutnov, I. Lezhava, A. Baburov, Z. Kharitonova, S. Sadovskii, and one sociologist, G. Diumenton.[44] Their new elements of resettlement consisted of interconnected units providing for all possible human activities within a settlement of about 100,000 people. The organic characteristics of the urban form are probably influenced by Japanese metabolist designs, while the linear spatial distribution of urban elements follows the tradition of the de-urbanist proposals of the 1920s. The NER theoretical scheme was followed by the "Kinetic System of Resettlement," a theory of urban form set forth during the late 1960s by Andrei Ikonnikov, S. Grechannikova, K. Pchelnikov, and A. Panin.[45] Both theories concentrated on the internal dependence between human activities, and on the continuous connection of the shelters that house these activities. Both were inspired by biological models demonstrating similarities with Metabolist theories and megastructure practices. The theoretical models were translated into imaginative architectonic forms especially appropriate to Siberian climatic conditions as illustrated by Ilia Smoliar's studies.[46] The grand scale of the design proposals, the technological complexity of the buildings, and their innovative forms expressed a new, diametrically different approach and design that were incompatible with that of the Stalin era. It symbolized the desire for change inaugurated by Khrushchev and the 1960 Party program. A new revolution was proclaimed, a scientific and technical revolution that, constrained by capitalism everywhere else, could only fully flourish under socialism.[47]

Most of the designers, however, broke slowly out of the rigid mold of trite solutions and out of the constraints imposed on them during the previous period. Architects were now faced with contradictory guidelines and incompatible demands. On one side, they were encouraged to be bold and imaginative; on the other, there were reminded to be practical within the economic realities. The designs and construction of the BAM towns provide numerous examples of ambiguities, conflicting directives, and discordant criticism. The first riddle designers had to solve was to create a unifying image for all fifty-eight railroad towns alongside the Baikal-Amur Mainline so that those towns could be recognized as belonging to a railroad 3,543 kilometers long. At the same time, each town and each settlement had to possess a unique appearance and identity. The housing in all towns was standardized by using prefabricated models as were most of the railroad stations. Yet homogeneity, uniformity, and monotony were to be avoided. Some projects were rejected for not complying with practical demands and for unjustified richness of form. Others were returned for their repetitious and mechanistic arrangement of trite patterns.

As has been the established practice in new town construction, the first workers arriving at the site were housed in temporary buildings. The harsh climatic conditions required even temporary housing to be well constructed. Furthermore, higher wages alone could not attract experienced workers and, above all, keep them on construction sites with poor living conditions. Therefore, many temporary settlements were improved with the addition of stores, club rooms, libraries, movie and entertainment halls, etc. Thus, temporary settlements often brought to the backward areas of Siberia unknown or unavailable products of civilization. Villagers traveled for hours to see a movie, eat in a restaurant, or simply walk under the first street lights of the region. Of the forty temporary BAM settlements, the best examples are the temporary settlements of Berkakit (begun 1974) at the northern end of the Little BAM (BAM-Tynda-Chulman) and of Urgal, the railroad junction at the confluence of the Urgal and Bureia rivers in the Far East. Both were not preplanned, but developed harmoniously with the natural environment; both were built of wood using local techniques and experiences. Berkakit and nearby Zolotinka were further enhanced with playgrounds, covered walkways, kiosks and benches, bus shelters, and supergraphics and wood carvings, designed and often executed by brigades of young architects from Moscow. Working independently, without the usual coordination reviews and approvals by numerous institutions, the architects could see their ideas immediately realized, while the settlers could directly participate in the improvement of their environment with advice, as well as with their labor.[48]

Urgal's temporary settlement was planned by the workers themselves. The wooden structures were arranged around courts with board walls and benches built over a heating pipe system that melted the snow. Instead of grass (recommended by Moscow's designers but impossible to grow in the cold climate), local moss was planted in wooden grids, a technique developed by local settlers. Post office, library, cafeteria, stores, and offices were all built simultaneously with the housing. When the plans for the school were delayed by Kharkov's designers (the Ukrainian urban design studio Ukrgorstroiproekt), the construction workers created their own design based on traditional practices of reconciling with the local climate.[49] In contrast, the permanent town was designed around a rigid, grandiose central plaza, lined by tall concrete structures, such as administrative buildings, stores, a hotel, club, and school. Five-story standardized housing blocks of concrete or of brick housed the first 7,200 inhabitants. The town, planned for 15,000 and for substantial future growth, has no identity and could hardly be distinguished from conventional Soviet new towns. Yet, the railroad station designed in the Ukraine by Kievgiprotrans is adorned with motives from Ukrainian folklore instead of complying with a unifying scheme.[50]

The dichotomy between the unique local characteristics of the old settlement and the new uniform structures imposed on the landscape is clearly evident in Tynda. The settlement Tyndinskii, founded in 1936, grew parallel to the motor route connecting the Trans-Siberian railroad with Iakutsk; it has traditional wood cabins (with carved window frames) that are located around an extinct volcano. These picturesque houses are to be destroyed after their nine-story concrete neighbors are completed. The design for Tynda, called the capital of BAM, began in 1972 at the same time as the start of the railroad's construction. The initial master plan was intended to serve as a model for the designers of the rest of the BAM towns and, therefore, was entrusted to Moscow's leading architectural planning organization, GlavAPU, in collaboration with Leningrad's Lengiprogor. The small settlement of Tyndinskii was transformed into a town of 35,000 by 1977, with a planned potential growth to 80,000 by 1990.[51] The master plan was revised several times, and other design organizations (Mosproekt-1 and Rostovgrazhdanproekt) were also included in the planning and designing. Yet the basic scheme, as codified during the 1930s and practiced ever since, remained unchanged. A wide thoroughfare bisects the town and forms a huge central plaza at its intersection with another, even wider mall originating at the railroad station. Administrative, commercial, and cultural buildings surround this central square whose primary purpose is the staging of political meetings and public celebrations. Housing is subdivided into large neighborhood blocks, with tall apartment buildings around a large open space for the usual location of the kindergarten, primary school, and neighborhood services. As construction progressed, the monotonous, tedious appearance of the future town, although evident already in the approved plans, became obvious, leading to further changes and new design proposals. Thus, the almost completed railroad station was totally modified in 1978 by a new design. The Soviet Union of Artists also suggested esthetic and artistic improvements for Tynda at its workshop in November-December 1983. The artists attempted to interrelate and synthesize the functional purpose of the buildings with elements of the natural environment and to transform the bare public spaces into informative, perceptually unique experiences.[52] They proposed the expansion of the railroad station as a cultural center to include concerts and exhibits commemorating the development of the BAM region. They insisted on the preservation of the old wood cabins as a link to the past. They designed sculpture-like elevated walkways to preserve the fragile soil and flora of the site. These projects, however, will probably remain dreams on paper, while blocks of prefabricated housing continue to be erected, disregarding natural or man-made beauty.

In August 1978, following Leonid Brezhnev's promotional trip to Siberia and the Far East in March and April of that year, Tynda hosted a conference on the planning, construction, and quality of life in the BAM towns and settlements. New qualitative criteria for the design of the BAM towns were established and several projects in the Khabarovsk region were reviewed and corrected accordingly. Yet the criteria were mostly quantitative. The projected population of most settlements was decreased, since 80 percent of the BAM inhabitants were to be concentrated in five towns: Komsomol'sk-na-Amure, Tynda, Ust' Kut, Udokan, and Urgal. For example, the settlement Dzhamku, originally planned in 1976 for 2,700 inhabitants housed in a variety of one-, two-, and four-story structures, was redesigned for 1,000 people residing mostly in prefabricated two-story flats. The monotony of the housing is interrupted by a large village green with the railroad station at one end and an administrative and commercial complex at the other. A solitary monument in the center of this square fulfills the requirement for quality through the "inclusion of the arts into the design."[53]

The Tynda conference decided that all plans for new BAM towns were to be reviewed and revised according to the new criteria, although most of the projects had already been revised according to similar criteria established in 1975 and approved after second and, sometimes, third submissions. The criteria were again vague, contradictory, and often irreconcilable. For example, settlements had to be compactly built for climatic reasons and infrastructure savings, yet many inhabitants were encouraged to raise food and tend poultry in their backyards. Multistory housing was criticized for deterring farming activities, while single houses were deemed wasteful. Architectural unity of all BAM towns was again demanded, yet "this unity had to be achieved also with the use of contrasts."[54] Functional zoning was to be uncompromised, but the separation of housing from social and commercial activities was also criticized. Decorative arts, painting, and monumental sculptures all had to be included in the design, yet stringent economy had to be observed.

The problem of the BAM towns, however, is neither esthetic nor economic but inherent in the institutional structure of the Soviet Union. The design of the railroad settlements was handled by six institutes for transportation design (Mosgiprotrans, Tomskgiprotrans, Sibgiprotrans, Lengiprotrans, Kievgiprotrans, and Dal'giprotrans), and sixty-four design organizations, some affiliated with the Ministry of Roads and Communication and the Ministry of Transport Construction, some with the Soviet republics, others with regional and city governments. Further-more, the Ministries of Heavy and Light Industries employed their own design and construction organizations for building their respective industrial plants. Wherever buildable land was limited, industrial plants were often built on the site allocated for the new towns. Moreover, the Ministry of Health was involved in the design, coordination, and management of its facilities, and the Ministry of Education was responsible for the schools located in the new towns. Local Party organizations and administrative institutions also participated in the evaluation of design proposals. Unless the representatives of all these institutions were guided by strict economic and planning norms and precise esthetic codes, they were apt to diverge in personal preferences and opinions. In April 1978, the position of a chief architect for BAM was created to coordinate the design and construction activities of the new towns. After his appointment as BAM's chief architect, Vladimir Butuzov, created yet another administrative unit, the section for architecture and construction of BAM, which included representatives of all parties involved in the process. The intangible design criteria Butuzov presented four months later in Tynda actually institutionalized inconsistencies and dissonance.

Conclusion

The Baikal-Amur Mainline is the most recent step in the continuous, centuries-long Russian pursuit of the conquest of Siberia's wilderness and exploitation of its natural resources. The planning and design of the settlements, not only alongside the 3,500-kilometer railroad, but also over the 1,600,000 square kilometers of BAM's hinterlands, demonstrate a half-century of Soviet commitment to the more even redistribution of its population. This policy entails the spreading of urbanization and its economic, social, and cultural benefits. The linear urban designs developed during the 1920s and early 1930s continue to inspire similar urban schemes, as evident in the creative proposals of the late 1960s and 1970s. Experimental design proposals, however, are persistently used as symbolic images for future possibilities and models for distant targets. They keep hopes high and provide direction and outlet for creative energies.

In contrast, designs approved for actual construction, with their trivial conventionality, demonstrate the restrictive role of governmental institutions. Agreement among the numerous participants in the design approval process is usually achieved for the lowest qualitative denominator. Therefore, continual changes retard environmental improvements and allow appreciation of every added amenity. The new BAM settlements, for example, are models of civilization and technical progress for the backward regions. They contrapoise nature with their straight streets, large open spaces, multistory concrete structures, electricity, central heating, and running water. Their significant design achievement, however, is in the reconciliation of two opposing ways of life: the farmers' and the urbanites'. Farming is allowed not only at the towns' edges, but also in the middle of housing blocks. Contrary to communist policies, individual family houses and land for personal production of food continue to sustain the relatively independent, freer way of life traditional to Siberia.

Continuity and contradictions have marked the history of Siberia and will probably persist in shaping its future.

Notes

1. Such settlements are abundant along the Amur and Ussuri rivers in the Far East, and along the Syr Dar'ia and the Caspian Sea in central Asia.

2. There are indications that prisoners had been sent to Siberia (Tobol'sk region) as early as the 1590s. From the 1640s on, exiles were permitted to take along wives and families.

3. Terence Armstrong, *Russian Settlement in the North* (Cambridge: Cambridge University Press, 1965), 82–83. The most detailed work in English on the tsarist exile system is still George Kennan's *Siberia and the Exile System* (New York, 1881).

4. The peasant migration centered around the fertile regions of western Siberia, Kazakhstan, and central Asia.

5. Between 1896 and 1916, over one million Russian peasants settled in Turkestan gubernia alone. The best English-language source on the migrations in Siberia is Donald W. Treadgold, *The Great Siberian Migration: Government and Peasant in Resettlement from Emancipation to the First World War* (Princeton: Princeton University Press, 1957).

6. Over one million people were deported to eastern Siberia during the nineteenth century alone.

7. V. I. Lenin, "The Immediate Task of the Soviet Government," *Collected Works* (Moscow, 1960–1970), vol. 27, 257.

8. Ibid., vol. 31, 483.

9. This was the first overall government plan. It called for the construction of thirty regional power stations during the next ten to fifteen years.

10. Construction of this power plant (named after M. Kalinin) began in 1924. It was to produce 2,400 kilowatts of electric power for projected industrial growth. See N. N. Lebedev et al., *Novosibirsk* (Novosibirsk, 1967), 132–134.

11. From the GOERLO report as quoted in N. P. Belen'kii and V. S. Maslennikov, "Design and Construction of the BAM," Theodore Shabad and Victor L. Mote, eds., *Gateway to Siberian Resources. (The BAM)* (New York: John Wiley and Sons, 1977), 123.

12. The idea of building a second railroad line connecting Taishet in western Siberia to Sovetskaia Gavan' on the Tatar Strait of the Sea of Japan was discussed during the early 1930s in conjunction with the location of Komsomol'sk-na-Amure in the Far East. Work on this Baikal-Amur Mainline began in the late 1930s, was interrupted by the war, but continued thereafter until the 1950s. Although the work was abandoned for over twenty years, the idea was never dropped, and in 1974 the construction resumed. For a complete treatment of the BAM line, see Shabad and Mote, *Gateway to Siberian Resources*.

13. Soviet military power in Asia is discussed in Geoffrey Jukes, *The Soviet Union in Asia* (Sydney: Angus and Robertson, 1973), 66–95; and in numerous articles in *The American Review on the Soviet Union*, especially issues published during the late 1930s and 1940s, and in its supplementary *Bulletin on the Soviet Union*, *"Russia at War", 1942–1946*.

14. *Istoriia uzbekskoi SSR* (Tashkent, 1957), vol. 2, 106.

15. Lenin's pre-revolutionary call for self-determination for the subject nationalities of the Russian Empire was directed against the empire in the belief that nationalist sentiments would lead to the empire's disintegration. But after the monarchy had been overthrown, he believed that nationalism should be subjected to the larger goals of socialist unity. Soviet nationalities policies are treated in T. Rakowska-Harmstone, *Russia and Nationalism in Central Asia* (Baltimore: John Hopkins University Press, 1970); and partially in Jukes, *The Soviet Union in Asia*, 30–65. For a different view on the subject, see Edward Allworth, ed., *Central Asia: A Century of Russian Rule* (New York: Columbia University Press, 1967).

16. B. S. Khorev, *Problemy gorodov*, 2nd ed. (Moscow, 1975), 247–270. While during the 1970–1975 period central Asia, Kazakhstan, and the Caucasian republics absorbed 30 percent of the natural population growth of the European territories, these regions are to receive all the natural population growth during the 1980s. See D. G. Khodzhaev, A. V. Kochetkov, and F. M. Listengurt, *Sistema zasseleniia v SSSR* (Moscow, 1977), 25.

17. Robert A. Lewis and Richard H. Rowland, "Urbanization in Russia and the USSR, 1897–1970," Michael F. Hamm, ed., *The City in Russian History* (Lexington, Kentucky: The University Press of Kentucky,

1976), 209.

18. During the census of 1926, the definition of a "town" was changed to reflect size and nonagricultural occupation. Of the 675 towns inherited from prerevolutionary Russia, 142 converted back to village status while urban status was given to another 176. See Oleg A. Konstantinov, "Izmeneniia v geografii gorodov SSR za sovetskii period," *Voprosy geografii*, vol. 6 (Moscow, 1947), 11–46; and B. S. Khorev, *Gorodskie poseleniia SSR* (Moscow, 1968), 215.

19. Ginsburg, who traveled to the central Asian republics in 1924 to found a museum of folk art in Bukhara and to study the indigenous housing, translated the traditional oriental house organization into contemporary Constructivist form. The center of the project is an interior court, an oasis of greenery, through which one enters different governmental departments.

20. The revival of classical planning and the garden city movement in Russia at the beginning of the twentieth century are the subject of S. Frederick Starr, "The Revival and Schism of Urban Planning in Twentieth-century Russia," in Hamm, *The City in Russian History*, 222–242.

21. The theories of urbanization and de-urbanization are discussed in Milka Bliznakov, "Urban Planning in the USSR: Integrative Theories," in ibid., 243–256. Both movements, but especially the de-urbanist achievements, are covered and well-illustrated in Anatole Kopp, *Ville et revolution* (Paris, 1967 and London, 1970). Unfortunately, no mention is made of Nikolai Ladovskii and his organization ARU. For this, see Milka Bliznakov, "Nikolai Ladovskii: The Search for a Rational Science of Architecture," *Soviet Union/Union Sovietique*, vol. 7, parts 1–2 (1980), 170–196.

22. N. Poliakov, *Gradostroitel'stvo* (Moscow, 1946), 50. The town was originally planned for 100,000 with projected growth to 300,000.

23. Jack Underhill, "Soviet Policy for New Towns and Its Implementation, Achievements, and Problems," in Gideon Golony, ed., *International Urban Growth Policies: New Towns Contributions* (New York: John Wiley & Sons, 1978), 419.

24. There is no agreement among Soviet scholars about the exact number of new towns built before the war, although the census of 1939 indicated 234 new towns for the entire Soviet Union. This figure, however, includes many settlements where new industrial plants were located, thus changing the occupational composition rather than the size of the settlement. The number of new towns for the period 1926–1939 varies between 200 and 250, with the year 1938 accounting for 139 new towns. See Oleg A. Konstantinov, "Rol' novykh gorodov v razvitii sistem rasseleniia SSSR," *Problemy urbanizatsii i rasseleniia* (Moscow, 1976), 145. The author of this study collected data on only twenty-eight new towns constructed in Asia before 1939 and on another twelve built during the years 1939–1945. All these new towns were built either on virgin land or on the bases of existing, but very small, settlements. (This number

does not include four towns in the Tuva Autonomous Soviet Socialist Republic, which became part of the Soviet Union in 1945).

25. In 1935 Igarka, Bodaybo, Novaia Zemlia, Vaigach and Aldan (Nezametnyi until 1939) were but a few of the known sites of labor camps. This same year, Poles from occupied eastern Poland began to be counted among the camps' inmates, to be joined during the 1940s by a large number of German prisoners-of-war. See Armstrong, *Russian Settlement*, 151. The forced labor camps were large establishments with the inmates engaged mainly in mining or construction. These activities were coordinated by DAL'STROI, located since 1939 in Magadan. It is quite possible that the difference between the small number of Asian new towns discussed in Soviet sources and the much larger number shown in statistics denotes the inclusion of labor camps and military installations.

26. Theodore Shabad, "Siberian Resource Development in the Soviet Period," in Shabad and Mote, *Gateway to Siberian Resources*, 13.

27. Irkutsk, for example, with hardly a quarter-million inhabitants in 1939, tripled in size by 1942. During the war years, thirty-four new towns were built in the Soviet Union and seventy-two settlements achieved the status of towns. See Oleg A. Konstantinov, "Novye gorodskie poseleniia perioda velikoi otechestvennoi voiny," *Nauchnye zapiski leningradskogo finansovo- ekonomicheskogo instituta*, vyp. 12 (1956), 67–137. Actually, the government tried to stop the massive exodus to Asia by its decree of 7 February 1942 empowering local authorities to appropriate the housing and belongings of those who had left without permission and to redistribute them among those who stayed. This decree was discussed in the *New York Times*, 18 February 1942.

28. William Mandel, *The Soviet Far East and Central Asia* (New York: Dial Press, 1944).

29. The evacuated war industries required an ample supply of energy. During the war years, many new power plants were constructed in Asia, for example in Novosibirsk, Krasnoiarsk, Tashkent, the Farkhad hydroelectric station on the Syr Dar'ia at Bakabad, etc.

30. The town was begun in 1947, according to V. M. Karro, et al., *Novye industrial'nye goroda* (Leningrad, 1975), 28; and in 1949 according to M. V. Posokhin, ed., *Gradostroitelstvo SSR 1917–1967* (Moscow, 1967), 327.

31. It has been suggested that forced labor has been used for the construction of the dam. See Gaia Servadio, *A Siberian Encounter* (New York: Farrar, Straus and Giroux, 1972), 55. It is interesting to note that 170 Jews, 84 Lithuanians, 58 Germans, 43 Poles, 30 Gypsies, and many other nationalities are named as working on the dam construction in 1960. See V. T. Luk'yanenko, *Goroda rozhdeniia volei partii* (Irkutsk, 1973), 92.

32. This railroad line was in construction during the third five-year plan (1938–1942), as reported in William Mandel, "The Soviet Far East," *The American Review of the Soviet Union*, vol. 5, no. 1 (February-March 1942), 7.

33. The known natural riches of Soviet Asia sounds like a list of the chemical elements. Virtually every raw material required by contemporary industry has been discovered there, from oil and natural gas (in western Siberia, central Asia, and the Far East) to ferrous (iron ores in Kazakhstan and the Siberian Platform) and nonferrous ores (copper in Kazakhstan and northern Siberia, tin, tungsten, molybdenum, lithium, beryllium, etc., in Transbaikal and Chita oblast'), gold (the Far East), silver (the Altai Mountains), and diamonds (Iakut ASSR). There are excellent studies in English on Soviet Asian natural and economic resources. See, for example, Violet Conolly, *Beyond the Urals: Economic Development in Soviet Asia* (London: Oxford University Press, 1967); and also her *Siberia Today and Tomorrow: A Study of Economic Resources, Problems and Achievements* (London: Collins, 1975); Theodore Shabad, *Basic Industrial Resources of the U.S.S.R.* (New York: Columbia University Press, 1969); and also his *Gateway to Siberian Resources.* For central Asia, see Alec Nove and J. A. Newth, *The Soviet Middle East: A Communist Model for Development* (New York: Praeger, 1966).

34. See Servadio, *Siberian Encounter,* 91–100; Lebedev, et al., *Novosibirsk;* and A. O. Kudryavtsev, *Ratsional'noe ispol'zovanie territorii pri planirovke i zastroike gorodov SSSR* (Moscow, 1971), 21–22.

35. The migration from Siberia to the Western regions that had marked the 1960s "appears to be related to the fact that living standards here are relatively low, especially in terms of real wages and climate." See Lewis and Rowland, in Hamm, *The City in Russian History,* 215.

36. For new towns proposals for the Arctic and the tundra, see L. K. Panov, ed., *Prognozy rasseleniia i planirovki novykh gorodov krainego Severa* (Leningrad, 1974), 185–192.

37. Ibid., 29.

38. See Khorev, *Problemy gorodov,* 88–140.

39. In addition to unattractive wages and harsh climate, population migration has been ascribed to the limited options for employment, especially for wives, teenagers, and the elderly, and to the limited choice of goods, entertainment, and cultural activities—all characteristics common to small and medium-size specialized towns built around one type of industry. See Panov, *Prognozy rasseleniia,* 36–130.

40. N. Nekrasov, *The Territorial Organization of Soviet Economy* (Moscow, 1974), 274.

41. See Paul E. Lydolph, *Geography of the U. S. S. R.* (New York: John Wiley & Sons, 1977), 420. The Abakan wagon plant has been operating since 1976. It produces eight-axle, 125-ton capacity freight cars that "will help to modernize the country's rolling stock fleet" (Nekrasov, *Territorial Organization,* 268–269). The new town of Saianogorsk, located close to the Saiano- Shushenskaia hydroelectric power station, owes its initial growth to a large aluminum plant. See Conolly, *Siberia Today and Tomorrow,* 85–86. This work contains abundant information on the problems of Siberian industrialization.

42. If one looks for precedents, Arturo Soria y Mata's work in Madrid

comes to mind. But no connection between the Spanish linear city of the 1880s and the de-urbanist theories of 1920s has been uncovered to date by this author. North American suburban growth, however, has been an inspiration.

43. Linear growth in Siberia occurred in many locations along railroad lines: Omsk, Novosibirsk-Barnaul, Kemerovo-Novokuznetsk, Krasnoiarsk, Cheremkhovo-Irkutsk, Khabarovsk, and Vladivostok are but few examples of such growth.

44. See Aleksei Gutnov and I. Lezhava, "Formirovanie structurnoi edinitsy v sisteme rasseleniia," *Arkhitektura SSR*, no. 11 (November 1970), 42–48. Some of the group's work was displayed at the 1968 Triennale in Milan. See Aleksei Gutnov, A. Baburov, G. Diumenton, S. Kharitonova, I. Lezhava, S. Sadovskii, *The Ideal Communist City* (New York: George Braziller, 1970). For in-depth publication of the theory, see Aleksei Gutnov and I. Lezheva, *Budushchie goroda* (Moscow, 1977).

45. The work of this group was displayed in the Soviet pavilion in Osaka at Expo 1970. See S. Grechannikova, A. Ikonnikov, A. Panin, and K. Pchelnikov, "Preryvnaia kineticheskaia sistema rasseleniia," *Arkhitektura SSSR*, no. 8 (August 1970), 39–43.

46. Ilia M. Smoliar, "Novyi gorod i nauchno-tekhnicheskaia revoliutsiia," *Arkhitektura SSSR*, no. 9 (September 1968), 18–24; Ilia Smoliar, K. Neustroev, "Novyi gorod v sisteme rasseleniia," *Arkhitektura SSSR*, no. 6 (June 1970), 8–13; and I. Smoliar, *Novye goroda* (Moscow, 1972).

47. The "Program of KPSS" as quoted in Smoliar, *Arkhitektura SSSR*, 18.

48. Tatiana Malinina, "Molodye arkhitektory BAMy," *Dekorativnoe iskusstvo SSSR*, no. 10 (November 1978), 2–4.

49. Konstantin Neustroev, "Vremennoe i postoiannoe v poselkakh BAMa," *Dekorativnoe iskusstvo SSSR*, no. 4 (April 1979), 2–6.

50. O. Iaitskii, "Urgal," *Arkhitektura SSSR*, No. 6 (June 1980), 7–8.

51. The master plan for Tynda is discussed in the editorial "Moskva-BAMu: proektiruetsia gorod Tyndinskii," *Stroitel'stvo i arkhitektura Moskvy*, no. 11 (November 1975), 34. For the conference in Tynda, see V. Butuzov, "Na stroike epokhi: nasushchnye problemy i perspektivy," *Arkhitektura SSSR*, no. 1 (January 1979), 4–12; and also his "Na stroike epokhi," *Arkhitektura SSSR*, no. 6 (June 1980), 1–2.

52. The proposals are discussed and illustrated in E. Rozenblium, V. Gudkov, "Tynda: khudozhestvenno-proektnaia kontseptsiia," *Arkhitektura SSSR*, no. 4 (April 1984), 54–55.

53. The first approved project for Dzhamku is illustrated, although not discussed, in V. Peterburzhtsev, "Perspektivy kompleksnogo razvitiia BAMa," *Arkhitektura SSSR*, no. 11 (November 1976), 4. For the revised project, see S. Briskin, "Dzhamku," *Arkhitektura SSSR*, no. 6 (June 1980), 14–15.

54. See the statement by V. Butuzov, chief architect of BAM, in *Arkhitektura SSSR*, 5.

JOHN M. KRAMER

8

The Environmental Crisis in Poland

In addition to its well-known political and economic problems, Poland confronts another crisis with profound implications for its physical, material, and social welfare: a massive deterioration in the quality of the environment.[1]

Western readers, accustomed to the sometimes hyperbolic rhetoric of their own environmentalists, might assume that Polish accounts of environmental deterioration are exaggerated. Thus, publications on this subject in 1982 speak of the "specter of disaster that looms before the entire Polish coast," of how the Upper Silesian Industrial Region (which the authorities themselves admit "has been hit by an ecological natural disaster") is in the "hands of the pollution shark," and of the "critical point" that environmental pollution has reached in the Kraków region where "there is a direct threat to human life."[2]

Yet such characterizations, while seemingly hyperbolic, appear justified by the data now available. Indeed, one source estimates that Poland annually incurs at least "300 billion zlotys in damages from environmental pollution," and some experts suggest that these damages may be even "twice as large."[3] If anything, these data understate the magnitude of the problem. In part, this is because Poland is only now developing a national network to monitor levels of environmental pollution; to date, such measurements have occurred "sporadically, unsystematically, and incompletely." Further, officials have not always been forthcoming in disclosing the state of the environment. Censorship regulations have prohibited any published reference to pollution of Polish rivers by sources in the Soviet Union. Polish environmentalists also allege that officials traditionally "would not admit that there was anything wrong" with the environment and that "across Poland, Party people in the factories were falsifying their reports on pollution levels." "They accused us of trying to stop the building of socialism," one environmentalist asserted, and "even journalists met with censorship when they tried to write about pollution."[4]

The environment became a prominent subject of public debate in the period of liberalization that preceded the imposition of martial law on 13 December 1981. Representatives for the Solidarity trade union movement demanded that the authorities publicly reveal the full extent of environmental deterioration. Several groups (each with the active support of members of Solidarity) also arose during this period with the express purpose of protecting the environment. The Polish Ecology Club, the most prominent of these groups, was founded in Kraków on 23 September 1980. The club enrolled 20,000 members in fourteen regional branches, and its vice-president claimed that membership could easily have been "perhaps ten times greater" but we "did not want to make the government nervous." Members of the club published an open letter to the Sejm, the Polish parliament, claiming that environmental pollution "threatened the cultural and biological life of the nation," and the club later called upon the Sejm to accord Kraków, a city "threatened by an ecological catastrophe," a "privileged status" in the fight against pollution. Club members also led campaigns of public protest that forced the closing of several highly polluting plants, including the nation's largest producer of aluminum, the Skawina works, located near Kraków.[5]

Just before the imposition of martial law, a group of well-known scientists, students, and activists in Rural Solidarity founded the "Association for the Protection of People and the Environment—the Green Movement." Its founding manifesto identified its adherents as "not just members of their nation, but also as Europeans and world citizens" who are part of a "powerful new movement that respects no geographic or political boundaries"—obvious references to similar movements in several West European countries, particularly the Federal Republic of Germany. The group, claiming that in Poland the "ecological threat is now a biological threat," sought to ensure that the public's interests were reflected in all decisions "affecting the physical and mental environment, including city planning and

military armament.[6] Needless to say, these and other manifestations of incipient political pluralism that arose in Poland
have been little heard from since December 13, 1981. On the other
hand, the government, perhaps realizing the value of a "safety
valve" for Polish citizens to vent their anger and frustrations, has
continued to permit the relatively free dissemination of
materials concerning the environment in both the popular and
specialized press. In particular, it permitted the publication in
1982 of a detailed (and highly critical) report on the state of
Poland's environment compiled by numerous researchers working
under the auspices of the Polish Academy of Sciences. One
account, summarizing the materials in the report's nine volumes,
found its overall conclusions "unambiguous": "If the present
trends, which are an expression of [a] peculiar voluntarism by
decision makers, their lack of consideration of the laws of nature
and endeavors to industrialize the nation at any price, continue, it
will bring about disaster throughout Poland."[7]

To deepen our understanding of these issues, the following
analysis focuses upon, respectively, (1) the scope and costs of
pollution, (2) factors causing it, and (3) responses to air and water
pollution in Poland.

Dimensions and Costs

Air Pollution

Poland's air is one of the most intensively polluted in the world.
Thus, the deputy chair of the State Council of Environmental
Protection estimated that emissions of sulfur dioxide in Poland
were the highest of any country in Europe. Overall, in 1975 atmospheric emissions (excluding emissions of carbon dioxide) totalled
almost 11 million tons, i.e., approximately 3 tons of air pollutants
per capita and (according to 1978 data) 22 tons of air pollutants
per square kilometer. Air pollution in several regions is even more
intense. Kraków voivodship and the Upper Silesian Industrial
Region, which between them occupy less than 3 percent of
Poland's territory, but where one-third of the nation's particulate
and one-half of its gaseous emissions occur, annually receive 548
and 476 tons of air pollutants per square kilometer, respectively.
Finally, these data understate the extent of air pollution, since
most of the nation's heaviest industrial air polluters either
"never" or only "sporadically" measure their emissions.[8]

Indeed, industrial polluters generate about two-thirds of all air pollutants; in 1978, these polluters emitted 8 million tons of wastes into the atmosphere—a figure that would surely be higher if industrialists accurately reported the full extent of their emissions. During the 1970s, increased purification held emissions of particulate matter almost constant, but emissions of gaseous wastes (whose purification is negligible) almost doubled between 1975 and 1980. The overwhelming reliance upon coal, which is heavily polluting, as a source of power for industrial (and household) units accounts for much of this pollution. Poland's atmosphere would be even more polluted if it possessed—as do its neighbors, Czechoslovakia and the German Democratic Republic—primarily soft coal and lignite of low calorific and high sulfur content, rather than the less intensively polluting hard coal with which it is mostly endowed. Yet one source estimates that Poland's already announced plans for increased utilization of soft coal (to provide more hard coal for export) is likely in the 1980s to raise the national average concentration of sulfur dioxide to over 20 tons per square kilometer and increase its concentration in Warsaw's atmosphere fivefold.[9]

Poland's three million motor vehicles (after the German Democratic Republic's, the largest such stock in Eastern Europe) are also significant polluters. Thus, traffic policemen in Gdansk, after only an hour's exposure to exhaust fumes at heavily travelled intersections, have experienced "symptoms of poisoning." In Warsaw, exhaust fumes account for over 70 percent of the toxic gases in the atmosphere. By 1990, 90 percent of Warsaw's surface may be contaminated with levels of carbon monoxide above the permissible norm, with 60 percent of the surface having levels at least double the norm. That most motor vehicles do not posses pollution control devices and are old and poorly maintained, and that the absence of beltways compels motorists to travel through urban centers, where narrow twisting streets require frequent starts and stops, have all exacerbated the impact of motor vehicles on atmospheric quality.[10]

Finally, what one might label transnational air pollution— pollution emanating from sources beyond a state's boundaries— undoubtedly contributes to Poland's air pollution. While the dimensions of such pollution are impossible to determine precisely (in part, because the official media have rarely acknowledged its existence, especially if it originates in another socialist country), it is probably considerable since the prevailing winds in Europe blow from west to east. Indeed, the 1982 report on the environment published by the Polish Academy of Sciences estimates that more than one-half of all air pollutants in Poland may originate from sources in Czechoslovakia and the German Democratic Republic. In turn, transnational air pollution from Poland has heavily damaged timber resources in those two countries, leading to the destruction of their forests at an "even much more advanced rate than in Poland itself."[11]

Air pollution has imposed substantial costs on Poland. The media have particularly focused upon air pollution's threat to public health. Naturally, many factors, including pollution, can contribute to a deterioration in one's health, but the data available suggest that those who see pollution as posing a "biological threat" to the nation may not be completely guilty of rhetorical excess. For example, in Kraków voivodship rates of malignant cancers per 100,000 inhabitants far exceed worldwide averages. Infant mortality rates in this voivodship are more than three times greater than the national average. In the Upper Silesian Industrial Region, 2.5 million persons are living under conditions harmful to human health and one-half of them are living under "hazardous" conditions where they are directly exposed to emissions containing carcinogenic substances. Two conditions exacerbate air pollution's deleterious impact on public health. First, most polluting plants are located in heavily populated regions: enterprises responsible for over two-thirds of all industrial air pollutants are concentrated in areas where one-half of Poland's population resides. Second, climatic conditions—characterized by frequent temperature inversions and long periods of meteorological calms—prolong the impact of emissions by trapping them above polluted areas.[12]

Air pollution has also entailed considerable economic costs. In the Upper Silesian Industrial Region it is "practically impossible" to expand heavy industry without a concomitant reduction in air pollution. In this same region, air pollution has so contaminated the land that only 50 percent of the soil is suitable for growing foodstuffs fit for human or animal consumption. On several occasions, officials have had to issue public warnings not to serve contaminated milk to children. Indeed, one source estimates that air pollution is the "primary reason" why 20 percent of all foodstuffs in the nation are too contaminated for human consumption. Table 8.1 provides additional data on this circumstance. Air pollution has also caused enormous damage to buildings and other structures. Emissions of sulfur dioxide that accelerate corrosion and the crumbling of buildings and other

Table 8.1 Foodstuffs Contaminated by Air Pollution, 1979

Commodity	Percent of Samples Too Contaminated for Human Consumption
Butter	19.4
Meat	31.4
Milk	36.8
Vegetable fats	20.9

Source: Data from State Inspectorate for Environmental Protection as reported in *Życie Warszawy*, 24 November 1982, in *Joint Publications Research Service*, no. 82733, 26 January 1983, 17.

structures reportedly cost the economy over $1 billion annually. Finally, in several instances, intense air pollution near residential areas necessitated their relocation at a cost of billions of złotys.[13]

Water Pollution

Pollution of Polish waterways, according to an official report, is "very high" with only a few rivers in western Pomerania and the extreme northeastern part of the country remaining relatively uncontaminated.[14] Table 8.2 presents data demonstrating the dramatic diminution in water quality that occurred in Poland overall and in its most important waterway, the Vistula River, during the 1970s.

The limited extent of waste purification in both the industrial and municipal sectors accounts for much of this pollution. In 1980, about 45 percent of all sewage from these sectors was completely unpurified upon emission, and most of the remainder received only mechanical treatment that cannot remove impurities soluble in water. The purification of municipal sewage is especially inadequate. Over 450 cities, including 20 cities with over 50,000 residents (among them, Kraków, Łódź, and Warsaw) still lack municipal treatment facilities; Warsaw is one of only two national capitals in Europe without such facilities.[15]

The agricultural sector also generates considerable pollution. No comprehensive data exist on the magnitude of pollution from this source, but one recent account asserts that chemical fertilizers and pesticides utilized in agriculture are the "principal cause" of pollution in inland waters. Further, the recent report on the environment by the Polish Academy of Sciences concludes that the "fast rate" at which many species of wildlife are dying out is due "most of all" to the improper application of chemicals to the environment. Finally, what one source delicately describes as "improper manure management" causes many case of "so-called catastrophic pollution" when uncollected animal wastes spill or seep into adjacent waters.[16]

Transnational water pollution also contaminates Polish waterways. A Czechoslovak source provides one of the few available accounts of such pollution. It admitted that the Polish city of Wrocław had to ration water, because polluters in Czechoslovakia had intensively contaminated the city's principal source of potable water, the Oder River. The Soviet Union is also a probable transnational polluter. First, Poland and the Soviet Union have agreed to combat the extensive pollution of the Bug River whose headwaters are in the Soviet Union and which demarcates long stretches of the Polish-Soviet frontier. Second, as noted, Polish censors prohibit any mention of pollution emanating from the Soviet Union, thereby implicitly confirming the existence of such pollution. Poland itself is a source of transnational water pollution; thus, Poland is a major, albeit certainly not the only, polluter of the Baltic Sea, called by one study the "world's most polluted sea."[17]

Water pollution has entailed a multitude of costs. First, of course, are the sums expended for waste treatment: between 1961 and 1980, over 50 billion złotys were spent for this purpose. Yet waste treatment is still relatively limited so that huge sums (one source "cautiously" estimates an additional 100 billion złotys) would have to be spent to reduce pollution levels to the present targets for water quality. Water pollution is also creating severe shortages of pure water that inhibit the further expansion of industry. As Table 8.2 indicates, pollution has made almost 50 percent of the nation's waters completely unusable, and in the Vistula River the comparable figure is over 80 percent. In the Upper Silesian Industrial Region (where only 19 percent of the industrial sewage and 11 percent of the municipal sewage receives "proper treatment"), over 60 percent of the water is unusable for industrial purposes since it would have a damaging effect on machinery and instruments. Water pollution has extensively damaged aquatic life. Commenting upon this damage, one account gloomily predicted that "before long nothing will remain of

Table 8.2 Water Purity in Poland

| | | Percent of Total | | | |
| | | Overall | | Vistula River | |
Class	Appropriate Utilization	A 1970[a]	B 1979[b]	C 1967[a]	C 1976[a]
I	Communal economy	24.8	1.0	0.0	0.0
II	Recreation	29.2	19.0	17.7	0.0
III	Industry and agriculture	17.6	21.0	44.6	19.1
IV	Unusable	28.4	49.0	37.7	81.9

Sources: A. *Gospodarka planowa*, March 1980, in *Joint Publications Research Service*, no. 76022, 10 July 1980, 38.
B. *Życie gospodarcze*, 12 December 1982, in *Joint Publications Research Service*, no. 82733, 26 January 1983, 11.
C. *Nowe drogi*, July 1980, in *Joint Publications Research Service*, no. 76690, 24 October 1980, 18.

[a]Data do not consider bacteriological or physicochemical pollution.
[b]Data do consider bacteriological and physicochemical pollution.

marine life except pictures in biology text books." Finally, Polish citizens personally became aware of these costs when water pollution forced the closure of many popular vacation beaches along the Baltic coast.[18]

The Causes

In one sense, of course, Poland suffers from the same factors creating polluted water, contaminated air, and cacophonous sound in all modern societies. The private automobile stands as the ubiquitous symbol of modern society's seemingly relentless assault upon the quality of the environment. Yet a complex of political, economic, technological, and geographic factors within Poland also contribute to its environmental ills.

First, Polish officials traditionally concentrated their efforts upon rapid economic growth and evinced little interest in minimizing the massive ecological damage attendant upon these initiatives. The postwar years have been ones of "unconcerned and destitute fancy" toward the environment, *Trybuna ludu*, the official organ of the Polish United Workers party, recently explained. Another source alleges that authorities dismissed warnings from environmentalists as "hysteria from our comrades in the countryside," but now "the dismal visions" of environmentalists "are being verified to the last iota."[19]

Industrialists have been especially indifferent to the environment. They typically view pollution control as "distant, indirect, and not always comprehensible." This perception derives from the well-known impact of economic planning criteria that emphasize the production of goods and assign a low priority to activities (e.g., environmental protection) not directly serving this end.[20]

This circumstance helps explain the inadequate state of waste purification. First, industrialists often divert to production tasks funds designated for environmental protection. Thus, a "glaring contrast" annually develops between planned and actual capital investments in waste treatment facilities: in the 1976–1980 period, a "bare" 40 percent of the funds allocated for waste treatment were spent on their intended purpose. Contractors exhibit similar attitudes so that deadlines for commissioning waste treatment facilities are rarely met. Consequently, existing facilities are rapidly aging and/or becoming technologically obsolete. Of the facilities operating in 1977, over 20 percent were built before 1945, more than 45 percent were capable only of mechanical treatment, and less than 20 percent reduced wastes to the stipulated norms. Finally, the operation of treatment facilities is a "particularly difficult and ticklish matter" since industrialists usually assign this task as an ancillary function to production workers ill-trained to perform it, make little effort to attract qualified personnel to this work by making salaries competitive with other specialties, and, most damaging, frequently shutdown such facilities in an effort to conserve energy.[21]

Fiscal constraints also inhibit efforts to protect the environment. Political elites in any society, confronted with innumerable demands upon their scarce fiscal resources, often find it difficult to justify the great sums necessary to control pollution not only because the benefits from this effort may not be readily apparent, but also, as a Polish source explains, "it is impossible to put a price on many of the effects brought about by the improvement in environmental conditions." Poland's well-known fiscal crisis has only exacerbated this circumstance. As Table 8.3 indicates, a considerable reduction in spending on pollution control accompanied the steadily worsening economic situation in the 1970s.[22]

The acuity of Poland's economic problems provides little hope that investments for pollution control will increase in this decade. One source bluntly predicts that in the "lean years" of the 1980s "outlays for environmental protection will be almost nil." That a major effort to control pollution would necessitate the expenditure of hard currency to acquire purification equipment available only in the West intensifies the fiscal dilemmas. Fiscal constraints may even engender political controversies as environmentalists clash with other groups over the limited funds available for investment.[23]

The legal system has also failed to protect the environment. Part of the problem is that most environmental legislation is merely hortatory and contains many goals that are unobtainable because the fiscal and/or technological resources are unavailable to realize them. For example, the "Law Concerning the Protection and Development of the Environment" (1980) forbids new

Table 8.3 Investment Outlays for Pollution Control, 1975–1979 (in billions of 1982 złotys)

	1975	1976	1977	1978	1979	Percent Decrease 1975–1979
Water pollution control	25.1	19.0	19.8	17.8	18.0	28.2
Air pollution control	8.9	10.2	13.4	8.8	7.1	20.2

Source: Gospodarka planowa, October 1982, in Joint Publications Research Service, no. 80939, 28 May 1982, 21.

production facilities from operating without the requisite purification installations. Yet environmentalists wonder if this provision will be vigorously enforced, since to do so in the present state of severe budgetary constraints would effectively preclude most new plants from ever opening.[24] Further, the dictates of environmental protection often clash with the imperatives of plan fulfillment so that industrialists ignore environmental regulations because they find the "stimuli encouraging realization of plan tasks" more compelling. That fines for violating environmental regulations are levied infrequently (and then rarely for large sums) helps explain this circumstance. Finally, Poland is only now developing a comprehensive body of environmental law that subjects all polluting activities to legal regulation: e.g., before 1980, polluters could almost with impunity contaminate the atmosphere because standards specifying maximum permissible concentrations existed for only a few pollutants.[25]

Environmental agencies also exhibit considerable short-comings. Their organization "cannot be described as anything but chaotic," one critic charged. Thus, agencies attached to six different central ministries and authorities are responsible for the management of water resources. Environmental agencies lack both the personnel and the material resources necessary to perform their duties effectively. It is said that the numbers engaged in such work are "microscopically small" and that there are "severe shortages" of instruments needed to determine sources and levels of pollution. Even more serious, environmental agencies lack the requisite political resources to successfully challenge politically powerful industrial polluters. This circumstance constitutes the "main flaw" in such agencies, one source contends, explaining that their work "does not have a high status." In reality, these agencies have little incentive to pursue their duties vigorously because they are attached to ministries that themselves are major polluters. Calling this arrangement a "sham," one environmentalist suggested that it "brings to mind the story of a hare who was entrusted with taking care of a head of cabbage—and, from all accounts, this did not work!"[26]

Finally, several factors exacerbating Poland's pollution problems are largely beyond the capacity of authorities to alleviate. That Poland finds itself, as an accident of geography, the recipient of transnational air pollution represents an obvious example. Climatic conditions such a temperature inversions or meteorological calms that intensify the deleterious consequences of pollution provide another example. Most important, Poland must rely overwhelmingly upon coal, rather than less intensively polluting liquid fuels, for its primary energy.

The Response

Polish authorities have responded to environmental pollution in ways that will evoke *déjà vu* among observers of the environment in Western political systems. They have displayed a strong rhetorical commitment to protect the environment but have evinced little enthusiasm for allocating the requisite political and material resources to implement this commitment. A Polish source describes the government's response as one of "holding conferences and seminars, shuffling statistics, and general moaning and groaning over the situation." "The alarm bells have been rung dozens of times," this source continues, "for the sake of appearances, to make things look dramatic, to state a phony pantomime that mimics a real ecological reform movement."[27]
  Legal and organizational measures predominate in the response to pollution. These measures include laws regulating atmospheric (1966) and water (1974) quality, and the establishment (1972) of the Ministry of Communal Economy and Environmental Protection (currently the Ministry of Administration, Communal Economy, and Environmental Protection) that contained a Central Office for Water Management and a Bureau for the Protection of Atmospheric Air. In addition, inspectorates to monitor compliance with environmental regulations were attached to voivodship councils throughout the country. Then in 1980, Poland passed a comprehensive law to protect the environment. Its provisions cover all facets of the environment, establish a State Inspectorate for Environmental Protection under the Ministry of Administration, Communal Economy, and Environmental Protection, invalidate any administrative decision conflicting with environmental regulations, prohibit new production facilities from opening without purification equipment, and provide for penalties of up to eight years imprisonment for violations of the law.[28]
  Despite this seemingly impressive body of measures, we have noted substantive defects in the legal regulation of the environment. In fact, Polish environmentalists now question whether legal initiatives are even an appropriate means to

protect the environment. As one of them has bluntly asserted, the Polish experience demonstrates "that even the best legal regulations will not be the proper remedy." Hence, several environmentalists are echoing the argument of Western economists that it is far more effective to provide polluters with economic incentives to reduce pollution than to coerce them into compliance with environmental regulations. The 1980 comprehensive law on the environment sought this end by establishing an Environmental Protection Fund whose monies will come primarily from fees charged for the use of natural resources, including the introduction of pollutants into the environment. These monies will then be disbursed for various projects—e.g., the construction of purification installations—to enhance environmental quality.[29]

Poland has taken other steps to combat pollution. It is establishing a national network to monitor levels and sources of pollution. Since 1971, it has ordered (not always successfully) its most intensively air-polluting plants to keep records on the extent of their emissions. Planners have incorporated these data in long-range and annual plans for the conservation and rational utilization of natural resources. Educational institutions have developed curricula to train specialists in environmental protection. In the 1976–1980 period, these institutions planned to graduate over 3,500 students in this specialty. Initiatives designed to restrict the utilization of automobiles, although motivated primarily by a desire to conserve energy, also serve to reduce pollution. As noted, before the imposition of martial law the authorities also closed several highly polluting plants, but the public pressure that prompted their action is unlikely to reappear soon.[30]

Finally, Poland cooperates with other countries to protect the environment. The Council for Mutual Economic Assistance (CMEA) provides the principal forum for multilateral cooperation with socialist states. CMEA environmental initiatives include a comprehensive program of environmental cooperation among the member states, national centers for the coordination of research on environmental protection, plans for the creation of organizations to design and produce purification equipment, and efforts to control transnational air pollution. Poland has also concluded bilateral agreements with Czechoslovakia, the German Democratic Republic, and the Soviet Union for the conservation of national resources and control of transnational pollution.[31]

Poland cooperates as well with nonsocialist states in environmental protection. It has hosted symposia on environmental issues sponsored by the United Nations, and it participated actively in preparation for the 1972 United Nations Conference on the Human Environment (although Poland, like all the other states of Communist Europe, except Romania and Yugoslavia, boycotted the conference itself to protest the exclusion of the German Democratic Republic from full participation in the proceedings). Several United Nation agencies have awarded Poland grants to pursue environmental efforts, including one that enabled Poland to purchase purification equipment from capitalist states, hire foreign experts, and train Polish specialists abroad to combat environmental deterioration in the Upper Silesian Industrial Region. Efforts to control the extensive pollution of the Baltic Sea have involved Poland with both socialist and nonsocialist states. In September 1973, the seven states bordering the Baltic— Denmark, the Federal Republic of Germany, Finland, the German Democratic Republic, Poland, the Soviet Union, and Sweden— concluded an agreement to conserve the marine resources of the sea, and the following year they signed a convention to cope with the sea's pollution.[32]

Prospects

Commenting on the difficulty of mitigating Poland's environmental ills during the present (and likely future) economic and political crisis, an environmentalist remarked that:

> Now a generation has come of age that will have to pay for the mistakes and misguided notions of its predecessors, and this is a generation that finds itself in the midst of a major economic and political crisis. This is not an easy bill to pay when you are surrounded by creditors with outstretched palms. But we are going to have to pay the bill anyway.[33]

One need not doubt the commentator's sincerity nor deny the severity of Poland's environmental problems to question whether Poland possesses the political will "to pay the bill" for its pollution. Certainly, Poland has been unwilling to date to allocate the fiscal resources needed to arrest—let alone reverse—the decline in the quality of its environment: one source estimates that Poland annually spends less than one-half as much of its national income on environmental protection as do developed Western nations. As noted, outlays for environmental protection in the 1980s are likely to decline even more rapidly than they did in the late 1970s. For example, official projections assign the "highest preference" to combatting gaseous emissions only "after 1990"; consequently, one critic contends, "virtually no facilities" to control these emissions will be built in the present decade.[34]

To be sure, Poland's disastrous economic situation presents even dedicated environmentalists with severe problems in saving the environment. That Poland does not possess the hard currency needed to purchase sophisticated pollution control equipment available only from Western manufacturers provides an obvious example of this circumstance. The country's announced intention to free hard coal for export by using more soft coal domestically presents another example. On the one hand, increased utilization of soft coal will inevitable undermine even more the quality of the environment. On the other hand, the environment undoubtedly benefits from the utilization of such relatively "clean" fuels as oil and natural gas—but these fuels are mostly imported and paid for with, among other items, Poland's most valuable export commodity: hard coal.

To achieve their ends in the current era of economic stringency, environmentalists have argued that environmental protection and economic development are mutually compatible goals. They are not, as some would assert, mutually exclusive. Pursuit of the former requires initiatives (e.g., the reprocessing of secondary wastes or the introduction of low-waste or waste-free technologies) that serve the imperatives of the latter.[35] Obviously, such arguments have merit, but they are unlikely to elicit more than a rhetorical commitment to the environment from the political elite or, if a recent newspaper account can be believed, from the public at large:

> Were passersby on a street to be polled, the answer would be negative. Most, if not all, people asked at random would have answered that we cannot afford such protection for the time being.[36]

In sum, decades of neglect, an energy base composed overwhelmingly of highly polluting solid fuels, severe economic problems, and a political elite and a public more interested in economic welfare than in protection of the environment have all contributed in Poland to a massive decline in the quality of the environment that is unlikely to be reversed soon.

Notes

1. Few accounts of environmental pollution in Poland have appeared in English. For a recent study of environmental pollution in Eastern Europe that includes material on Poland, see John M. Kramer, "The Environmental Crisis in Eastern Europe: The Price for Progress," *Slavic Review*, vol. 42, no. 2 (Summer 1983), especially 208–209. An earlier account of the environmental situation in Poland as of 1972 appears in Radio Free Europe (hereafter cited as RFE), *Situation Report*, no. 18 (Poland, May 26, 1972). I. A. Pavliak, *Vklad stran-chlenov SEV v okruzhaiushchei srede* (Moscow, 1982), 61–70, provides an analysis in Russian by a Polish official of the scope and responses to environmental disruption in Poland.

2. *Życie gospodarcze* (Warsaw, 2 May 2, 1982), translated in *Joint Publications Research Service* (hereafter cited as *JPRS*), no. 81659 (August 30, 1982), 18; *Slowo powszechne* (Warsaw, April 29, 1982), translated in ibid., 28; *Narodowa gospodarka administracja* (Warsaw, May 17, 1982), translated in ibid., 23.

3. *Życie Warszawy* (Warsaw, November 24,1982), translated in *JPRS*, no. 82733 (January 26, 1983), 17. One zloty was worth $.0125 at the 1982 official rate of exchange.

4. *Czasopismo geograficzne* (Warsaw, October-December 1978), translated in *JPRS*, no. 73050 (March 21, 1979), 25. Material on Polish censorship practices from *The New York Review of Books* (August 17, 1978), 16–18; *The Wall Street Journal* (July 24, 1981).

5. See *The Wall Street Journal* (July 24, 1981), for a detailed account of the activities of the Polish Ecology Club.

6. Material on the "Green Movement" from *Dagens Nyheter* (Stockholm, 4 December 1981), translated in *JPRS*, no. 79972 (January 28, 1982), 19.

7. *Nauka Polska* (Warsaw, April 1983), translated in *JPRS*, no. 83910 (July 18, 1983), 16–17.

8. *Trybuna ludu* (Warsaw, December 13, 1983); *Gospodarka planowa* (Warsaw, March 1980), translated in *JPRS*, no. 76022 (July 10, 1980), 32. Data on air pollution in Kraków voivodship and the Upper Silesian Industrial Region from *Narodowa gospodarka administracja* (May 17, 1982), *JPRS*, 23. *Nowe drogi* (Warsaw, July 1978), translated in *JPRS*, no. 72225 (November 14, 1978), 18, reports on the indifference of industrialists to the measurement of their emissions.

9. Among the numerous treatments of air pollution from industrial sources, see, for example, *Gospodarka planowa* (Warsaw, March 1980), *JPRS*, 24–45, especially 31–35. Estimates on the impact of increased utilization of brown coal from the "Green Movement" as reported in *Dagens Nyheter* (Stockholm, December 4, 1981), *JPRS*, 19–20.

10. *Przeglad morski* (Warsaw), no. 4 (1981), translated in *JPRS*, no. 80741 (May 5, 1982), 50; *Przeglad techniczny innowacje* (Warsaw, June 10, 1979), translated in *JPRS*, no. 74142 (September 7, 1979), 28.

11. *Nauka Polska* (Warsaw, March 1983), *JPRS*, 24; *Życie Warszawy* (Warsaw, November 24, 1982), *JPRS*, 21.

12. Data on Kraków voivodship and the Upper Silesian Industrial Region from *Narodowa gospodarka administracja* (Warsaw, May 17, 1982), *JPRS*, 24; and *Slowo powszechne* (Warsaw, April 29, 1982), *JPRS*, 28.

13. *Przemysl chemiczny* (Warsaw, February 1977), provides a detailed account of the impact of air pollution in the Upper Silesian Industrial Region. Data on pollution of the soil and foodstuffs from *Slowo powszechne* (Warsaw, April 29, 1982), *JPRS*, 29; *Życie Warszawy* (Warsaw, November 24, 1982), *JPRS*, 17. The "Green Movement" provides the estimate of the impact of air pollution on buildings and other structures. For details, see *Dagens Nyheter* (Stockholm), *JPRS*, 20. See *Przeglad techniczny* (Warsaw, September 3, 1971), translated in *JPRS*, no. 54392 (November 1, 1971), 57, for examples of intense air pollution forcing the relocation of residential areas.

14. As reported in *Nowe drogi* (Warsaw, July 1978), *JPRS*, 20.

15. *Nauka Polska* (Warsaw, April 1983), *JPRS*, 20; *Aura* (Warsaw, November 1978), translated in *JPRS*, no. 72619 (January 15, 1979), 21.

16. *Gdansk glos wybrzeza* (Gdansk, May 29–30, 1981), translated in *JPRS*, no. 78799 (August 20, 1981), 48. *Nauka Polska* (Warsaw, March 1983), *JPRS*, 25; *Aura* (Warsaw, November 1978), *JPRS*, 20.

17. See RFE *Situation Report*, no. 15 (Czechoslovakia, May 17, 1972), for details of Czech pollution of Polish rivers. See *Gdansk glos wybrzeza* (Gdansk, May 29–30, 1981), *JPRS*, 46–51, for a particularly detailed account of Polish pollution of the Baltic Sea.

18. *Aura* (Warsaw, April 1978), translated in *JPRS*, no. 72346 (December 1, 1978), 11; *Nowe drogi* (Warsaw, July 1980), translated in *JPRS*, no. 76690 (October 24, 1980), 15–16; *Slowo powszechne* (Warsaw, April 29, 1982), *JPRS*, 28; *Życie gospodarcze* (Warsaw, May 2, 1982), *JPRS*, 19.

19. *Trybuna ludu* (Warsaw, June 5, 1981); *Gdansk glos wybrzeza* (Gdansk, May 29–30, 1981), *JPRS*, 46.

20. *Sovetskoe gosudarstvo i pravo* (Moscow, November 1973), 92. Among the numerous criticisms of the indifference of industrialists to pollution control, see, for example, *Gospodarka planowa* (Warsaw, October 1982), 444–449; *Narodowa gospodarka administracja* (Warsaw, May 17, 1982), *JPRS*, 37–38; *Nowe drogi* (Warsaw, July 1980), *JPRS*, 116–126; *Życie gospodarcze* (Warsaw, December 12, 1982), 1, 4, translated in *JPRS*, no. 82733 (January 26, 1983), 16.

21. On the practice of industrialists diverting funds intended for pollution control, see *Życie Warszawy* (Warsaw, 25 November 1982), *JPRS*, 20. *Aura* (Warsaw, April 1978), *JPRS*, 10, discusses the low priority that contractors assign to building purification facilities. According to this source, in 70 percent of the cases the construction of these facilities "exceeded the stipulated deadline," and in "some plants" the construction of these facilities took as much as eighteen years. On the inefficient operation of purification equipment, see, in particular, *Nowe*

drogi (Warsaw, July 1978), *JPRS*, 85–97. *Problemy* (Warsaw, October 1981), translated in *JPRS*, no. 79719 (December 23, 1981), 21, reports that orders to conserve energy by idling machinery "apply first to protection equipment." On this subject, also see *Gospodarka planowa* (Warsaw, October 1982,) *JPRS*, 25.

22. *Gospodarka planowa* (Warsaw, October 1982), *JPRS*, 24. Commenting upon the diminution in expenditures for pollution control in the 1970s, one source noted that the decrease appears "even more drastic" when one considers the impact of inflation on investment outlays. *Problemy* (Warsaw, October 1981), *JPRS*, 21.

23. *Problemy* (Warsaw, October 1981), *JPRS*, 18. *Gospodarka planowa* (Warsaw, October 1982), *JPRS*, 34, discusses the "impossibility of importing pollution control equipment in Poland's current economic situation. Ironically, Poland is an exporter of pollution control equipment despite persistent shortages of this equipment on the domestic market. For details of these exports, see *Przeglad techniczny* (Warsaw, November 30, 1975), 27–29, translated in *JPRS*, no. 66948 (March 11, 1976), 18. The following quotation suggests the clashes that may erupt between environmentalists and other groups over the allocation of scarce fiscal resources.

> In light of the alarm [about pollution] it is hard to explain to residents of Silesia where the money is going to come from for the construction of a subway in Warsaw when no money is available to pay for the construction of garbage incinerators and composting plants in the Upper Silesian Industrial Region.

Slowo powszechne (Warsaw, April 19, 1982), *JPRS*, 28.

24. One environmentalist bluntly predicts that "personally, I doubt that facilities scheduled to open will have their ribbon-cutting ceremonies delayed for lack of such an incidental—in the opinion of many decision makers—matter as environmental protection equipment." *Problemy* (Warsaw, October 1981), *JPRS*, 19.

25. For a general treatment of defects in environmental legislation, see *Życie gospodarcze* (Warsaw, May 2, 1982), *JPRS*, 18–19. I. A. Pavliak, "Vklad stran-chlenov," 64, reports that before 1980 Poland had established only sixteen standards for maximum permissible concentrations of different pollutants; by 1982, Poland had elaborated fifty-four such standards.

26. *Życie gospodarcze* (Warsaw, December 12, 1982) *JPRS*, 16, provides a scathing critique of the organization and performance of environmental protection agencies. On this subject, also see *Gospodarka planowa* (October 1982), in *JPRS*, no. 80939 (May 28, 1982), 25.

27. *Slowo powszechne* (Warsaw, April 29, 1982), *JPRS*, 30.

28. For a general discussion of legal and organizational initiatives to protect the environment, see I. A. Pavliak, "Vklad stran-shlenov," especially 61–66.

29. *Problemy* (Warsaw, October 1981), *JPRS*, 18–19. *Gospodarka planowa* (Warsaw, October 1982), *JPRS*, 20, provides information on the new environmental protection fund.

30. For accounts of such measures, see *Aura* (Warsaw, November 1978), *JPRS*, 26, and *Wiadomosci statystyczne* (Warsaw, July 1975), translated in *JPRS*, no. 66011 (October 28, 1975). John M. Kramer, "The Energy Gap in Eastern Europe," *Survey*, vol. 21, no. 1–2 (Winter-Spring 1975), 75–76, discusses measures to restrict the utilization of motor vehicles in Eastern Europe, including Poland. For examples of highly polluting plants that have been closed, see *Gospodarka planowa* (Warsaw, October 1982), *JPRS*, 37. This source notes, however, that while these closings were "doubtless right and warranted from the viewpoint of environmental protection," they nevertheless had "major economic consequences."

31. See Kramer, *Slavic Review*, 218, for a discussion of CMEA environmental initiatives. *Voprosy ekonomiki* (Moscow, April 1978), 68–76, also discusses this subject.

32. Ibid.; RFE *Situation Report*, no. 18 (Poland, May 26, 1972), 15. For details of initiatives to control pollution in the Baltic Sea, see *The New York Times*, (March 23, 1974).

33. *Slowo powszechne* (Warsaw, April 1982), *JPRS*, 29.

34. *Nauka Polska* (Warsaw, April 1983), *JPRS*, 21; *Zycie Warszawy* (Warsaw, November 25, 1982), *JPRS*, 21.

35. For a typical example of this argument, see *Nauka Polska* (Warsaw, April 1983), *JPRS*, 18.

36. *Życie Warszawy* (Warsaw, November 24, 1982), *JPRS*, 17. The following quotation probably expresses the sentiments of many Polish citizens who see environmental pollution as inevitable, albeit regrettable, concomitant of economic progress: "Environmental pollution is the price that has to be paid for industrial development and the development of civilization. Arresting and eliminating these processes is extremely costly, and we do not always have the means at our disposal for necessary action."

Kurier Szczecinski (Szczecin, June 9, 1981), translated in *JPRS*, no. 78799 (August 20, 1981), 42.

9

FRED SINGLETON

Czechoslovakia: Greens Versus Reds

The Czechoslovak Republic, which was created from the ruins of the Habsburg Empire, was proclaimed on October 28, 1918, but it was not until the signature of the Treaty of Trianon (June 4, 1920) that the frontiers of the new republic were internationally endorsed. The new, landlocked state was composed of disparate elements that had previously been ruled under a variety of political dispensations. The Czech lands of Bohemia and Moravia had been under Austro-German Habsburg rule and were linked to the government in Vienna. Part of the historic province of Silesia was also attached, although only 20 percent of the population of the area incorporated was of Czech origin, the majority being Poles and Germans. Slovakia had been governed from Budapest, as part of the Hungarian territories of the empire. Finally, the eastern boundary was extended in 1919, almost as an afterthought, to include the region known as Subcarpathian Ruthenia, which had a mixed population of Magyars, Romanians, Germans, Slovaks, and, above all, of Ruthenians, who made up 60 percent of the population and who were akin linguistically and in other respects to the Ukrainians across the Soviet border. The various minorities within the borders of the new state, of whom the Austro-Germans (with 3.2 million in a total population of some 13 million) were the largest single group, proved a great source of weakness to the Czechoslovak state, and eventually contributed to its enforced disintegration on the eve of World War II.

The Czech lands had been among the most industrialized

regions of the Habsburg Empire. They contained the largest coal basin, which provided 85 percent of all the coal mined in the empire. More than half of the coal was in the form of lignite, which contains a high proportion of sulfur. Since World War II, the proportion of lignite to bituminous coal has increased, and is now over 70 percent of total coal production.[1] This has serious environmental consequences today, but in the nineteenth century, when industrialization began, this fact was not considered to be of importance.

The iron ore, non-ferrous metals, and other minerals that occurred in the Czech lands provided a basis for a wide range of industries. The abolition of internal tariffs within the empire in 1850 gave Czech industry a home market of over 60 million people. Beginning in the nineteenth century and growing rapidly in the interwar period, French capital was heavily invested in the iron, steel, and engineering industries, so that on the eve of World War II, Czechoslovak manufacturing was among the most technically advanced in Europe. Other industries that began under Austro-Hungarian rule—textiles, woodworking, shoe manufacture, glassware, and ceramics—gave the new republic of 1918 a strong industrial base, and by 1938 over one-third of GNP was derived from manufacturing. Where foreign capital was not involved, German-speaking operatives had a disproportionate share of control over native Czech and Slovak speakers. Also, in many cases, they held managerial positions in industry, regardless of the ownership of capital.

The Czech lands were not only important as an industrial base, but they also had the most developed and efficient agriculture in Eastern Europe.[2] Slovakia also had rich agricultural land, which formed an extension of the loess-covered Hungarian Plain. The Slovak lands, however, were less developed industrially, although there were large deposits of iron ore and other minerals. These were largely untapped until after World War II. Some industrial development occurred in Slovakia during the war, encouraged by the Germans, who took advantage of the comparative immunity from Allied bombing to build a base for the supply of essential war materials in Monsignor Tiso's puppet Slovak republic. Since the war, and especially since the assumption of power by the Communists in 1948, there has been a conscious effort to stimulate industrial growth in Slovakia, with the expansion of the long-established iron and steel center at Podbrežova in the Hron valley, the development of the Bratislava region, and the opening up of the east Slovakian iron works at Košice. The loss of Ruthenia to the Soviet Union in 1945 did not have a major impact on Slovakia's economic development, as it was mainly a rather backward agricultural region, although it was also an important source of timber and salt.[3]

The rapid expansion of Slovakia's industries—especially of heavy industries—was carried out with little thought for the impact it would have on the environment. One problem, which has not yet been fully overcome, is that the rail and road links between Slovakia and the Czech lands were poorly developed, because Slovakia's system looked towards Budapest, while the Czech lands were integrated with Austria and Germany.

During the war, there was a shift of emphasis toward heavy industry in response to German demands for war materials, and the internationally known Czech consumer goods industries—textiles, footwear, furniture, etc.—suffered a decline. This tendency continued into the postwar period, especially after 1948, when the new communist leadership adopted a Soviet-inspired economic strategy. The decline of the consumer goods industries—especially textiles—was further accelerated by the mass deportation of Sudeten Germans, many of whom had been managers and skilled technicians in the industries of Bohemia. The pattern of foreign trade also changed, because the Czechoslovak economy was tied to that of the Council for Mutual Economic Assistance (CMEA). Czechoslovakia quickly became an exporter of capital goods to the Soviet bloc, and a net importer of oil and foodstuffs, especially grain, from the Soviet Union (see Table 9.1).

The prewar pattern, in which the brand names of Czechoslovak consumer goods were household words in Western Europe and North America, was broken by the war and its aftermath. The momentum of its past industrial supremacy carried on into the postwar world however, and Czechoslovakia, along with the German Democratic Republic, remained one of the most industrialized regions within the CMEA orbit; but there was a sad decline in efficiency, in the quality of goods produced, and in the morale of the work force. The Soviet type of norms, in which sheer volume of output was the yardstick of success, replaced the former pride in workmanship of the skilled operators. The economic machine was controlled by a muscle-bound central bureaucracy that stifled initiative and killed enthusiasm. Even *Rudé právo*, the party newspaper, had to admit that an examination of the clothing industry in 1959 revealed

Table 9.1 Composition of Exports and Imports, 1937–1953

| | Percent of Exports | | Percent of Imports | |
Products	1937	1953	1937	1953
Machinery and equipment	6.4	42.4	9.8	14.1
Raw materials and fuels	47.0	36.8	68.0	54.2
Manufactured consumer goods	36.8	12.2	5.9	1.5
Foodstuffs	9.8	8.6	16.3	30.2

Source: G. R. Feiwel, *New Economic Patterns in Czechoslovakia* (New York: Praeger, 1968).

that "65 percent of the checked merchandise was deficient and should not have appeared on the market."[4]

The economy failed to live up to the optimistic forecasts of the party leaders, who had boasted in 1960 that, by 1965, "Czechoslovakia will be far ahead of the United States, Great Britain, the German Federal Republic and France, and she will be a model for these states, not to speak of other capitalist countries, insofar as the standards of living are concerned."[5] In fact, the regime patently failed to deliver the goods, and only kept itself in power by a machinery of repression that was backed by the might of the Soviet Union. The techniques used varied from the naked use of terror, under Klement Gottwald, whose death shortly after that of Stalin in 1953 marked the end of the era of show trials, to the more subtle methods of his successor, Antonín Novotný. Economic and political reforms were already under way in the early 1960s. The replacement of the old Stalinist premier, Vilem Široký, by the younger Slovak leader, Josef Lenart, in 1963, was the first important sign that the Stalinist edifice was beginning to crumble. The economy was stagnant; planning at national level was little more than a set of *ad hoc* reactions to crisis situations, with no overall concept of long-term targets.[6]

Further economic reforms were instituted in 1967, and political reform followed in 1968 with the removal of Novotný in January. Alexander Dubček became first secretary of the party, and the respected wartime military leader, General Ludvík Svoboda became state president. The progress of reform was not immediately halted by the Warsaw Pact invasion of 20–21

August 1968. Dubček was reelected as first secretary on 2 September, and in January 1969 the constitutional change granting equality of status to Slovakia within a federal system was enacted, but the writing was on the wall for Czechoslovakia's experiment in "socialism with a human face." Dubček was replaced in April 1969 and a new party leadership, led by Gustáv Husák, came into office with a pledge to carry out policies more in keeping with Soviet wishes.

By 1970, it seemed as if the "Prague Spring" of 1968 had been a waking dream, which had been followed by a return to the nightmare reality of the previous two decades. Many of the prominent figures in the reform movement—like Ota Šik, the economist, Eduard Goldstücker, the former rector of Prague University, and a host of younger men and women—had gone into exile in Western Europe and North America. Those who remained in Czechoslovakia were subjected to harassment by the authorities, losing their jobs and homes, and eventually being put on trial on political charges. For example, Jaroslav Šabata and Jiří Müller were arrested in November 1971, under Article 98 of the Penal Code, which contains the vaguely worded charge "subversion of the Republic," motivated by "hostility to socialism." Šabata had been a leading member of the Communist party; and Müller the most prominent student leader of the sixties. Both had spoken out against the invasion of 1968. In the summer of 1972, Šabata was sentenced to six and a half years' imprisonment, and Müller to five and a half years. Professor Věnek Šilhan, one of the authors of the economic reform program of 1966, and a close associate of Alexander Dubček, was forced to take a job as a laborer, and his daughter was denied entry to the university medical faculty, although she had passed the entrance examinations with high marks. Dubček himself was comparatively lucky. After a brief period as an ambassador in Turkey, he returned to his job as a forester in Slovakia, on the strict understanding that he would keep out of public life. There were many other examples of repressive measures being taken against any who had played a part in the reform movement, and it seemed outwardly that the Husák regime was firmly in control of all aspects of Czechoslovak life. New party statutes were introduced in May 1971 that were designed to restore Leninist orthodoxy and "to prevent a resurgence of reform communism within the ranks of the CPCz."[7]

Despite the victory of Husák and the pro-Soviet elements within the Czechoslovak Communist party, not all of the former adherents to the concept of socialism with a human face were cowed into submission or forced into exile. There remained in Czechoslovakia a group of reformers who continued to struggle for the ideals of the Prague Spring. In the 1970s, their ranks were enlarged by younger people, who embraced the ideals of socialist humanism and who were repelled by the dead hand of bureaucratic orthodoxy represented by Husák.

It is difficult to gauge the full extent of the influence of the opposition to the regime within Czechoslovakia. After the purge of 1970, when party membership fell to 1.2 million, there was a recovery. By 1980 the numbers were back to the 1968 figure of 1.5 million, or 14 percent of the adult population—a higher figure than in any other Soviet bloc country. It is impossible to know how many of the new members, who had been subjected to more rigorous entry procedures than had those who applied in the 1960s, were cynical opportunists rather than genuine party activists.[8] Some of the communist reformers who were expelled in the post-Dubček purges formed the nucleus of an organized opposition, which others joined—such as Christians and liberal intellectuals who had no communist connections. The non-communists eventually came to form a majority among those who were courageous enough to defy the authorities and publicly to declare their opposition.

The most dramatic sign that the spirit of 1968 was still alive came with the issuing in 1977 of the Charter 77, an impressive declaration of human rights. Charter 77 signatories had been subjected to sustained harassment by the authorities, and many of its members had been imprisoned under various articles of the Penal Code, which is drawn up in such a way as to permit the widest interpretation when the authorities choose to use it. Thus, Ladislav Lis, a former spokesperson of Charter 77, was sentenced to fourteen months imprisonment in July 1983 for "the distribution of materials of an inciting character against the socialist state system." On his release he was placed under "preventive surveillance" for three years, This required him to report to the police daily, to inform them of his movements and his income, and to allow them entry to his flat without a warrant at any time of day or night.[9]

Although Charter 77 has been primarily concerned with problems of human rights and with peace, it has also been active in protesting against the misuse of the environment. The reasons for the rapid deterioration in the quality of the environment are manifold and complex, but there is no doubt that the policies of the various Czechoslovak governments during the postwar period have been a major contributory factor. The view widely held in official circles is that the primary purpose of economic policy is to stimulate growth. Expenditure on environmental protection, especially if it involves a slowing down of the rate of growth, is a luxury that cannot be afforded. There is a vague optimism that, at some point, the rise in living standards will have reached a sufficient level to enable society to turn its attention to the problems of the environment, and that, at this stage, a scientific *deus ex machina* will appear, to provide necessary weapons with which to restore the balance of nature. A Swedish observer recently summarized this attitude thus: "Under the socialist system, the development of science and technology is said to be able to correct the negative effects on nature and even to be a precondition for the solution of the problem.[10]

The Czechoslovak economic strategy since the war has been based on the primacy of heavy industry, in contrast to the prewar "bourgeois" emphasis on consumer goods. This has been particularly the case in Slovakia, where iron and steel, chemicals and heavy engineering industries have been established in an attempt to raise the living standards of the Slovaks to a level closer to that of the more affluent Czechs.[11] Ironically, this policy has resulted, in the short term, in a slowing down of the rate of growth of the Czechoslovak economy, but it seems that this is acceptable for sociopolitical reasons, while a diversion of resources for ecological reasons is considered to be unacceptable.

Although hydroelectric stations have been constructed along the Váh River in Slovakia and the Vltava in Bohemia, the main source of energy is from domestic coal and lignite supplies. In 1975, over 80 percent of Czechoslovakia's energy needs came from this source.[12] Since then, imported oil and natural gas from the Soviet Union have played a growing part, and there has been some development of nuclear power, although most of Czechoslovakia's uranium (from the Soviet-controlled Jáchymov mine in Bohemia) is exported to the Soviet Union. The dependence on coal, especially lignite, creates problems because of its heavy sulfur content, and emissions of sulfur dioxide are a major contributory factor to the creation of "acid rain," which has made such inroads into the country's forests. In 1983, Charter 77 published information derived from a report prepared by the Czechoslovak Academy of Science, which had been suppressed by the authorities. The report stated that, before the end of the

century, between 45 and 60 percent of the forests in Bohemia and
Moravia would be irreparably damaged; and that more than 50
percent of all plants and a third of the birds, fish, and mammals
would be in danger of extinction.[13] In a letter to the prime minister
on 12 December 1983, the spokespersons for Charter 77 wrote:
"Where animals, fish and birds cannot live today, man will not
be able to live tomorrow."[14]

Czechoslovakia, according to the International Centre for the
Investigation of Atmospheric Pollution, produces more sulfur
dioxide than any other country in central Europe, including both
Germanies and Poland. North Bohemia, where one-third of the
nation's thermal power stations are situated, is the worst
affected area, with the highest concentration of sulfur dioxide in
Europe.[15] The effect is not only catastrophic for the natural flora
and fauna, but it also has serious effects on agricultural yields and
human health. The production of potatoes and cereals has been
affected, and there have been significant increases in respiratory
diseases, digestive ailments, heart problems, and birth defects in
the industrial regions of Bohemia, which can be traced to the
pollution of the atmosphere by industrial wastes.[16]

In Slovakia, the growth in sulfur dioxide emissions has been
recorded in official publications as being especially high near the
iron and steel plants at Košice and Gemer and the chemical
industries of Bratislava.[17] Another hazard arising from the rapid
growth of industry since the war is derived from the uncontrolled
spread of magnesium dust in certain areas. The village of Jelšava,
a community of 4,000 inhabitants, was virtually abandoned
according to Bratislava TV.[18] The aluminum factory at Gemer
pays fines of one million crowns (kčs) a year for violating air
pollution regulations, but cannot find the money to install filters,
even if it had access to the technical staff and equipment to make
such measures effective. There are many cases of factories
installing filters, which soon become useless because there is no
adequate backup to ensure that the equipment is kept in working
order. One of the problems is that Czechoslovakia has not
maintained the high level of technology for which it was once
famous. Equipment for pollution control must be imported, and
there is a shortage of foreign currency for this purpose. The giant
Slovnaft petrochemicals enterprise at Bratislava, for example,
was forced to spend one million kčs in order to buy antipollution
equipment from Japan.

The threat to the rivers, streams, and lakes of
Czechoslovakia is as serious as that arising from air pollution. As

with air pollution, there is an international dimension. Just as polluted air from both Germanies and Poland can be blamed for some of the acid rain in Bohemia and Moravia, so also the Austrians and Hungarians may accuse the Slovaks of polluting their air space.

The Danube is now an open international sewer. The Czechoslovak section near Bratislava receives pollution from Germany and Austria, and adds to it with the contribution of Bratislava's sewage and the chemical effluent from its factories before passing it on to Hungary. The rivers of Slovakia, which drain towards the Danube, add their quotas. The Vltava and its tributaries flow into the Elbe, and their pollution passes into both Germanies. In June 1982, Slovak radio reported that almost half of the republic's 3,750 miles of rivers were polluted by industrial wastes, agricultural chemicals, and sewage, and in the whole of Czechoslovakia over 4,300 miles (28 percent) of the rivers had no fish life.[19] Along the Váh River in Slovakia, no bathing is allowed, and several tourist centers have been shut down because the rising level of pollution has forced the closure of bathing beaches. The drinking water supply in many areas is suspect, and prudent citizens boil their drinking water and use mineral water to clean their teeth. Many parts of Czechoslovakia report water shortage problems, some of which arise from the non-availability of water because of pollution.

The water problem is not simply a matter of chemical pollution. There are also serious environmental problems that arise when large-scale hydroelectric schemes are undertaken. The disruption of the drainage pattern and the change in the level of the water table over large areas, as a result of such projects as the proposed hydroelectric dams at Hainburg in Austria and at Gabčíkovo-Nagymaros on the Hungarian border, have led to international complications, which have included protests by environmentalists. The cascades of dams on the Vltava and Váh rivers are less damaging to the environment, but even here there are problems arising from the disregard of environmental factors in the construction of the dams.

In the aftermath of the Chernobyl explosion in the Ukraine in April 1986, attention has been focused on the plans of Eastern European countries to develop their nuclear power programs. Czechoslovakia has a strong incentive to invest in new sources of power. The existing thermal power stations are dirty. Many are technologically backward, and the use of lignite as fuel gives rise to serious pollution problems. There are limited domestic supplies of oil. The progress of the economy depends on the availability of cheap sources of power. The hydroelectric potential is limited. The two sources favored by the authorities are natural gas, imported from the Soviet Union, and nuclear power. There is a program to build twelve atomic reactors to supplement the present stations at Jaslovské Bohunice, Mochovce, and Dukovany. Czechoslovakia has a domestic supply of uranium and the blessing of the Soviet Union, which controls the mines at Jáchymov, to embark upon an enlarged nuclear program. Its experience in the past with nuclear power has not, however, been very encouraging. The first plant, opened in 1973, was closed down after barely three years because of design faults and leakages.[20] The current program, which will take 37 percent of all new industrial investment in the period 1986–1990, is already behind schedule. Delays have been caused by bad management, shortage of trained personnel, and the need to reexamine safety procedures and waste disposal techniques after the Chernobyl disaster. The risks are admitted, as a broadcast on Prague radio a week after Chernobyl stated:

> The rapid programming of science and technology brings with it not only successes but also material losses, as well as loss of life. . . . Mankind has to pay for every advance, and this also applies to the nuclear power industry...there can be no exemption from the risks of scientific progress.[21]

The attitude of Czechoslovak environmentalists to the proposed expansion of nuclear power is far from united. Charter 77, in a statement on May 6, 1986, appealed to the authorities to give more information and to improve safety measures, but the new Anti-Atom Group launched a campaign, openly opposing the plans for a nuclear power station at Temelín, in southern Bohemia.[22] They were more outspoken than Charter 77 in drawing attention to the environmental hazards, now and in the future, and to the military implications. They warned that Czechoslovakia is to become the Warsaw Pact's atomic base.[23]

Charter 77 has frequently raised "Green" issues in its publications, and several of its members have been punished for "antistate" activities because of their activities in defense of the environment of their homeland. The degree of severity with which they are treated varies from time to time, and it seems to be related, in part, to the extent of publicity abroad that their protests have aroused, as well as to the preoccupation the authorities may have at a particular time with other dissident groups.

In the winter of 1985, two young environmentalists were tried and sentenced at Pardubice. Pavel Křivka, a young botanist who studied at Martin Luther University in Halle between 1978 and 1983, wrote letters to friends in the German Democratic Republic and to a Bavarian magazine for nature conservation. He drew attention to the deterioration of the forests in Bohemia. In the winter of 1984, "he pinned up two wall charts in the display window of the Velorex Science Club, in which he tendentiously, and in an inciting manner, criticized and evaluated the protection of nature and the environment in the Czechoslovak Socialist Republic."[24] Another letter written by Křivka was intercepted by customs officials in the luggage of one of his friends, who was traveling to Yugoslavia. The letter, which was to be posted in Yugoslavia for onward transmission to West Germany, was considered to "defame conditions in the Republic." Křivka was subjected to a psychiatric examination and was judged to be sane. "He has an anomalous personality, with higher than normal intellectual faculties, although he also displays certain symptoms of hypersensitivity, schizophrenia and a tendency towards non-conformist attitudes and behavior."[25]

Křivka's friend, Pavel Škoda, was charged with similar offenses. In November 1985, Křivka was sentenced to three years imprisonment and Škoda to twenty months. It should be stated that the charges against Křivka and Škoda related not only to their reporting of environmental atrocities committed by the Czechoslovak regime. They were also charged with writing a parody on J. Ryba's "Czech Christmas Mass," in which the state systems of Czechoslovakia and the Soviet Union, as well as the leaders of those states and the Czechoslovak and Soviet parties were "unscrupulously and scandalously defamed and disparaged." Křivka also sang parodies in front of fellow prisoners in Hradec Králové prison, and compiled crosswords "which included hidden words of an inciting character." It would seem that the spirit of the Good Soldier Švejk lives on in Křivka, and his accusers appear to have inherited the mantle of the old Habsburg bureaucracy.

Less than two months after the trials of Křivka and Škoda, a former Czechoslovak citizen, Milan Horáček, who later became a Green Bundestag representative in West Germany, was allowed to visit his home village and also to have talks with members of Charter 77.[26] It seems that the attention of the authorities in 1986 was directed more toward attacks on the resurgence of religious activity than toward the Greens, although police action was taken to disband unofficial environmentalist groups in northern Bohemia.[27]

There is, of course, some recognition of the environmental problems in official circles. They cannot be unaware of the various threats to the environment that are regularly reported to them by their own scientific institutes. They may suppress the reports of these bodies, but they must take note of them. There are a number of permitted environmental groups, such as the Slovak Association of Guardians of Nature and the Homeland. This body has undertaken campaigns to clear up polluted areas, using brigades of youth volunteers, and there have been tree-planting exercises. In the Košice area, workers in factories where manganese dust and sulfur dioxide pollution are particular problems have made efforts to organize clean air programs. There have even been protests by trade unions against the health hazards that arise from working in polluted conditions. The Czech Union of Protectors of Nature claims 20,000 individual and 100 institutional members, and has taken action to protect endangered species.

In the current five-year plan, (1986–1990), provision is made for the investment of a large sum on environmental protection, but most experts say that this is too little to affect the situation, and many doubt if it will in fact be spent. Past experience suggests that money voted for environmental protection is often diverted to other purposes by local people's committees and that exemptions to the water pollution laws are often granted on a wholesale basis.[28] An article in Rudé právo refers to "gross carelessness, indifference and nonobservance of basic duties," and also hints that some environmental disasters are "deliberately committed calamities."[29]

The exceptions permitted to the inadequate legislation are referred to by Ingmar Oldberg, quoting from Czechoslovak sources. Although the law permits factories to be exempted from the obligation to purify waste water in "exceptional cases, justified by the special interests affecting the entire community," there appears to be a widespread evasion of the rules wherever powerful party and economic interests can put pressure on those responsible for enforcing environmental legislation.[30] Even where it can be clearly seen that short-term economic gain is prejudicing longer-term interests, the machinery of regulation is inadequate. In some of the tourist resorts in the High Tatras, for example, emissions of car and bus exhausts because of the hundreds of thousands of tourists who drive to the mountain holiday centers and the "people pollution" of uncontrolled numbers of visitors are visibly degrading the environment, and no one seems to be in a position to stop it.

There have been recent attempts through the machinery of CMEA and through bilateral agreements—for example, between Czechoslovakia and the German Democratic Republic—to organize some form of international action to deal with air and water pollution, but so far these efforts have yielded little practical result.

The basic problem is that there is no sense of urgency among the decision makers, no overall plan in which the protection of the environment is given a high priority, and no adequate mechanism to coordinate efforts at national level, still less at the international level. There is also no free flow of information within the society. Those who attempt to draw attention to the steady deterioration of the environment and the ineffective measures of the authorities to enforce even their own laws are treated with contempt, as "enemies of progress," and may even be persecuted as traitors to the socialist state. There is no doubt that the position will get worse in the short run, even if the scale of the impending calamity does not, in the long run, force a change of attitude.

Notes

The author acknowledges the helpful comments made by Jan Kavan and the Palach Press, London, although the author is, of course, responsible for the interpretation of the facts and for any expressions of opinion.

1. N. J. G. Pounds, *Eastern Europe* (London: Longmans, 1969), 449.

2. Ibid., 439.

3. Jan M. Michael, "Postwar Economic Development," in V. S. Mamatey and R. Luza, eds., *A History of the Czechoslovak Republic, 1918–1948* (Princeton: Princeton University Press, 1973), 16.

4. Cited in F. B. Singleton, *Background to Eastern Europe* (Oxford: Pergamon, 1965), 183.

5. Article in the Slovak Právda, January 1960, quoted in ibid., 179.

6. Ladislav Jeník, ed., *New Trends in the Czechoslovak Economy* (Prague, 1967). In a chapter by Ing. B. Šimon, head of the Economic Department of the Central Committee, it is admitted "that the national economy in the years 1962 and 1963 lost its dynamic, and the national income dropped."

7. Gordon Wightman, "Czechoslovakia," in W. B. Simons and S. White, eds., *The Party Statutes of the Communist World* (The Hague: Martinus Nijhoff, 1984), 151.

8. Ibid.

9. Ján Kavan, "Ladislav Lis Rearrested," in *Across Frontiers*, Berkeley, (Summer 1984), 10.

10. Ingmar Oldberg, "Planned Economy and Environmental Problems: Eastern Europe from a Comparative Perspective," *Bidrag till Öststatsforskningen* (Uppsala), vol. 11, no. 2 (1983), 44.

11. R. E. H. Mellor, *Eastern Europe: A Geography of the Comecon Countries*, (London: Macmillan, 1975), 276–278.

12. Ibid.

13. This document is summarized in detail in *Summary of Available Documents*, no. 21 (Palach Press, July 1984).

14. The text of the letter is published in *Across Frontiers* (Summer 1984), 11–12.

15. *Práca*, 17 August 1985.

16. Charter 77, document 26/38. On the situation in northern Bohemia, see Bulletin 24 (Palach Press, April 1984).

17. Christine Zvosec, "Environmental Deterioration in Eastern Europe," *Survey*, vol. 28, no. 4 (Winter 1984), 119–120.

18. Reported in *Radio Free Europe*, vol. 11, no. 7 (February 1986).

19. Zvosec, *Survey*, 118.

20. Charter 77, document 22, on nuclear safety measures, in Summary of Available Documents, no. 11 (Palach Press, August 1979).

21. Radio Prague, May 4, 1986.

22. Charter 77, document no. 15/86 (London: Palach Press, 1986).

23. *Radio Free Europe*, vol. 11, no. 23 (June 6, 1986), where a copy of the anti-Temelin postcard issued by Anti-Atom is reproduced.

24. Text of the indictment is published in *Across Frontiers* (Spring/Summer 1986), 17.

25. Ibid. 18.

26. For Václav, Havel's letter on Horáček's visit, see *East European Reporter*, vol. 1, no. 4 (Winter 1986).

27. *Planovane hospodarstvi* (Prague), no. 8 (1983).

28. See Bulletin 26 (Palach Press, October 1985).

29. *Rude pravo*, June 11 1983, quoted by Zvosec, *Survey*, 126.

30. *Oldberg, Bidrag till Öststatsforskningen*, 25.

FRED SINGLETON

10

National Parks and the Conservation of Nature in Yugoslavia

The idea of a national park is not in itself a socialist concept, although it does imply the intervention of the state in order to prevent the commercial exploitation of certain areas within a country. It is so that they may be preserved for the benefit of the people, for the preservation of landscapes, flora, and fauna of scientific interests, and for the recreation and aesthetic pleasure of this and future generations. In the sense that these objectives are often in conflict with the short-term objectives of Western industrial society, based on the pursuit of private profit, they can be said to contain an element of socialist thinking.

The Concept of National Parks

National parks are one element in a wider concept of environmental protection that involves the planned use of natural resources. This involves not only conservation, but also the elimination of waste, the control of pollution, and many other aspects of economic and social policy. It might be expected, therefore, that the "socialist" countries of Eastern Europe would be in the forefront of the ecological movement, and would have been pioneers in the development of national parks, nature reserves, and other areas of conservation.[1] In fact, the first steps were taken in Britain and North America, and the socialist countries have not been conspicuous leaders in the fight for environmental protection.

The Origin of National Parks

The idea that certain areas should be given special protection to prevent the exploitation of their natural beauty for commercial or state purposes was first put forward by the poet William Wordsworth, when he suggested in 1810 that the Lake District of northwest England, where he lived, should be regarded as "national property," to be preserved for the enjoyment of both his contemporaries and future generations. The idea was taken up in the United States by George Catlin, in 1833, when he spoke of "A nation's park, containing men and beasts in all the wild freshness of their nature's beauty." In 1864, Congress designated the Yosemite Valley as an area to be preserved for the citizens of California, "for public use, resort and recreation," which was to be "held inalienable for all times." In 1872, President Grant signed the Yellowstone National Park Act, which was the first use of the term in an official document.

In Britain, at about the same time, a movement was gathering strength that attempted to ameliorate the worst ravages of the industrial revolution and to preserve certain areas—like Wordsworth's beloved Lake District—from the encroachments of the industrial juggernaut. As in many nineteenth century social movements in Britain, the impetus came from concerned members of the middle and upper classes who were prepared to spend some of the abundant leisure time in "good causes," whether for the promotion of religion among the lower classes, the protection of pauper children or endangered species of animals and plants, or the preservation of beautiful landscapes and buildings. One of the most effective of these pressure groups was that led by the socialist poet, craftsman, and artist, William Morris, whose efforts led to the formation of the Society for the Protection of Ancient Monuments, which in 1895 merged with the Commons Preservation Society, to form the National Trust. Morris had some success in drawing working people into his movement, but on the whole, conservation, whether of buildings or of nature, remained the preserve of an educated elite. The mass of workers were too concerned with the daily struggle for subsistence to be able to afford the leisure to enjoy the countryside, let alone to campaign for its preservation.

Paradoxically, it was in the period of mass unemployment following the Wall Street crash of 1929 and the subsequent world economic recession that many workers found themselves with the time to enjoy the countryside. Organizations like the Youth Hostels Association (YHA) and the Ramblers Association were founded, partly with the aim of keeping unemployed youth "off the streets" by providing cheap facilities for recreations such as walking, rock climbing, and cycling. Although the leadership remained in the hands of the middle-class reformers, among whom there was a high proportion of intellectual and religious leaders—especially Quakers—awareness of the value of perserving the countryside was seeping down the social scale. Something that could be called perhaps optimistically, a mass movement was developing; for example, there was the mass trespass on the grouse moors of Derbyshire, organized by the Ramblers Association in 1935. Awareness of the value to the individual and to society of protecting the environment and providing access to the countryside for ordinary people was sufficiently strong to be accepted as part of the program of the Labour party, so that when a reformist Labour government was elected in 1945 it soon introduced a law establishing "national parks," and the present ten national parks in England and Wales were founded under this legislation. Separate arrangements for conservation exist in Scotland and Northern Ireland.

National parks in Britain are unlike those in North America and in most European countries, where geographical and economic conditions and historical experiences are different. In countries where large tracts of land are virtually uninhabited, it is possible to designate areas of mountain and forest as national parks, which are available solely for recreation and for the preservation of natural landscapes and habitats. The potential for the creation of such areas does not exist in Britain, except perhaps in some parts of the Scottish Highlands. In international terms, the national parks in Britain are more like the European regional parks, where a measure of protection and planning control is exercised over an area in which the existing rural economy is maintained. This usually comprises a mixture of farming, quarrying, forestry, and tourism, which is practiced by a resident population of several thousands, in villages which have existed for centuries.

The Yugoslav term *nacionalni park* (or in Slovenia, *narodni park*) refers, in some cases, to an area with characteristics closer to the North American type, while other national parks appear to occupy an intermediate position between the British and North American types. In addition to the areas designated as national parks, there are several other types of protected areas that include natural and regional parks (of which there are twenty), special nature reserves, protected landscapes, and horticultural gardens. In addition, the law gives special protection to 75 plant and 370 animal species.[2]

The first measures for nature conservation that were taken on the present territory of the Socialist Federated Republic of Yugoslavia were introduced in the nineteenth century in the areas of the Austro-Hungarian Empire that are now in the republics of Slovenia and Croatia (e.g., the Triglav area of Slovenia and the Plitvice Lakes region of Croatia). In 1893, a Hunting Act attempted to control the indiscriminate shooting of certain birds in the Plitvice area, and in 1910 a Cave Protection Act was passed, which protected some of the more important features of the Croatian Karst. The more accessible cave system of Postojna (Adelsberg) in Slovenia was explored by Austrian scientists in the early nineteenth century[3] and was later developed as a tourist attraction by a Slovene nobleman, Josip Jeršinovič, who acquired special rights over the cave system from the Austrian authorities.[4] The Italians, during their period of occupation between the wars, further developed the tourist potential.

The term "national park" was first used in Yugoslavia in a proclamation in 1928, by the royal government, which designated several areas in Croatia, including the Plitvice Lakes and the Paklenica area in the Velebit Mountains. However, the legal status of these parks was unclear, and little active work was done to implement the intentions of the legislation. What preserved them from exploitation was the sparseness of their population and their inaccessibility. In some cases, the devoted work of private individuals and voluntary societies also played a part in protecting these and other areas from abuse. In the case of the Julian Alps in Slovenia, bodies like the Slovene Alpine Club (Planinska sveza) and the Museum Society promoted conservation. Elsewhere in prewar Yugoslavia, especially in the former Turkish areas south of the Sava-Danube line, nothing was attempted.

The situation changed after World War II, when the new regime passed constitutional enactments, declaring it the responsibility of the federal, republic, and local government bodies, as well as of individuals, to protect the environment. As the experience from the Soviet Union and other Eastern European societies since the war has shown, the passing of resolutions, at whatever level, does not in itself solve environmental problems. The greatest problem in a society undergoing a rapid process of industrialization is to reconcile short-term economic interests with the long-term objectives of conservation and environmental protection. It is regrettable, but understandable, that where there is a direct conflict between these two forces, the economic interests usually win. Other interest groups, which often deliberately or unwittingly frustrate the objectives of environmental protection, especially in national parks, are local farming communities and those involved in tourism and recreational activities. There are signs that in Yugoslavia there is a growing recognition that there need not be a conflict between economic interests and environmental protection, and that the long-term interests of both can be served by cooperation and compromise. In some cases, pressure groups both from within Yugoslavia and from outside (as in the case of the Tara Gorge in Montenegro) may have an effect.[5]

The Constitutional Framework

The Yugoslav Federal Constitution (Ustav Socijališticke Federativne Republike Jugoslavije), which was promulgated on February 21, 1974, contains several clauses relating to the rights and duties of individual citizens and collective bodies concerning the protection of the environment. Article 192 states that:

> Man shall have the right to a healthy environment. Conditions for the realization of this right shall be ensured by the social community.

Article 193:

> Anyone who utilizes land, water or other national goods shall be bound to do so in a way which ensures conditions for man's work and life in a healthy environment.

> Everyone shall be bound to preserve nature and its goods, natural landmarks, and rarities and cultural monuments.[6]

Similar provisions were written into earlier constitutional laws from 1946 onward.[7] The most recent constitutional enactment, the Law on Associated Labor, which deals with the relations between self-managing organizations, includes Article 44, which states:

In performing their activities, organizations of associated labor should safeguard environmental values and provide for the protection and improvement of the human environment, and shall prevent the causes and eliminate the harmful consequences of anything that threatens the natural and man-made values of the environment.[8]

Within the framework of these broad constitutional guidelines, the federal assembly and the assemblies of the individual republics and autonomous provinces are empowered to enact specific laws concerning the protection of the environment. These include the establishing of national parks, regional parks, and other conservation areas, as well as measures to control air and water pollution.

As with every other aspect of Yugoslav life, there is a great variety in the methods adopted from one republic to another. This is partly an appropriate response to the geographical diversity of the country. Measures fitting to a group of rocky islands in the Adriatic (the Kornati National Park) are not appropriate to a linear park along the Danube (the Djerdap National Park—Nacionalni Park Djerdapska Klisura) or to an area containing an Alpine mountain mass like the Triglav National Park in Slovenia. There are also historic, economic, and social reasons why the methods of dealing with conservation vary from republic to republic.

In each of the republics and autonomous provinces there are institutes for the protection of the environment. These institutes are staffed by professional workers—geomorphologists, economists, botanists, zoologists, etc.,—who conduct research and submit reports and recommendations to political and administrative bodies, usually at the request of the decision makers. In some cases, as in Slovenia, the same institute is concerned with the protection of both nature and the cultural heritage;[9] in others, the two functions are separated, as in Macedonia and Kosovo.[10] In addition, each republic and province has a council (savet or savez) for the protection of the environment, and these are federated in the Jugoslovenski savez za zaštitu i unapredjenje čovekove sredine. The institutes and councils have no executive functions. They can advise when asked, or may independently submit reports, issue warnings, and made recommendations. They may even initiate legal action to prevent breaches of the laws protecting the environment. The administration of the national parks bears responsibility for the day-to-day running of the parks, the provision of wardens and guides, the control of visitors, and the technical management of the park. They work under the policy control of self-managing bodies, representing the local authorities in the areas in which they operate and many other local and national bodies that have an interest in the running of the park. For example, the "Self- managing Community of Interest" (Samoupravna interesna zajednica, or SIZ), which governs the Sutjeska Park at Tjentiste in Bosnia-Herzegovina, has representatives from the veterans' organization SUBNOR at federal and republican level and the People's Army, as well as the usual local political, cultural, and economic organizations. This is because a major reason for establishing the Sutjeska Park was to honor the dead heroes of the epic battle that took place there in 1943.[11] The park is centered on a huge Partisan memorial and a museum dedicated to memories of the battle. Similar considerations apply in the affiliation of other organizations to the Lovčen Park in Montenegro, which is dominated by Meštrović's memorial to the nineteenth century national hero, Petrović Njegoš.

The elaborate machinery of self-management and the multiplicity of organizations concerned with the running of the national parks is designed to resolve the conflicts of interest that inevitably arise within the parks. It is appropriate at this stage to examine specific cases where such conflicts have arisen and to note the outcome.

Triglav National Park

The largest and the oldest national park is the Triglav National Park, in northwest Slovenia. The first protection plan was proposed in 1908, and in 1924 a decree protecting the Valley of the Seven Lakes, known as the Alpine Protected Park (Alpski Varstveni Park), was promulgated. This decree expired in 1944, but before that time its practical effects had been nullified by the outbreak of World War II. The change of the frontier with Italy brought the whole of the Triglav massif and the adjoining Soča (Isonzo) Valley within Yugoslav jurisdiction. It was necessary to reorganize the park, and it became possible to extend its boundaries. The original protected park had contained no permanent residents, although there were some summer pastures and mountain refuges that had temporary residents. The new arrangement, completed in 1961, provided for protection for a larger area, covering 2,000 hectares, and the new official name, Triglav National Park.[12] Experience during the next decade convinced the environmentalists that there was a case for enlarging the park and including within it a zone of less stringent protection, which would give the park authorities some control over the peripheral areas where tourism, forestry, and quarrying were beginning to affect the environment.

Proposals to extend the park boundary even further, to include the upper Soča Valley, were fiercely contested by local inhabitants and by more distantly located Slovene economic enterprises, including hydroelectric concerns and tourist interests. A Ljubljana hotel company actually laid the foundations of a new hotel near the village of Stara Fužina, at the eastern end of Lake Bohinj, before protests from the park administrators and some local inhabitants prevented its completion. The neighborhood of Lake Bohinj, which is close to the original core area of the park, has a population that was once devoted to Alpine pastoralism and craft industries, but in the postwar period was becoming more and more dependent upon tourism. It also contains many summer cottages that have been owned since prewar days by professional middle-class people from Ljubljana and Kranj. There was little local opposition—in fact, some strong support—for the extension of the park boundary here. The real fight came in the Soča Valley, where there were plans to build three hydroelectric dams to supply power for new industries: cement making, plastics, saw milling, furniture making, etc. If they had been built, a twenty-kilometer stretch of the upper Soča Valley would have been flooded. The extended boundary took in territory belonging to the commune of Tolmin, which resisted the proposals, fearing that its economic potential would be reduced. There were stormy public meetings and a fierce political battle, eventually drawing the intervention of the republic's government. In 1981, legislation was passed by the Slovene assembly, which authorized an extension of the park to include an area of 85,805 hectares, in which there are twenty-five settlements with a total permanent population of over 2,000 inhabitants.[13] The extended zone will be protected from some economic activities that are considered to be environmentally harmful, but tourism (including winter sports) and some forestry will be permitted. The government has decreed that the proposed dams will not be built at least for the rest of this century.

The laws promulgated in May 1981 regulate in some detail the uses to which the park can be put.[14] In the strictly controlled zone, no permanent residences can be built; hunting, collecting wild flowers, and the use of herbicides and pesticides are forbidden, (article 12, paras. 1–35); and in the peripheral areas, agricultural practices and the erection of buildings will be controlled. The park authorities, who employ twenty-four full-time administrative staff and eighteen full-time wardens, plus many voluntary wardens from the Alpine Club, have powers to fine offenders.

The economic interests have not given up the fight, however. There is resistance from town dwellers, many of whom have local family connections in the villages, to the ban on the conversion of farm buildings into *vikendice*, or holiday cottages, and in 1985 a local forestry enterprise defied the regulations by attempting to bulldoze an access road along the north shore of Lake Bohinj, to cull trees growing at the foot of the scree slopes. This case was the subject of a series of articles in the Slovene press, and the public clamor resulted in the halting of the operation and in talk of prosecutions. It seems that in Slovenia public opinion can be roused to promote environmental causes.

Montenegro

There are three national parks in Montenegro: Lovčen, Durmitor, and Biogradska Gora. The last is a small forested area, surrounding a lake, near Kolašin. Its main purposes are to protect the trees—beech, maple, and spruce—and to preserve the lake. Rowboats are permitted on the lake, and there is a discreet development of other recreational facilities, with a few wooden chalets, which may be hired for holiday accommodation, and a small hotel. Cars are forbidden, although there is discussion of a plan to site an "autocamp" about two kilometers away, and to provide electric-powered cars to give access to the lake. This might destroy the unique feature of Biogradska Gora as an area of tranquility, now frequented only by walkers. It might also open up a conflict of interest between the conservationists, anxious to protect the trees and the lake, and the catering interests who see the encouragement of tourists as a method of increasing the income of the park, which receives only a small subvention from the republic's authorities.

This conflict of interests is glaringly obvious at Lovčen, where an asphalt road takes car-borne tourists to pay their respects at the Petrović Njegoš mausoleum and to refresh themselves at the smart modern restaurant, tastefully designed by a Slovene architect in the Montenegrin popular style. The motor road passes through several alpine pastures and protected forests, but the main purpose of the park is to encourage visitors to the national monument. The SIZ that runs the park includes representatives from the local commune and several factories, as well as from the Montenegrin Institute for the Protection of Nature. A separate organization is responsible for the restaurant and tourist facilities, however, and its interests are in encouraging as many visitors as possible in order to increase its income, which is kept separate from the funds of the park. These are provided by subventions from public authorities and donations from local enterprises, and there is a contrast between the relative poverty of the SIZ and the affluence of the profitable catering enterprise. Another conflict of interest arising in the Lovćen Park is between the owners of small houses on the alpine pastures (*katuni*) and the park authorities. A few of these pastures are still used as traditional seasonal grazing grounds, but they are under increasing pressure from those seeking to own *vikendice*. Although planning regulations prevent this, several have been converted and legal cases are pending that could result in the demolition of the offending buildings.

The cause célèbre in recent years in Montenegro, however, has been the fight to save the Tara Gorge. This is an awe-inspiring chasm cut by the Tara River, a tributary of the Drina. The gorge is over 1,000 meters deep and several miles long, and it lies within the Durmitor National Park. Its spectacular beauty has been recognized by its inclusion in the UNESCO list of World Heritage areas. Twenty kilometers upstream from the gorge is a lead mine and processing plant, "Brškovo," near the town of Kolašin. At a symposium organized by the Montenegrin Academy of Sciences and Arts, held at Hercegnovi in October 1976, it was stated that the Tara River would be threatened with biological death if action were not taken to protect it from pollution by lead wastes, which were discharged at that time into settling tanks.

> Construction of appliances for refinement of "Brškovo" mine waste waters will protect the Tara from pollution, but only for eight years, and on condition that waste waters do not penetrate the walls or bottom of deposit pools and flow into the river. After eight years it will be necessary to build new walls on top of the existing ones, or to build a new deposit tank, or to change the technology of refinement of waste waters rich in heavy metals, which have a disastrous effect upon life in the river.[15]

This was the first public warning, and the conservationists prepared for a battle with the local authorities in Kolašin and with the workers' council at "Brškovo." The conservationists knew that little success had been achieved from efforts to prevent the pollution of the Morača River by red mud from the aluminum refinery near Titograd and of Lake Skadar from Titograd's industries, a local food processing plant, household wastes, and agricultural chemicals.[16] The first reaction of the local bodies was apparently one of indifference. Eight years is a long time in Montenegro, where the guiding principle in local government appears to be "never to today what can be left until tomorrow." The economy of Kolašin depends, to a large extent, on the 2,000 jobs provided by the lead industry. The workers' council at "Brškovo" was not able or willing to find the sums needed to provide the new antipollutant equipment, and there seemed no possibility of help from republic or federal funds. The local environmentalists exhausted the official channels of protest at republic and federal levels without success. As time passed and the deadline approached, they became more desperate. The story leaked out to a wider audience when a delegate of the 1983 assembly of the Federation of Nature and National Parks, which met that year in Plitvice, wrote to a leading British environmentalist, Professor David Bellamy, and to the International Union for the Conservation of Nature (IUCN). The IUCN had also received protests from other countries, and wrote to the Yugoslav authorities in 1984. It is impossible to say whether these representations had a significant effect, and it may be pure coincidence that in 1985 the federal government announced that action would be taken to save the Tara Gorge.

The danger of lead pollution was not the only threat to the Tara, however, as a scheme for building a hydroelectric dam was also under discussion, which would have flooded a large part of the gorge. Cheap electricity is an important factor in the development of industry in a country that is deficient in fossil fuels. If the scheme for a dam on the Tara is realized, it would presumably lead to the expansion of industry in this remote and virtually unspoiled area of Montenegro.

The Durmitor National Park authorities are keen to expand tourism in the area for which they are responsible, and the Tara Gorge is one of its attractions. In recent years, an exciting and potentially profitable enterprise has provided rafts on which tourists can be transported for several miles through the gorge's spectacular scenery. Access roads have been improved and some facilities for accommodation and catering have been provided. At the Black Lake, in the center of the Durmitor Park, the park authorities have leased to a catering enterprise the right to provide refreshments and sell tourist souvenirs. They have also built an administrative center that includes a museum and a cinema where educational activities related to the ecology of the park are provided. Nearby is a residential hotel and a restaurant.

If the river is polluted, or the gorge flooded, much of the expenditure incurred in trying to attract tourists will be set at nought, and the conservation of several species of wildlife— including the black pine and the imperial eagle—will be made more difficult. The debate between the protagonists of rival interests is still proceeding. As far as the hydroelectric project is concerned, it is fortunate for the cause of conservation that the processes of Yugoslav industrial self-management are slow and cumbersome. In the case of Durmitor Park, they involve republic and federal authorities, as well as the local SIZ machinery. It is unlikely, therefore, that any firm decision will be reached governing the construction of a dam or dams for some time to come. Concerning the threat of lead pollution, however, delay would be fatal.

It seems that the intervention of the federal government has at least put the dam project into abeyance, and that something is being done to lessen the danger of lead pollution. The conservationists, however, must remain eternally vigilant, and prepare for battles ahead.

Plitvice National Park

The Plitvice Lakes, surrounded by forests of beech, fir, spruce, and pine, form an area of outstanding natural beauty that is a great tourist attraction. They are also of great scientific interest. The travertine dams that contain the echelon of sixteen lakes are unique geomorphological formations. Many of the lakes spill over the lip of the dams in waterfalls, scores of meters high. When the Plitvice National Park was reestablished in 1949, there was only the ruin of prewar hotel to indicate that some tentative efforts at tourism had been made. At that time a poor road, with a water-bound macadam surface in great need of repair, passed the park, connecting it to Zagreb, 120 kilometers road journey to the northeast. Today, with an improved road connecting Zagreb to the coast, Plitvice is on a main commercial and tourist route. This has created additional problems for the park authorities, who have tackled them in such a way that has given the Plitvice administration a well-deserved reputation for skill and competence. Moreover, the merging of the park and hotel administration into one authority in the mid-1970s has avoided the conflicts of interest that are found in places like Lovčen and Durmitor, where the two are separate.

There are three sets of problems that could threaten the park. The first is the opposition of the local population to the planning restriction and the denial to them of their traditional access to the park area for timber cutting, hunting, and fishing. The park authorities have succeeded in drawing the teeth of local opposition by demonstrating in practical ways that the rural economy, in an area extending as far as Ličko Polje some thirty kilometers away, has benefited from the development of the park. There are hundreds of local inhabitants employed directly by the park authorities as guides, wardens, and administrators, and also as workers in the tourist hotels along the boundaries of the park. Visitors' purchase of food and handicrafts has stimulated the economy of the local villages, which were notoriously poor and overpopulated in prewar days. The park has entered into agreements with local farmers by which loans and grants have been made to improve farm buildings and modernize methods of farming. In return, the hotels receive regular supplies of fresh produce.

The problem of pollution from the 10,000 vehicles a day that pass through the park is being dealt with by seeking permission to divert the road. This is a slow process of negotiation with the republic's authorities, who have to be persuaded to give priority to a project that has no immediate economic benefit in a republic where the inadequate road system is still a brake on economic development. Other areas in Croatia could claim that their prosperity is more important than the loss of an endangered species of plant or animal.

The third problem concerns the regulation of tourism so that the visitors may enjoy the natural beauty and contribute their share to the costs of running the park without damaging the environment. This is achieved by limiting the parking space to the capacity with which the park can cope. Admission is charged to enter the park (about $5 per visit) and cars are banned within its boundaries, but free electric buses and boats are provided to carry visitors around and across the lakes. The income from visitors is a major source of revenue, which contributes to the scientific and educational work that is a prime purpose of the park's existence. Some local people, including park employees, feel that more income could be generated, for example by exploiting the timber resources.

In 1983 the director Ivan Movčan wrote:

> There is continuing pressure, especially among new employees, to use and exploit the existing natural resources....There are also problems with the village population, since they too crave rapid growth and developments which eventually lead to urbanization. Great efforts have been made to stop such tendencies. . . .[17]

> Not only is Plitvice one of the few national parks that is self-supporting, but "apart from its primary activity of nature conservation it involves a self-sustaining regional economy, based on services offered to park visitors."[18]

It would be pleasant if the overall picture in Yugoslavia was as satisfying as it appears to be in Plitvice. Alas, this is not so, either within the parks themselves, or in the country at large. Part of the problem is, of course, finance. Plitvice has solved this by combining ecological objectives with a sound business sense and a skillful political technique in handling the local population. Movčan sums up the position thus:

> The exceptional beauty of the area, its favourable geographical position, good management and long-term bank loans have all contributed. . . .[19]

The Triglav Park does not charge admission and is not involved in catering and hotel management, but it has been successful in obtaining 80 percent of its running costs from the Slovene government.

Many of the others are underfinanced from public sources and have to raise what they can for financing their conservation work from tourism, forestry, sporting, and recreational activities, which are often in conflict with the ecological purposes for which they were ostensibly established. The island of Mljet, for example, has suffered ecological damage from the sheer volume of tourists walking over it and trampling the vegetation.

Those that are near industrial sites or have rivers like the Tara, which flow past industrial sites before entering the park, suffer from the appalling lack of concern for environmental issues that Yugoslav industry has displayed during its period of rapid growth since the early 1950s. Self-managed, decentralized economic management has proved no better than the centralized administration of the soviet type in curbing the pollution from rapid industrial expansion. The state of most Yugoslav rivers, many lakes, and even the Adriatic Sea is an ecological disgrace. Air pollution, even in such places as Jajce, the ancient capital of Bosnia, where a steel works of doubtful economic value has been built, is a danger to public health and a threat to the natural environment.

There is, however, some hope for the future. There is a growing body of concerned citizens who are voicing their protests, and, unlike the situation in some other socialist countries, public opinion in Yugoslavia can have an effect on the decision makers. The "Greens" are not seen as a politically dangerous group of dissidents, to be harassed or suppressed. The examples given above show that the environmentalists can sometimes win, but there is still a long way to go.

Notes

1. The term "socialist" is used in this paper to refer to the Soviet Union and to the countries of Eastern Europe. Many who believe that socialism and democracy are inseparable would question whether the term is justly applied to them.

2. "Natural Conservation in Yugoslavia," a paper prepared for the Assembly of International Union for the Conservation of Nature, Plitvice, October 1983.

3. A. Schmidl, *Die Grotten und Höhlen von Adelsberg, Lueg (Predjama), Planina und Laas (Lož)* (Vienna, 1854).

4. A. Šerko, and I. Michler, *The Cave of Postojna*, 2nd ed., revised (Ljubljana, 1958), 44–46.

5. One important group is the Jugoslovenski savez za zaštitu i unapredenje čovekove sredine, which publishes a bimonthly journal *Čovek i životna sredina*. The late Aleš Bebler, who was appointed to the Savet federacije (Federal Council) after his retirement from the diplomatic service, appointed himself as a one-man environmentalist lobby in the upper strata of the federal administration, using, among other media, the journal of which he was editorial chairman.

6. The constitution of the Socialist Federal Republic of Yugoslavia (English text), published by Dopisna delavska univerza, Ljubljana, for the Secretariat of the Federal Assembly Information Service (Belgrade,1974).

7. Constitution making is a popular occupation in Yugoslavia. Since the first postwar constitution, based on the 1936 Soviet model, there have been five major constitutional statutes promulgated in Yugoslavia—in 1958, 1967, 1971, 1974, and the Law on Associated Labor (*Zakon o udruženom radu*) of November 1974.

8. English text in B. Bošković and D. Dašić, *Socialist Self-management in Yugoslavia, 1950–1980* (Belgrade, 1980), translated from *Službeni list SFRJ*, no. 53, 1976.

9. The Slovene institute is the Zavod SR Slovenije za varstvo narave in kulture dediščine.

10. Nature conservation in Macedonia is the responsibility of the Republički zavod za zaštitu na prirodnite retkosti. Cultural monuments are the responsibility of other institutes, as in Kosovo, where nature conservation is dealt with by the Pokrajinski zavod za zaštitu prirode. There are, as yet, no national parks in Kosovo.

11. This is clearly stated in the regulations establishing a self-management agreement (*Samoupravni sporazum*). "Samoupravni sporazum o osnovaniju samoupravni interesne zajednice Sutjeska, Tjentište, April 1983 godina," 3.

12. Y. Fabian, "Triglav National Park," in *European Bulletin* of the Federation of National and Nature Parks, vol. 22 (1984), 31.

13. Ibid.

14. "Zakon o Triglavskem narodnem parku, Skupščina SRS" (Ljubljana, 1981).

15. K. Zunjić, "Uticaj industrijskih i komunalnih otpadnih voda na slatkovodne ekosisteme Crne Gore," in *Zaštita čovekove sredine u Crnoj Gori* (Titograd, 1978), 44–46.

16. D. Kažić, "Zaštita riba Skadarskog jezera od zagaćenja," in ibid., 81–82. See also Stanka Filipović, "Effects of Pollution on Lake Skadar," in *The Biota and Limnology of Lake Skadar* (Titograd, 1981), 97–99.

17. J. Movčan, "Development and Economics in Plitvice National Park," mimeographed report to the Assembly of the Federation of European Nature and National Parks (Plitvice, October 1983), 3.

18. Ibid., 4.

19. Ibid.

Index

Tsentral'no–chernozemnyi reserve. *See*
Central Black Earth Biosphere
Reserve
Tynda, 135, 139, 140
Tyndinskii, 138–139

Udokan, 140
Ukraine, the, 19, 35, 86, 88; drainage,
83–84; soil erosion, 72, 73, 86,
92(n29)
UNEP. *See* United Nations
Environmental Program
UNESCO, 15, 33, 60–61, 192
United Nations; pollution control
programs, 161–162
United Nations Conference on the
Human Environment, 161
United Nations Environmental
Program (UNEP), 15
United States, 184
Upper Silesian Industrial Region, 149,
151, 153
Ural–Kuznetsk Combine, 129, 131
Ural River, 18, 48
Urbanization, 6; Siberia, 125–126, 130,
131, 134, 136, 140, 144–145(nn 18, 24,
27), 147(n43); town planning,
136–138, 139, 140–141
Urgal, 138, 140
Ust' Kut, 135, 140

Váh River, 177
Valley of the Seven Lakes, 189
Vil'iams, V. R., 78
Virgin lands scheme, 4, 133
Volga River, 18, 44; diversion, 48, 49;
irrigation, 84, 88
Voronezh Reserve (USSR), 62, 65
Voropaev, G. V., 49–50

Warsaw, 152
Waste materials, 157; forestry, 27;
Soviet use, 18, 19–20, 22, 119(n4),
120(n9)
Water; Czech pollution, 176–177;
Polish pollution, 154, 156, 160;
Soviet management, 19, 22, 27;
Soviet transfer projects, 47–51
West Amur Territorial–Production
Complexes, 135
Wildlife, 10, 65; Soviet Union, 20, 21,
28–29, 30–31, 32, 33, 44
Wood products. *See* Forestry industries
World Heritage sites, 192
Wrangel Island Reserve (USSR), 30,
60, 63
Wrocław, 7

Yugoslavia, 198(n10);
environmentalism, 192–193, 197;
environmental protection, 188–189;
legislation, 187–188, 190–191;
national parks, 9, 185–187, 189–197;
pollution, 7–8; tourism, 193–194,
195–196

Zakazniki (USSR), 29, 30–31
Zapovedniki, 59, 68(n3); function,
60–61; research, 61–62; scientific
work, 62–67; sizes, 64–65, 68(n4).
See also Biosphere reserves;
Nature reserves
Zeia River, 23, 135
Zeisk, 135
Zestafoni, 20
Zhiguli Reserve (USSR), 29
Zhigulev Reserve (USSR), 64
Zolotinka, 138
Zubr. See Bison, European

Contributors

Book Editor
Fred Singleton *University of Bradford*

General Editor
The Third World Congress for Soviet and East European Studies
R. C. Elwood *Carleton University*

Brenton M. Barr *University of Calgary*

Milka Bliznakov *Virginia Polytechnic Institute*

Kathleen E. Braden *Seattle Pacific University*

Elisabeth Koutaissoff *Oxford*

John M. Kramer *Mary Washington College*

Philip R. Pryde *San Diego State University*

Ihor Stebelsky *University of Windsor*

Publications of the Third World Congress for Soviet and East European Studies

Social Sciences   Published by Cambridge University Press, The Edinburgh Building, Shaftesbury Road, Cambridge CB2 2RU, England

> *Planned Economies: Confronting the Challenges of the 1980s: Selected Papers from the III World Congress for Soviet and East European Studies*, edited by John P. Hardt (Library of Congress) and Carl H. McMillan (Carleton University)

> *The Soviet Union, Eastern Europe and the Developing States: Selected Papers from the III World Congress for Soviet and East European Studies*, edited by Roger E. Kanet (University of Illinois at Urbana-Champaign)

> *USSR: Party and Society: Selected Papers from the III World Congress for Soviet and East European Studies*, edited by Peter J. Potichnyj (McMaster University)

Social Sciences   Published by Lynne Rienner Publishers, 948 North Street, No. 8, Boulder, Colorado 80302

> *Environmental Problems in the Soviet Union and Eastern Europe*, edited by Fred Singleton (University of Bradford)

> *Religion and Nationalism in Eastern Europe and the Soviet Union*, edited by Dennis J. Dunn (Southwest Texas State University)

Literature and History   Published by Slavica Publishers, P.O. Box 14388, Columbus, Ohio 43214

> *Issues in Russian Literature before 1917: Selected Papers from the III World Congress for Soviet and East European Studies*, edited by J. Douglas Clayton (University of Ottawa)

East European History and Politics, edited by Stanislav J. Kirschbaum (York University)

Aspects of Modern Russian and Czech Literature, edited by Arnold McMillin (University of London)

Imperial Power and Development: Papers on Pre-Revolutionary Russian History, edited by Don Karl Rowney (Bowling Green State University)

Essays on Revolutionary Culture and Stalinism, edited by John W. Strong (Carleton University)

Special Volumes

Books, Libraries and Information in Slavic and East European Studies: Proceedings of the Second International Conference of Slavic Librarians and Information Specialists, edited by Marianna Tax Choldin (University of Illinois at Urbana-Champaign).   Available from Russica Publishers, 799 Broadway, New York, N.Y. 10003

Soviet Education Under Scrutiny, edited by N. J. Dinstan (University of Birmingham). Available from Jordanhill College Publications, Southbrae Drive, Glasgow, Scotland, G13 1PP

The Distinctiveness of Socialist Law, vol. 37 in the series *Law in Eastern Europe*, edited by F. J. M. Feldbrugge (Rijksuniver-siteit te Lieden). Available from Martinus Nijhoff Publishers, P.O. Box 566, 2501 CN The Hague, The Netherlands

Problems of European Minorities: The Slovene Case, special issue of *Slovene Studies*, vol, VIII, No. 1 (1986), edited by Tom M. S. Priestly (University of Alberta). Available from W. W. Derbyshire, Slavic Department, 324 Scott Hall, Rutgers University, New Brunswick, New Jersey 08903

Special issue on linguistics in *Folia Slavica*, vol. 8, edited by Benjamin A. Stolz (University of Michigan). Available from Slavica Publishers, P.O. Box 14388, Columbus, Ohio 43214